IMPOSSIBLE DANCE

IMPOSSIBLE DANCE Club Culture and Queer World-Making ≋ FIONA BUCKLAND

Wesleyan University Press   MIDDLETOWN, CONNECTICUT

Published by Wesleyan University Press, Middletown, CT 06459
Printed in the United States of America
5 4 3 2 1

Library of Congress Cataloging-in-Publication Data

Buckland, Fiona.
    Impossible dance : club culture and queer world-making / by
Fiona Buckland.
        p.   cm.
Includes bibliographical references.
    ISBN 0-8195-6497-4 (cloth : alk. paper)—ISBN 0-8195-6498-2 (pbk. :
alk. paper)
    1. Gay clubs—New York (State)—New York. 2. Gay communities—New
York (State)—New York. 3. Lesbian communities—New York (State)—New
York. 4. Gays—New York (State)—New York—Identity. 5. Lesbians—New
York (State)—New York—Identity. I. Title.
HQ76.3.U5 B83 2002
305.9'0664'09747—dc21   2001004768

For Christine

CONTENTS

Acknowledgments   ix
Timeline   xi

Introduction: Impossible Dance   1

1. The Theater of Queer World-Making   16

2. The Currency of Fabulousness: Fashioning the Self,
Fashioning the Lifeworld   36

3. Slaves to the Rhythm? Using Music, Space, Dance, and the
Ideas of the Body   65

4. The Order of Play: Choreographing Queer Politics   86

5. Only When I Lose Myself in Someone Else: Desire,
Mimesis, and Transcendence   111

6. Closer: Crackdown, Community, and the Physicality
of Queerness   128

7. Mr. Mesa's Ticket: Memory and Dance at the Body
Positive T-Dance   159

Appendixes   185
    A. Method
    B. Informants
    C. Locations of Clubs Mentioned
    D. How the City Planning Commission of the City of New York
    Defines "Adult Establishment"
    E. Regulations and Licenses
Notes   201
Bibliography   207
Index   215

ACKNOWLEDGMENTS

I would like to thank José Esteban Muñoz, Barbara Kirshenblatt-Gimblett, Randy Martin, Thomas De Frantz, and especially Barbara Browning for all their invaluable advice and support. I would also like to thank Marcia B. Siegel for instilling in me the importance of looking at what people actually do. In addition, many thanks to Joe Simmons, Todd Rheinhart, and all at the Department of Performance Studies, Tisch School of the Arts at New York University for their great patience with me on my rare visits, often with late and vital paperwork in hand. I would also like to thank the Fulbright Commission and the Institute of International Education for the opportunity to study for my doctorate in the United States and for making sure I did not get thrown out of the country until I had completed it.

I am grateful for all the help received from all those at Wesleyan University Press, especially Suzanna Tamminen, and also Kathy Kattenburg Astor. Thanks to my U.K. support connection: Christine, Simon, and Philip; Peter, the unsinkable Larry Brown, Jess Tyrell, Rebecca Johnson, and Chris Lavers.

I want to thank the following people for their invaluable support: Aitor Barabator, Mark Cicero, Ephen Glenn Colter, Andy Ingall, Paul Likens, James Polchin, Lori Ramos, and Thomas Weise; Ari Gold and Paul Scolieri for their advice on an early version of the final chapter and for being so damn handsome; Kai Fikentscher for his insight into music and DJ technology and technique; Tito Mesa for loving me more than Jesus; Nancy Olsen for being the fiercest babe north of the border; Peter Mazza for his integrity and magical ways with a fret board; Mary Ann and Eric Allison for being visionaries and introducing me to Cambodian food; Paul Smentek, Jeffrey Stephens-Prince, Richard Green III, and Mark Seaman for shining their love on me; Madeline Acton for opening up her home to me; Ana Medeiros for fixing me cocktails hourly; and Mark Lipton for his unwavering friendship and intellectual inspiration. Finally, a heartfelt thanks to all the informants who moved me time and time again with their generosity.

F. B.

TIMELINE

1920s and 30s

- Gay speakeasies flourish and tend to be very safe because they have to be clandestine. After Franklin Roosevelt ends prohibition in 1933, they are replaced by a constantly changing constellation of gay bars, which, because they are more open, are more prone to harassment by the police.
- During this period the clubs of Harlem are popular destinations for nighttime fun seekers.

1944–54

- During the 1940s, Park Avenue gays—wealthy and white—hold lavish private parties or congregate at the old Metropolitan Opera House on Broadway just below Times Square, the Oak Room at the Plaza, and at the Astor Hotel at Seventh Avenue and 45th Street, while in the theater district around Times Square, gay bars and restaurants are part of a thriving gay scene.
- According to the State Liquor Authority, the mere presence of gays in a bar makes it disorderly—no one opposes this. Many gay bars in the city feature lights warning of a raid. When the warning light comes on, people stop dancing with each other.
- The U.S. recording industry enjoys rapid postwar growth.
- At Ocean Beach, and then later at Cherry Grove and the Pines on Fire Island off the south shore of Long Island, gays and lesbians forge summer communities sixty miles from Manhattan.

1950–51

- The Mattachine Society starts in Los Angeles. The name was meant to symbolize that gays were a masked minority, and its opaqueness is typical of the homophile movement in which open proclamation of the purpose of the society was seen as too radical and impudent. Its founders analyzed homosexuals as an oppressed minority. From January

1953 it publishes the monthly periodical *ONE Magazine,* which eventually achieves a circulation of 5,000. Eventually it changes its aims to the assimilation of homosexuals into general society. Up to 1965, it is the leading gay organization in the United States; then the San Francisco Society for Individual Rights becomes dominant. Mattachine fails to adapt to a more radical militantism after the Stonewall rebellion and fades away.

1955

- Daughters of Bilitis, a lesbian organization designed to promote a sense of community and political unity for women, starts in San Francisco. Although members work on *ONE,* there are sometimes tensions between gay women and men as a result of male chauvinism. Both Mattachine and Daughters of Bilitis have chapters in U.S. cities by the mid-1960s.

1960

- The Twist takes the United States by storm. The dance craze liberates social dancing from formalized partnering, steps, and the need for training of some sort. Dancers can dance as part of a crowd, rather than having to find a partner, thus allowing anyone to dance. Conservative elements rail against its associations with blackness and sex. It is followed by numerous dance crazes, such as the Frug, the Mashed Potato, the Pony, and the Monkey. These are disseminated even more through television. The dance floor is no longer a space for tightly policed rituals.

1965

- A New York State law is passed against deviant sexual intercourse, applying to all oral and anal sex. It remains on the statute books at the time of writing.

1969

- Drag queens fight back after the Stonewall bar in New York City is raided by police.
- At small illegal after-hours clubs such as Haven in Sheridan Square, DJ Francis Grasso—a straight Italian-American—is developing the lexicon of mixing techniques that will become the standard basis for the form. He recognizes that the power to create a performance lies

with the DJ, not records, and that he can work with dancers to create energy. Haven is one of the last places to be smashed up with impunity by the police simply because it is a gay club.

1970

- David Mancuso starts the Loft dance club with rent parties held from 1970–74 at 647 Broadway between Bleecker and Houston, before moving to 99 Prince Street in 1982. The Loft is the blueprint for a club experience in which dancers share a spirit of joy and liberation through identifying with music. It also sets the standard for the precision of its sound system. Mancuso and other DJs such as Nicky Siano use tracks with lyrics of hope, pride, and love to build a narrative. The club is racially and sexually mixed.
- Sanctuary opens in the shell of an old German baptist church at 407 West 43rd Street—one of the first open gay discotheques in the United States. DJ Francis Grasso goes to work there.
- First celebration to commemorate the Stonewall riot.

1972

- Siano and his brother open the Gallery on 23rd Street; later it moves to Soho in Manhattan. It quickly becomes one of the key clubs in the rise of disco. Siano hires Larry Levan and Frankie Knuckles to assist in DJ duties. While working with Siano, the two learn beat mixing. All are still teenagers.
- Other gay dance clubs of this era include Better Days at 316 West 49th Street, a small black club, and Galaxy 21 (1972–76) a black, Latino, and gay underground club on 23rd Street with a restaurant, chill-out room, and an X-rated movie theater.

1973

- Levan and Knuckles go to work for the Continental Baths, an upscale gay bathhouse in the basement of the Ansonia Hotel on 73rd Street and Broadway with regular performances, best known for launching the careers of Bette Midler and Barry Manilow.
- Le Jardin, another upscale club, opens in the basement of the Diplomat Hotel at 110 West 43rd Street. It attracts crowds and celebrities, including Diana Ross, who attends the opening. Disco is starting to go aboveground.

- On December 15, the American Psychiatric Association removes "homosexuality" from its list of mental illnesses.

1974

- Banks refuse to lend to New York City. Decades of mismanagement and the middle class taxpayer exodus to the suburbs have left the city in a fiscal crisis.

1974–80

- Disco is embraced by the entertainment industry, and dominates both the airwaves and the club scene.

1975

- New York City's fiscal crisis deepens. President Ford tells the city no federal help will be forthcoming; the famous *Daily News* headline reads "Ford to City: Drop Dead."

1976

- Afrika Bambaataa DJs his first party at the Bronx River Community Center.
- Paradise Garage opens at 84 King Street with Larry Levan DJing at Michael Brody's new club. Unlike some other famous clubs of the time, the Paradise Garage has a majority clientele of color. "Garage" music has a strong, heavy beat, with hard percussion and, most important, a soaring lead vocal.

1977

- Studio 54 opens at 254 West 54th Street.
- At the height of disco, DJ Frankie Knuckles leaves his successful DJ work in New York to help open a new club called Warehouse in Chicago, not a dance music city at that time. He helps begin "house" music by reconstructing and remixing records live.
- Looting during NYC blackout.

1978

- Federal government finally comes through with $1.65 billion in federal loan guarantees to stabilize the city's finances.

- Mudd Club opens downtown with a more punk aesthetic than the chi-chi Studio 54.
- Harvey Milk, an openly gay San Francisco city council member, is murdered. In 1979 the convicted murderer receives a verdict of voluntary manslaughter and a sentence of seven–eight years.
- Gallery closes.

1977–79

- Street parties featuring not only dance music but rapping DJs become increasingly popular in the New York area.

1979

- The Sugarhill Gang (a pre-fab group assembled by record mogul Sylvia Roberts) records "Rapper's Delight," the first commercial rap record.
- Roxy opens at West 18th Street.
- The Chicago White Sox and Detroit Tigers schedule a doubleheader featuring a "disco demolition" in which people burn disco records between games.
- Amii Stewart's "Knock on Wood" and Patrick Hernandez' "Born to Be Alive" are produced. With an increase in the speed of dance cuts coupled with very strong vocals, melody lines, and a purposeful sense of joy and excitement, Hi-NRG is heartily embraced in the early 1980s by the gay-club community. It becomes the music of choice for leading clubs such as the Saint in Manhattan.
- On October 14, the first National March on Washington, D.C. is held with over 100,000 people in attendance.

1980

- Studio 54 closes.
- The Saint opens on Fifth Street between Third and Fourth Avenues on September 20th. A private, men-only club on Saturdays and Sundays, the Saint is the culmination of three years of development by owner Bruce Mailman (owner of the Saint Mark's Baths gay bath house) and architect Charles Terrel. On the opening night several thousand men attend and dance together on the 4,800-square-foot circular dance floor under a dome larger than the Hayden Planetarium's.

1981

- Juan Atkins and a college friend, Rick Davis (also known as 3070), release a self-financed single under the name Cybotron in their home city of Detroit. Derrick May, one of the lead producers of Techno, described the budding music genre as "George Clinton and Kraftwerk stuck in an elevator with only a sequencer to keep them company."
- Pyramid Club opens at Avenue A and 7th Street.
- MTV launched in August.
- With the growing isolation of dance music from the musical mainstream, the dance music business becomes more narrowly focused and moves underground. The 12-inch single returns as a preferred format for dance music.
- The *New York Times* runs an article on a July report from the Centers for Disease Control about a mysterious "gay cancer," mentioning a pattern among those afflicted of amyl nitrite and LSD use "to heighten sexual pleasure."
- Alarmed by the report, eighty men gather in New York writer Larry Kramer's apartment to hear a doctor speak about "gay cancer." Passing the hat, the men contribute $6,635 for biomedical research. Six months later, this fundraising group becomes Gay Men's Health Crisis.
- Dec. 31, 1981: 422 cases of the mysterious new disease have been diagnosed in the United States; 159 people die of it.

1982

- Studio 54 reopens.
- Dec. 31, 1982: 1,614 cases of AIDS have been diagnosed in the United States; 619 people are dead.

1983

- The New York City Limelight opens on Sixth Avenue and 20th Street. Mudd Club closes.
- Dec. 31, 1983: 4,749 cases of AIDS have been diagnosed in the United States; 2,122 people are dead.

1984

- April 23, 1984: the U.S. government tells the world that the probable cause of AIDS is the virus now known as HIV.

- GMHC publishes and distributes its first safer sex guidelines.
- Dec. 31, 1984: 11,055 cases of AIDS have been diagnosed in the United States; 5,620 people are dead.

1985

- Palladium opens on 14th Street between Broadway and Third Avenue.
- Empowered with a newly passed Sanitary Code, city officials close the St. Mark's Baths on St. Mark's Place as a health hazard, along with many adult venues, bathhouses, and backrooms in bars and clubs.
- At the Saint, heterosexuals are allowed to join for the first time to bolster declining membership rolls, and the club begins serving liquor.
- Actor Rock Hudson's public announcement of his AIDS diagnosis puts the epidemic on the front pages of newspapers and magazines throughout the country.
- The first International Conference of AIDS is held in Atlanta, Georgia.
- Polls show 72% of Americans favor mandatory testing; 51%, quarantine; and 15%, tattoos for those infected with HIV.
- Dec. 31, 1985: 22,996 cases of AIDS have been diagnosed in the United States; 12,592 people are dead.

1986

- Studio 54 closes.
- Tunnel opens on 12th Avenue and 27th Street.
- Run-D.M.C. releases a hip-hop version of Aerosmith's "Walk This Way," and hip-hop breaks into the pop charts, MTV, and mass media all at once.
- Farley "Jackmaster" Funk releases "Love Can't Turn Around," the first house record to have a major chart impact.
- Dec. 31, 1986: 42,255 AIDS cases have been diagnosed in the United States; 24,669 people are dead.

1987

- AZT—the first drug approved to fight HIV itself—is marketed for use by people with AIDS. The cost of a year's supply—$10,000—makes AZT the most expensive prescription drug in history.
- Outraged by the government's mismanagement of the AIDS crisis, a "wake-up call" speech by playwright-author Larry Kramer galvanizes the first of a series of Monday night meetings in New York, March,

1987, from which ACT-UP (AIDS Coalition to Unleash Power) forms. Their first demonstration takes place three weeks later on March 24th on Wall Street, the financial center of the world, to protest the profit-eering of pharmaceutical companies (especially Burroughs Well-come, manufacturer of AZT). Seventeen people are arrested. Shortly after the demonstration, the Food and Drug Administration (FDA) announces it will shorten its drug approval process by two years. By the early 1990s, ACT-UP has over 100 chapters worldwide from Seat-tle to Paris.

- Paradise Garage holds its last party September 26th. It closes because Soho residents opposed the renewal of the lease. The final flyer to members reads:

Every so often, something beautiful in our lives passes on. We find sadness in this because we can no longer see it, or feel it, or be near it. However, we must remember that these things live on in our memory, and in spirit. We have sad news to share with you. The lease of Paradise Garage officially ends October 1st, 1987. Paradise Garage will come to an end at that time. We have had 11 beautiful and crazy, fun-filled years with you, which I and the staff will never forget. There is not a moment of regret. Our final weekends will be: Fri., September 11th, 1987 Sat., September 12th, 1987
Fri., September 18th, 1987 Sat., September 19th, 1987
Fri., September 25th, 1987 Sat., September 26th, 1987
The spirit of the Garage will always be there, and possibly one day in the future, we'll all be partying together again.
In love and hope,

Michael Brody and The Staff of Paradise Garage.

- October 11: Gay and Lesbian March on Washington, D.C. AIDS Quilt unveiled on the Capitol Mall in Washington, with 1,920 panels. ACT UP joins other national activist groups in civil disobedience at the White House in Washington, D.C. In a display of AIDS-phobia, the police wear rubber gloves while arresting protesters.
- Dec. 31, 1987: 71,176 are diagnosed with AIDS in the United States; 41,027 people are dead.

1988

- The Saint closes. The "Last Party" with Michael Fierman and Robbie Leslie in the booth, begins on Saturday April 30th and ends early afternoon May 2nd to Jimmy Ruffin singing "Hold On to My Love" and the last movement of Beethoven's Ninth.

- *Yo! MTV Raps* video show, launched in August, becomes a runaway MTV hit, a weekly (expanded to daily) dissemination of urban black modes of dress, speech, and music to the white suburbs.
- Dec. 31, 1988: 106,994 cases of AIDS have been diagnosed in the United States; 62,101 people are dead.

1989

- Junior Vasquez, a onetime record-store clerk, teams up with a former employee of the legendary Paradise Garage to create the Sound Factory at 530 West 27th Street between 11th and 12th Avenues. Vasquez's DJ style is raw and bass-heavy, and attracts a tribal following.
- Dec. 31, 1989: 149,902 cases of AIDS have been reported in the United States; 89,817 people are dead.

1990

- *Outweek* publishes Michelangelo Signorile's "The Secret Gay Life of Malcolm Forbes," a story that appears one month after the millionaire's death. Signorile's action—dubbed "outing" by *Time* magazine—engenders ferocious debates over journalistic ethics. The ACT-UP spin-off, Queer Nation, which Signorile helps found, plaster downtown Manhattan with posters declaring the homosexuality of public figures. One of Queer Nation's most radical gestures is their reappropriation of "queer."
- Voguing enters the public consciousness in 1990, when Madonna's dance track, "Vogue," climbs the charts. Voguing also encompasses a performance-oriented culture that grew out of the gay Afro-American and Hispanic drag balls held in Harlem, New York, since at least the 1950s.
- Eighty-seven people die in a fire at the Happyland club in the Bronx. In response, the New York Fire Department sets up a Social Task Force to ensure bars and clubs comply with city safety regulations.
- The first GMHC Dance-A-Thon draws a young, diverse crowd of 6,200, and raises over $1 million.
- Clit Club opens at 432 West 14th Street.
- AIDS deaths in the United States pass the 100,000 mark. Nearly twice as many Americans have now died from AIDS as died in the Vietnam War.

- In New York, AIDS deaths surpass those of the great influenza epidemic of 1918, making AIDS the worst epidemic in the state's history.
- Dec. 31, 1990: 198,466 cases of AIDS have been diagnosed in the United States; 121,255 people are dead.

1991

- *Paris Is Burning,* Jennie Livingston's 1991 documentary of the Harlem drag balls, debuts.
- Jackie 60 kicks off at the same venue as Clit Club.
- Dec. 31, 1991: 257,750 cases of AIDS have been diagnosed in the United States; 157,637 people are dead.

1992

- In the November elections, Colorado's voters approve Amendment 2—spearheaded by the Board of Colorado for Family Values—to deny gays the "special privileges" of Denver, Aspen, and Boulder laws guaranteeing civil rights for homosexuals in matters of employment and housing.
- Club USA opens on West 43rd Street.
- Larry Levan dies of an AIDS-related illness November 8th.
- Bill Clinton is elected 42nd President of the United States. His campaign promises include full funding of the Ryan White CARE Act; targeted and honest HIV prevention; an increase in the AIDS research budget; an end to discrimination against HIV-positive immigrants; and the appointment of a national "czar."
- Dec. 31, 1992: 335,211 cases of AIDS have been diagnosed in the U.S.; 198,322 people are dead.

1993

- The state Supreme Court declares the Colorado amendment unconstitutional.
- The Hawaii Supreme Court rules that a refusal to grant marriage licenses to same-sex couples violates the state constitution.
- In August, *Vanity Fair* shows supermodel Cindy Crawford "shaving" lesbian country crooner k.d. lang. *New York* magazine dubs it "Lesbian Chic."
- Rudolph Guiliani is elected New York City's first Republican mayor in two decades.

- Queens senator Frank Padavan helps pass a bill giving local community boards a greater say in the State Liquor Authority's awarding of liquor licenses.
- Dec. 31, 1993: 411,887 cases of AIDS have been diagnosed in the United States; 241,787 people are dead.

1994

- Stonewall 25 celebrations include the Gay Games IV in New York City.
- A Children's Aid Society report estimates that one-third of teen suicide victims are homosexual; 40 percent of homosexual youth are victims of violence from family or friends because they are gay; and half of New York City's 15,000 homeless youth are homosexual.
- Senator Jesse Helms proposes to ban federal money for any school district that permits school counselors to refer students to gay and lesbian support groups.
- The administration of New York City under Guiliani proposes zoning regulations for "adult establishments." In order to remain open in central locations, they have to purge themselves of all "adult" material and performances.
- There is a wave of closings of gay sex clubs such as He's Gotta Have It and Zone DK after the media stoke a moral panic about unsafe sex.
- Volunteers at Body Positive—a not-for-profit organization helping those with HIV and AIDS—start a T-dance for gay men with HIV and their friends on early Sunday evenings at Sound Factory Bar on 21st Street between Fifth and Sixth Avenues.
- *Roseanne* and *Beverly Hills 90210* both have episodes featuring lesbian characters.
- Bruce Mailman, owner of St. Marks Baths and the Saint dies of an AIDS-related illness in June.
- Queercore band Pansy Division support Green Day on a national tour in the fall and the queer punk phenomenon is widely reported and easily packaged by the likes of MTV and *Rolling Stone*.
- AIDS activist and openly gay member of MTV's third *Real World* ensemble, Pedro Zamora, passes away on November 11th, shortly after the series premiers.
- Dec. 31, 1994: 478,756 cases of AIDS have been diagnosed in the United States; 288,597 people are dead.

1995

- The Centers for Disease Control and Prevention reports that AIDS has become the leading cause of death for Americans aged 25 to 44.
- The first protease inhibitor, saquinavir, is recommended for approval by the Food and Drug Administration in November; by July 1996 there are three such compounds on the market.
- The Sound Factory's legendary status is cemented by its February swan song: a 16-hour blowout after community board complaints and extra police attention force its closure. The 27th Street space reopens nine months later as Twilo.
- The building that housed the Saint is demolished. A seven-story apartment building replaces it. Both the Saint and the Fillmore East are memorialized on a plaque on the front of the building.
- Dec. 31, 1995: 534,806 cases of AIDS have been diagnosed in the United States; 332,249 people are dead.

· 1996

- AIDS Quilt panels number over 37,000 (among 343,000 AIDS deaths), cover 16 acres, and weigh a collective 44 tons.
- Citing a lack of funds caused by overwhelming demand, New York State slashes 120 drugs from the AIDS Drug Assistance Program (ADAP). After an aggressive lobbying campaign by AIDS advocates, Albany lawmakers restore funding and establish an ongoing funding stream to guarantee ADAP dollars for the next three years.
- In the midst of both an election season and growing fear that Hawaii would one day export gay newlyweds, Congress rushes in the 1996 Defense of Marriage Act, which withholds federal marriage benefits from gay married couples and declares that no state must recognize another state's gay marriages. President Clinton signs it into law.
- Cover stories hailing AIDS breakthroughs and the "end" of the epidemic appear in *The New York Times Magazine, The Wall Street Journal,* and *Newsweek.*
- Police raids of the Tunnel and Limelight lead to federal racketeering charges. The press accuses owner Peter Gatien of running the clubs as "drug supermarkets," while a state suit claims $1.3 million in back taxes. The grisly murder of a Limelight regular, Angel Melendez, casts another shadow over the New York club scene. Club promoter Michael

Alig's guilty plea in that case, however, effectively deprives the government of its star witness against Gatien.

- Tunnel launches a Sunday hip-hop night. Police set up a roadblock across Eleventh Avenue at 27th Street to stop and search cars going toward the club looking for drugs, guns, and stolen property.
- After a young man falls into a GHB-induced coma and has to be evacuated by helicopter from the Fire Island Morning Party on Fire Island, columnists in the gay press including Michelangelo Signorile pressure its sponsors Gay Men's Health Crisis to stop holding it.
- Police crack down on prostitution. The Anti-Violence Project of New York reports a huge increase in arrests for public lewdness. Police arrest men caught necking or cruising on streets.
- June 30, 1996: 548,102 cases of AIDS have been diagnosed in the United States; 343,000 people are dead.

1997

- As part of Mayor Guiliani's high profile "Strategy '97" push to fight low level crime and insure his reelection, the mayor and police commissioner target dance clubs as "a magnet for drug sales, underage drinking, loud music, and other conditions, which create an atmosphere conducive to crime" (in Bastone 1997). Enforcement agencies crack down on bars and clubs, increasing raids and citations for fire regulations and identification searches. They also enforce current licensing laws restricting public dancing with new vigor.
- Midtown transvestite bar Edelweiss is padlocked after community accusations that it attracted prostitutes.
- Guiliani is reelected.
- After appeals objecting to the zoning laws, New York's highest state court rules that they are constitutional. Porn houses and strip clubs begin to be closed down.
- Cake, a small club on Avenue B between Sixth and Seventh Streets, closes under the weight of fines for offenses such as overcrowding and obstruction of view.
- After the closure of the Palladium, Junior Vasquez begins a residency at Twilo. His all-new Saturday night party is humbly named "Juniorverse."
- Gabriel Rotello argues that monogamy is the socially responsible response to AIDS and blames gay club lifestyles for its spread.
- American Airlines announces the end to its sponsorship of four gay

circuit parties, including the blossom season Cherry Jubilee in Washington, D.C. and the Easter Palm Springs White Party.
- In a March 1997 issue of *Poz* magazine covering ACT-UP's 10th anniversary, Kramer rails against complacency: "You cannot stop for one single minute. Or you'll die."

1998

- A Brooklyn jury, reportedly skeptical of the government's other drug-dealer witnesses, acquits Peter Gatien in February.
- The Palladium closes and this building of special architectural importance is bulldozed to make way for New York University residence halls.
- Body Positive ends its Sunday evening T-Dances for HIV positive gay men and their friends.
- Reported AIDS cases in the United States (CDC, July 1998): 665,357.
- Reported AIDS deaths in the United States (CDC, July 1998): 401,028.
- Americans living with HIV (1997 CDC Estimate): 650,000–900,000.
- Reported AIDS cases in New York City (November 1998): 109,392.
- Reported AIDS deaths in New York City (November 1998): 67,969.

IMPOSSIBLE DANCE

INTRODUCTION
Impossible Dance

≋ AS A TEEN, the most explosive fights I ever had with my mother were about footwear. She wanted me to have sensible—but feminine—shoes. I wanted boots. But not just any boots: ankle boots with strong laces and chunky rubber soles that sprung my energy back through me when my feet hit the floor. The kind of boots ideal for dancing; comfortably heavy to ground me, with a grip that made me secure that whatever I did with my body, I would not find myself sprawling facedown on the dance floor. So I worked hard, saved my pennies, and bought the boots. Now I had to find somewhere to dance. This book is about that search and about finding such a space. It's about finding movement, and sometimes crossing critical boundaries in order to do so. It is about community and individualism, politics and pleasure, past, present, and future, mourning and celebration, mimesis and difference. It's about why improvised social dancing was inspiring, tangible, beautiful, playful, and affective. How it held potential to transform and transcend. How it could link the everyday to the utopic. How it was a way in which participants both remembered the past and imagined possibilities for the future. How they composed and why the act of composition and its results articulated where they came from, where they were, and where they hoped to go.

I can't remember how I found out I could dance. I do have an early recollection of rummaging through my parents' record collection when I was about five, and discovering "Love Train" by the O'Jays and dancing around the room feeling its irresistible vibe: "People all over the world/ Join in/ Start a love train." Even from that early time, music and dance were integral parts of my life. They formed my play space, helped socialize me, and gave me an avenue of free expression. They also opened up

1

a new and effective method of control and punishment. My parents could most effectively punish me by taking away my record player.

When I started to dance at clubs, I reaffirmed the knowledge I had begun to accumulate in my parents' living room, but this time, it was a shared knowledge and a celebration of this exchange, which seemed to open possibilities in everyday life. But in gay, lesbian, or queer clubs, I noticed that the energy I shared burned bright from the fuel of knowing that this play was worked for against tough opposition and was achieved not only historically but night after night in clubs up and down the country in spite of the lack of social consensus about homosexuality. I sought out these spaces repeatedly, desiring new friendships and the now familiar pleasure of moving my body with the rhythm. I wanted to embrace the sound and communal energy, and feel again the sensation of those wings we all lost when we fell from grace.

Several years later I touched down in New York City with a few essential belongings (which included my dancing shoes—a pair of much worn, much loved rubber soled boots), a few hundred dollars, and a place in the doctoral program in Performance Studies at New York University. I had little idea then that I would go on to combine my pleasure in dancing at gay clubs with my peculiar leaning toward intellectual immersion. But at some point I realized that I and others who also chose to dance in these spaces were sharing cultural knowledge and sharing it physically. So in the fine twin causes of pleasure and knowledge, I decided to explore how improvised social dancing in queer clubs plays a role in queer world-making through its physicality and through its embodiment of experience, identity, and community. I did this partly to excavate my own personal archaeology (how *did* I learn to dance and what is the pleasure it gives me?) but also because the subject of improvised social dancing has been relegated to the sidelines in scholarship, not least because of its perceived impossibility—that is, its resistance to discursive description. The limitations of language render it impossible for me to convey in words exactly what I saw and experienced on dance floors. Dance is inherently difficult, and improvised dancing seemingly impossible, to write. It involves an act of translation from a physical, ephemeral medium to a discursive one. Formalized academic languages further shape the translation and analysis of dance. While understanding that in writing dance I can only translate my observations with the inevitable loss of some precision, meaning, and experience, the effort is worthwhile because social improvised dancing—at least in queer clubs— is so vital to the cultural life of individuals, groups, and lifeworlds and to how they make meaning and value. As a carrier of utopic imagination, the promises of freedom and egalitarianism in improvised social dancing may be impossible to realize in practice. So I attempt the impossible because it is there. The gap between what we desire and what we can achieve is defined only by our imagination and is bridged by our ambition to move.

This could never be a story with one voice. The dance floor is packed with stories all pulsating with their own experiences and needs. Any queer dance floor is a node in which many weaving, layered maps meet. Any one of these maps is part of a queer lifeworld: a mobile theater or map of common relations. A queer lifeworld can be created, articulated, embodied, performed, expressed, and contested. How might participation in improvised social dancing also be participation in these processes? I want to use the paradigm of theater to emphasize the dance floor as a space of performance in which all present participate. This focus on theater extends and challenges Jurgen Habermas' model of the public sphere as "a *theater* in modern societies in which political participation is enacted through the *medium of talk*. It is the space in which citizens *deliberate about* their common affairs, hence, an institutionalized arena of *discursive action* [my italics]" (Fraser 1993, 2). Rather than a "medium of talk," this project offers a window onto the medium of movement. Rather than "deliberating about their common affairs" in dance clubs, I suggest that participants performed, not discursive, but *embodied* action. More than this, back out on the streets, this embodiment of the public sphere or lifeworld contributed to self-fashioning: dance informed the walk. Movement described and achieved something: it constructed, articulated, and re-formed queerness in the everyday at a creative intersection of performance, embodiment, and the quotidian. Through embodied action, participants materialized the third body of recreation outside work and home, and performed an imagination of the potentials achievable through modeling a lifeworld on togetherness, individuality, pleasure, and movement.

As queers are often denied access to state, church, media, or private institutions, they constitute lifeworlds in a variety of sometimes contesting ways that cannot assume a taken-for-granted social existence. Many people who identify as queer are made worldless, forced to create maps and spaces for themselves, without the support of these more traditional realms. In such circumstances, any queer lifeworld is itself a critique as well as a place from where participants critique these realms. However, being queer in and of itself does not guarantee entry to queer clubs, or even the desire to go. Open access to queer dance clubs was problematic because although they may exist outside some traditional institutions, they are firmly situated within a market economy in which some clubs charge thirty dollars for entry. Clubs also operated within economies of desirability based on ideals of beauty, status, race, gender, sexuality, and age. Not all clubbers criticized these economies. Even my early pre-research experiences in dance clubs contained a few voices that wanted to exclude those who did not fit into communities based on identity politics. A friend of mine was beaten up by other lesbians in a club while they cried "Old against the young!" So my experience of queer nightlife already contained some questions about singular notions of gay or lesbian "identity" and utopian ideals of "community." World-making is articulated and dispersed through "incommensurate registers," and therefore may be unrealizable as community or identity (Berlant and Warner 1998, 558). Informants expressed these terms in very different and complex ways. For instance, some invoked them uncritically, even if they felt that a particular club or event failed to produce their desired effects. Appealing to one's sexual, gender, or ethnic identity as the ground of community and politics has inherent instabilities.[1] For instance, not all those who have same-sex attraction embraced similar notions of "gayness" or "queerness" as a way of being or of self-knowledge. Some informants spoke of their "SSL," short for same-sex lover, but never used the terms "gay," "lesbian," "bisexual," or "queer" to describe themselves or their peers. In addition, individuals and groups asserted other identifications such as race, ethnicity, gender, and class as central posts in the production of self-knowledge.

The concept of lifeworlds is useful for what are, after all, environments created by their participants that contain many voices, many practices, and not a few tensions. In their essay "Sex in Public," Lauren Berlant and Michael Warner assert that a lifeworld differs from community and group because it "necessarily includes more people than can be identified, more spaces than can be mapped beyond a few reference points, modes of feeling that can be learned rather than experienced as a birthright" (Berlant and Warner 1998, 558). By using the term "world-making," I am not referring to the creation of a bordered culture with recognizable laws, populated by homogenous subjects, but rather, I mean a production in the moment of a space of creative, expressive, and transformative possibilities, which remained fluid and moving by means of the dancing body, as it improvised from moment to moment. Bruce Robbins invokes this when he contends that the notion of a public sphere invokes "identity," but does so with "more emphasis on actions and their consequences than on the nature or characteristics of the actors" (Robbins, ed. 1993, xvii). Identity is not fixed, but tied to movement and its contexts. Actors made interventions in their self-fashioning through social improvised dancing: identity is a continuous, creative act of world-making. To this end, lifeworlds are useful paradigms, emphasizing the inventiveness of queer world-making and the contingency and fragility of queer lifeworlds. In short, I want to understand "queer lifeworlds" both as a definition and as an analytical paradigm. There is no single, monolithic, homogenous queer lifeworld.[2] The notion of a multiplicity of lifeworlds opens the way to understand the agency of individuals and groups to produce sites of interaction and intersection with other groups and concerns such as race, ethnicity, class, and gender. There are many queer lifeworlds, perhaps as many and as unique as each individual. Not everyone meets on the dance floor of a club in New York City. Not everyone meets on the same dance floor.

But what is this "queer" of which I speak? I write of "queers," "queer clubs," and "queer lifeworlds" knowing full well that the term comes oiled and ready for some slippery action. Unless it is spliced to some firm notions, it threatens to run riot all over meaning. Not all informants and clubs identified themselves as "queer." Many used "gay" or "lesbian." I use those terms as the people and clubs apply them to themselves, but describe many practices and lifeworlds as queer as they crossed the critical boundaries of the everyday and the utopian, the real and the imaginary, the private and the public, as well as those borders between insider and outsider that are crucial to both identity politics and to ethnography itself. Queer social practices include strategies and tactics that deconstruct heteronormativity.[3] But being gay or lesbian is not a conscious strategy, nor is a gay or lesbian club, in and of itself. However, to staple a fixed meaning on queerness as solely an undoing of normativity would reveal more about homophobic, racist, and patriarchal ideology than about the meanings and values of improvised social dancing in queer clubs to participants and how they constructed lifeworlds using these practices.

I sometimes use the term "queer" as a collective noun to include more subjectivities than gay or lesbian: for instance, bisexual and transgendered. But I doubt it would have been such a useful term if it had not already been reappropriated from a stigmatized interpellation to a badge of pride, and put to good use. As an academic discipline, queer theory has highlighted difference in order to expose, problematize, transgress, and hopefully transcend unmarked norms with the aim of challenging binarism and sexual and gender categories. As Teresa de Lauretis wrote in her groundbreaking introduction to the 1991 issue of the journal *differences* on queer theory, "From there, we could then go on to recast or reinvent the terms of our sexualities, to construct another discursive horizon, another way of thinking the sexual" (iv). Improvised social dancing in queer clubs also creates the possibilities for reimagining creatively. Political theorist Jacques Attali recognized that (music) composition held this promise:

> We are all condemned to silence—unless we create our own relation with the world and try to tie other people into the meaning we thus create. This is what composing is. Doing solely for the sake of doing, without trying artificially to recreate the old codes in order to reinsert communication into them. Inventing new codes, inventing the message at the same time as the language. Playing for one's own pleasure, which alone can create the conditions for new communication. [. . .] it relates to the emergence of the free act, self-transcendence, pleasure in being instead of having. (Attali 1985, 134)

This then is the queer world-making I define, by resisting the impulse to straitjacket the experiences of informants into an ill-fitting theoretical garment that hides all their bulges. The experiences and observations of participants and informants suggested this framework and I use it to get me a little further down the road towards understanding the power, potential, and frustrations of social improvised dancing in a queer club. Queer lifeworlds embodied utopic imagination and power whereby queerness occupied the center, in which the heterosexual couple was no longer the referent or the privileged example of sexual culture. They existed within and drew some energy from not always oppositional relationships to the field of hegemonic power that attempted repeatedly and contingently to normalize heteroorthodoxy. But only an impoverished, thin reading of these practices would deal lightly with the agency, meanings, and values participants drew from the pleasure of fitting in, as well as from resistance. Even in a dance club, at the end of the night when the music stopped and the lights came on, participants had to step back from the center stage of a queer lifeworld into a world that marginalized them.

This project contextualizes the deconstructive turn within a larger project of queer social *construction*. It asks, *How do people make pleasure to-*

gether? "Third spaces" of recreation (after home and workspaces) fuse both quotidian (for instance, dressing and traveling to a destination) and play practices (for instance, working with others in activities in which the imaginary is as concrete as the real). In clubs, dressing and looking, for instance, were vital play activities and expressive performance tools for self-fashioning. Through going to queer clubs, I learned the rules of a lifeworld: how to dress, how to interact, and the in-jokes, argot, values, and issues. Through word of mouth, I also discovered other places such as bars and coffee shops, community centers, workshops, newspapers and magazines, and other people's homes that made up constellations of sites within a lifeworld. I also learned to incorporate and embody a way of being that allowed me to interpret any environment through a worldview informed by queerness. A queer lifeworld is not only a stage outside of the body, but a state of consciousness and a way of deportment. Movement is central to understanding this. What was it that people actually did? How did they make pleasure? What was the relationship between the everyday and dancing in a club? Was it always the same relationship and how did that affect pleasure-making?

Dancers made pleasure together without a score. Improvised social dancing has no existence or agency outside of its participants. In this it is different from formal scores of social dance such as tango or even lindy hop. "Improvised social dancing" is a verb, rather than a noun, an activity rather than an object of knowledge. Dancing is a multivocal and flexible sphere of social activity. The same movements can generate a variety of meanings depending on the contingent historical, social, and psychological contexts in which they take place. Dance is not only a feature within the context of its creation, but also can key us in to understanding that context itself. As a playful practice that depends upon the agency of its performers, improvised social dancing produces queer club culture, not as a homogenous, transhistorical object, but as a process of counterpoint, contestation, and polyvocality. This more fluid model shifts agency away from culture and its structural forms, including dance, to participants who improvised movement in response to everyday experiences, which, in turn, influenced the experiences and understanding of everyday life. These dance-floor compositions interpenetrated and were interpenetrated by mass-mediated culture, and were influenced by the dance people saw in music videos on MTV (Music Television) and BET (Black Entertainment Television). Going to a club already affected how participants might be represented and how they might see themselves, and it's these representations that spawn both danger and pleasure as this book will often explore. One of the dangers and pleasures of social improvised dancing is its trivialization within "rational" postindustrial societies: those dance floor darlings are almost always suspect in some contexts. Dancing could be a queer business, as was already the case in New York City, at least.

I wrote this book during an emergency for some queer lifeworlds: namely, the rezoning of adult businesses in New York City. Improvised social dancing at a queer club was not simply an escape from these contexts. It existed within and dynamically responded to them. As a practice, improvised social dancing can not only be analyzed through its functions of release of tension, but also as an expression of both the tension and the release as well as an intervention. In 1994, the administration of New York City under Republican Mayor Rudolph Guiliani proposed zoning regulations for "adult establishments" that would radically affect the locations, forms, and content of queer lifeworlds. Gay spaces such as bars, bookstores, and clubs defined as adult establishments according to the definitions of the City of New York City Planning Council would be forced to relocate to areas less accessible for potential customers.[4] In order to remain open in their current locations, such establishments would have to purge themselves of "adult" material and performances, the presence of which would render them subject to the zoning laws. This proposal used the politics of space to curtail the existence and articulation of queer lifeworlds. In February 1997, New York's highest state court affirmed a lower court ruling that the law was constitutional.

Contemporaneously there was a noticeable crackdown on bars and dance clubs, including those catering to queer clienteles. This crackdown was propped up by licensing laws that restricted public dancing, which, while on the statute books for a number of years, were subject to unprecedented enforcement. These laws stated that go-go dancers could not perform at an establishment without a cabaret license and that three or more customers "moving rhythmically" in any establishment unlicensed for dancing constituted a violation. Although technically any businesses were subject to these licensing laws, in the perspective of informants as well as queer activists they were disproportionately enforced on queer establishments in New York City.[5] As well as using the politics of space, the authorities used the politics of the body and of movement to legislate and dictate how and where certain pleasures could be enjoyed. In the mainstream media, dance clubs were represented as dangerous, undisciplined spaces, the indices of the excesses of drugs, sex, and HIV infection. Because of these representations, queer dance floors were always contested and marginalized sites under scrutiny and constantly threatened by dominant social agencies, including some mainstream gay sources. For instance, commentators in the gay press objected to the Fire Island Morning Party. These representations relied upon the sensationalization and generalization of incidents of drug overdoses, violence, and what orthodox heteronormative morality views as deviant sexual behavior.

This book is another representation to add to the coverage of clubs. The effects of generalization that representation trigger carry particular weight in a discussion of queer social worlds and their practices. Historically, many gay rights activists have used notions of gay and lesbian culture to legitimate marginal groups as different, but "normal." In this project, it is difficult to speak of "queer culture" because it is anything but a monolithic unity. Anthropologists such as Lila Abu-Lughod (1993) have thrown doubts on constructing "culture" as a model of analysis because to do so inscribes an illusion of professional objectivity and a claim to legitimacy as an empirically based social science. A representation of a singular monolithic culture flattens out the differences between people and their experiences in order to discover its laws, while simultaneously fixing boundaries between self and other. The theater of this ethnography takes its cue from the dance floor. In this space of participation, the boundary between audience and actor is already blurred. My performance studies lens enables me to zoom in on what an actor does, and zoom out to explore its effects. Tensions are not smoothed out, but embodied in movement: tensions not only between constituents of lifeworlds, but between the real, imaginary, past, present, and future bodies of each participant. I have tried to keep these tensions in this book by letting people speak and move, and by saying, "This is what I saw happen in this space, in this moment," rather than stating that this is what happens in queer clubs everywhere, every time.

That I went to clubs in downtown Manhattan was not only determined by my access, but also because both historically and today, New York City is a crucible of queer lifeworlds, in which queerness, history, feminism, race, ethnicity, HIV/AIDS awareness, and capitalism are mixed. The dance floors of gay clubs in the city were also such crucibles. I was attracted to these spaces by the extraordinary energy and style of dancing I witnessed and experienced. The images of the improvising, dancing figure, enjoying the experience of power and creativity of his or her own body were affective, and the sensation of participation as pleasurable as it had always been for me. I stress not for the first or last time, that the only way to begin to get to grips with any physical practice is to do it. So I laced up my boots again and hit the dance floor. I immersed myself in a full and rich experience that engaged all my senses. I heard the sonic ebbs and flows created by the mixing, layering, and programming of music and sound samples over beats and felt the pull of the soundscape. I experienced the sight of other dancers and myself, often in a fragmentary and disorienting way as lights flashed and bodies moved in front of, behind, and around others within a mass of movement that made it difficult to isolate individuals. I felt the touch of my own body to the floor, to my own body, and to others'. I felt the impact of physical movement on my body, through my breathing and the sensations of heat, sweat, and exhaustion. The body was the prime reference point in these spaces: not only the bodies of others, but my own. My body provided constant feedback to judge spatial parameters, distance, and size. I perceived the position of body parts, and processed and stored information about laterality, gravity, verticality, balance, tensions, and dynamics, as well as integrating and coordinating rhythm, tempo, and sequences of movements. These sensations produced the body, rather than just the visual apparatus, as the location of experience and knowledge and the primary way knowledge was experienced and shared by participants and myself in the dance clubs. An ethnography that presents these experiences more faithfully reflects the realities of the field. I write what it felt like to be on a crowded dance floor and what it was like to "lose" myself in the flow of music and dance. I don't provide any conclusive analyses. But what I hope I do is offer a few snapshots of experience, as well as make the meaningfulness of these sensations vivid.

It would be naïve and disingenuous of me to suggest that my presence and actions did not affect the behavior of others in that space. I'm not invisible after all. Marking myself as an observer (an ethnographer rather than just another person watching the dance floor along with other participants) would have affected others' behavior. How would you dance if someone stood scrutinizing you and taking notes? I can only speculate how the effect of my presence might have been different in a male gay space in comparison with a lesbian space. However, in a few instances I was read in certain ways that affected people's behavior. As I stood on the bleachers at Twilo, a large gay club, to get a sense of the space and energy of the crowd, I was approached by a couple of people who asked if I was selling drugs. They intended—I suppose—to buy some from me. Another time, a clubber thought I was an undercover cop. Again in Twilo several men on different occasions either tried to cruise me or explain to me that they were not gay and had in fact not known this was a gay space. As a woman I suppose they felt I could bear convincing witness to their straightness. At the Body Positive T-Dance, a man wanted to dance with me. He explained that he was bisexual, that his wife and family had left him when he came out as bisexual and HIV-positive. He really wanted to dance with a woman again, not as a pick-up, but because, he explained gently, women knew how to follow in pairs dancing.

I did not sit at the side of the dance floor and take notes. I wanted to be immersed in the movement, rather than looking at a notepad, trying to think of the appropriate term. Field notes were written on my return home from the club or the next day. Therefore, in common with most ethnographers, my writing of the event is at a spatial and temporal distance from it. Throughout, I usually move fluidly from one site to another. This movement is part of a strategy of making connections between spaces that shifts the focus away from one practice and one space to clusters of practices and spaces. My approach emphasizes the use of these spaces, rather than their planning. People chose to go to one club rather than another and left one club at a certain time to go to another, knowing that each space was just one within a constellation of queer spaces. In a club itself, more than one thing happened. Human action and interaction shaped clubs, and participants shaped themselves by going to them.

It was outrageous even to think about writing this book without asking people what they thought they were doing in clubs. The meanings *they* made from these practices are more crucial than whatever meanings I impose with the theoretical tools in my standard issue doctoral utility belt. I carried out interviews in order to elicit the vocabulary that some clubgoers used to explain the significance of a club and their dance practices and experiences. I did not walk around the club looking for people to interview for several ethical reasons. A queer club is a "safe" space. How safe might someone consider it to be if approached by a stranger with a notepad or tape recorder? What's more, people go to clubs for pleasure. How much fun can you have when this fully equipped stranger keeps interrupting with a plethora of questions? And finally, the issue of consent gets murky. Participants may have taken alcohol or drugs, or may be in a particular affective state. I wanted all participants to give consent knowingly and with time to consider what they were being asked to do. After initially approaching people—usually through introduction outside of a club space by a person who played the role of point-of-entry—I

gave potential informants a cooling off period and answered any questions they had about what I was doing and why.[6] Within the club, I did
not want to mark myself as an outsider, which I felt walking around with
recording equipment would have done. Of course, it also would have
made it difficult to dance, separating me again into an observer rather
than a participant. Each interview lasted anywhere from forty-five minutes to three hours depending on how much the informant wanted to
say. I interviewed some informants more than once for the same reason,
based on their availability and willingness. I half-expected that my over-
tures to potential informants would be met with suspicion and demands
for justification. Instead, many warmly welcomed my interest.

While I cannot claim to have exorcised the ghosts of the ethnographic practice in which I have invested, I have attempted to draw attention to this project as a cultural representation. I do not pull myself out
of the picture. You already know that improvised dancing in queer clubs
was a way I made meaning and value in my own life. You'll soon encounter the informants, some of whom have become friends. We went to
clubs together and spoke about our experiences with each other. These
bonds are implicit in my very style of writing. I wanted to let them speak.
In interviewing, I rarely walked in with a set of questions I wanted answered. I usually started by asking participants to tell me a story and then
let them speak with little interruption. Then I would pursue some issues
and expressions that they raised, trying not to impose a pre-set agenda.
These experiences and the ways they were retold are the building blocks
of this book. Perhaps, on reading, you will see omissions, assumptions,
or strange elisions. Perhaps this disjunctive account comes closer to the
reality of these complex spaces and practices.

The narrative logic of the chapters takes readers on a journey from
the streets of New York City, into the dance clubs themselves, and the
practices within, before it pops out in the two final chapters to explore
particular themes and sites. In Chapter One, I develop the definition
and use of queer lifeworlds and discuss their constitution as ways of con-
textualizing the relationship of the quotidian to improvised social dancing in queer clubs. I explore how the embodiment and performance of
memory through storytelling contributed to the creation of queer lifeworlds. The juxtaposition of informants' stories and cognitive maps
against official histories of gays in New York City offers a compelling
framework of interpretation on the relations between the body, the city,
and memory that constantly create and recreate queer lifeworlds. In
Chapter Two I explore the currencies of fabulousness and fierceness

valued in clubs. The narrative moves from preparation for a night out to getting there to getting in and moving through the space. How was the space claimed and used? In Chapter Three, I enter the soundscape on the dance floor. How did dancers and DJs collaborate and with what effects? In Chapter Four, I explore the complex, sometimes contradictory texture of desire and reality-making that emerged from the stories of informants and their relationships—imagined and realized—with others in the club. What were the relationships between individual self-fashioning and notions of community and political agency through the relationships between bodies as they danced? How does meaning in and of a queer lifeworld get constructed not only by the individual dancing, but also by bodies dancing together? In what complex ways might participants be choreographing politics? In Chapter Five, I focus more specifically on bodies negotiating desire through exploring the role and influences of go-go dancers and strippers, common in many queer dance clubs I visited. As well as exploring dancers' interactions with each other, I also investigate the relationship of each participant's own body and the body she or he sought to achieve or fashion utopically through its transcendence. Next, in Chapter Six, I dig deeper into why, when clubs bring in so much capital—financial and cultural—to New York City, they were being cracked down on. I do this by looking at how these practices fitted into the "quality of life" agenda of the New York City mayor's office, which criminalized some activities and groups. How did the new defiantly queer and nonmainstream spaces respond to this and how might they also have been responding to the history of clubs in New York City and to dominant gay culture? Was it possible for new alliances to be formed, or were class and race distinctions, for instance, simply reproduced in seemingly utopian spaces? Were these spaces cultural laboratories and what might participants have been rehearsing? Finally, in Chapter Seven, I focus on the Body Positive T-Dance, a now defunct event that was unique in its time for being the only dance event for HIV-positive gay men and their friends. What were the problems of imagining an "HIV community"? How were memories of times and people passed on sedimented in the bodies of participants and performed in improvised social dancing? I explore the needs of people to dance in this space as part of a process of accepting themselves, releasing stress, healing, reclaiming their bodies from medical practice and knowledge, expressing sexual desire, sharing experience, and keeping the future open. Could participants transcend and transform their consciousnesses through the experience of dance?

In a way, this project is a dance floor. People enter and, drawing on their experiences, memories, hopes, and desires, move across these pages in unique ways. Their moves interact with the moves of others. There are similarities and differences, juxtapositions, counterpoints, polyrhythms. There is self-fashioning, queer world-making. This does not only apply to content, but to form. A space was opened, "Tell me a story . . . ," and they started with their cognitive maps of the city, and so does this project. They told me how they got ready to go clubbing, how they met friends and traveled there, how they felt when they saw the line, how they got in, and so does this project. They told me how they met people, what they did, what they thought, and why any of this mattered to any of them. They told me what pissed them off. They told me how they made pleasure. They told me how politics shaped the spaces and practices within clubs and how these in turn shaped their politics. They told me about people who were no longer around, but who were remembered on the dance floor through movement. They performed their knowledge and their memories. And this project is a dancer. Even now it's checking out the floor, getting a sense of the environment into which it has entered, looking for a rhythm to ride. It's looking for pleasure; it has fashioned itself; it has learned the rules, and wants to use them to find a space in which to offer an intervention on the crowded dance floor. It incorporates the moves of its peers and adapts them, spinning out a few moves of its own. It wants to go home having done its damndest to be fabulous.

Finally, why study improvised social dancing? I want you to recognize its importance, but this does not mean that I see it as a utopian achievement. Although participants criticized these spaces and practices, I do not think that they render them any less important. I'm not sure how I first learned to dance, but I explore what I learned by doing it. The impossibility of fixing improvised social dancing is its power as queer world-making in its production of multiple, fluid possibilities.

I like being a part of the early Sunday morning gang walking home after a night dancing. I pay more attention to people on the street than I would if I had just got up. Who are these good folk coming out of stores with a pack of smokes and the paper, waiting for the walk light? Where are they coming from and where are they going to? A friend once told me that most people in New York are from somewhere else; some coming to find their feet; some, like him, queers from Middle America who came to live where they could be themselves and with others, and who we leave like dancers at the end of the night with a kiss goodbye and a promise to call.

I get home and rummage around in piles of accumulated junk to grab a clean towel. How much crap can one person accumulate in five years in New York City? There are a lot of boots; some with worn holes where once deep textured rubber had been; some with dark slits where the leather has separated from the sole. I keep promising myself to have a good clean out one day. But not today. Today I need to sleep. I kick off my boots, fling them on top of the pile and fall into bed, with the shadows of people going to work outside my window flickering across the insides of my eyelids.

《《 1

THE THEATER OF QUEER WORLD-MAKING

I'll never forget that first sight of the city from the bus. I was thrilled and appalled at myself. "Oh, fuck . . . what have I done. I don't know anybody. How am I going to figure all this strangeness out?" But I was excited, after everything I was leaving behind. And this was New York City—the promised land. I remember the bus went into the Midtown Tunnel and everything was dark. Then we were through and this was it, all around me. I craned my neck to see round each corner, and each turn was a new adventure, each street a mystery to unravel. What would be my favorite places, where would I go, which streets would become my streets? Could I see them from the bus? Could I make a home here? Would I be happy? And it scared the shit out of me and it was exactly where I wanted to be.

(Catherine, age 26)

《《 EVERYBODY IN NEW YORK seems to come from somewhere else. It gives the city its energy and a living library of stories. Roberto "Tito" Mesa came to New York City in the early 1970s from his native Argentina, where he was persecuted for being gay. Now in his fifties, he is a talking and dancing book of gay club history in the city. Soon after his arrival, he immersed himself in the gay scene from the drug-fueled hedonism of the Saint dance club in the East Village and the city's gay sex clubs such as the Mineshaft in the west to the celebration of survival and memorial of the Body Positive T-Dance for HIV-positive gay men. I interviewed him several times in 1997 and 1998. His physicality was a striking feature of our conversations. In our first interview, I asked him to describe some of the changes he had witnessed in the city since arriving. He jumped up from his chair and scampered to the middle of the room where there was more space. Fired up with the anticipation of his performance and my audience, he continued his story in his thick Argentinian accent, dramatizing his narrative with both vocalized and physicalized tone, stresses, and pauses, as he built toward its climax:

> Chelsea was not always like it is today, oh no. Today it's the gay area, but this is recent. It used to be a Latino area. No English spoken. To get to the leather bars on the West Side, you had to walk through Chelsea. And that was no fucking picnic. You would try to disguise you were gay. If you had a leather cap, you tucked it into your jacket [he mimes]. You took chains off your shoulders—'cos that was a sign. You just zipped up your leather jacket and hoped nobody bothered you. One time, these boys came after me. I just ran. They laughed 'cos they thought I was running away. [He enters into the moment and mimes his actions.] I go to the nearest trash can, find a bottle, smash it, turn, and I'm standing there, threatening them to try to hurt me, "'Cos I will fucking cut you." [He pauses and breaks the moment, returning to the moment of retelling the story.] And they are so surprised. I don't think they ever expected a faggot to turn and say—like Joan Crawford said to the board of Coca-Cola company—"don't fuck with me boys." They backed off. [He pauses.] I was so scared. When I got up to the bar [he "arrives" at the bar, still holding the memory of the bottle in his shaking hand], I'm shaking and holding this bottle. The bar man, he takes one look at me and says, "Rough journey, eh?"

Tito's performance gathers together many of the threads of this chapter. In performing this memory, he restored a moment that evoked the tensions between changing social conditions and a marginalized sexuality. This chapter begins to trace some ways in which performances such as his cloaking of the signs of his gayness on the street, his performance of aggression when challenged, and the performance of his restored experience in the retelling of his story mapped the space of New York City as a personal cognitive map. This cognitive map was retained, interpreted, and retold through the body in an intersection between memory, play, embodiment, and the quotidian, which, if it was worked cautiously on the streets in light of the possible dangers, released its potential on the dance floors.

Tito's performance in his apartment in the moment of retelling indicated some important features of embodied memory. His performance in the moment of retelling fluidly embodied two "presents." The "I" acting out the story on a January evening in 1998, and the "I" trying to escape his pursuers on a street in Chelsea in the early 1980s were present in the same body. The present and the remembered body were one and the same. In the same moment of performance Tito embodied physical memories and through that embodiment interpreted the past through the present body, and interpreted and experienced the present in what I call the *theater of memory*. In such a theater of memory, the past was restored and reinterpreted through movement in two ways. First, in the performance between performer and audience—in this case, informant and ethnographer—in which the performer restored a prior experience using the theatrical conventions of space, by using choreographic elements such as directions or floor patterning, levels, shape, and focus, as well as characterization of self and others, and the dramatic and choreographic conventions of dynamic high and low points, stillness and activity. Tito's use of theatrical conventions indicated a consciousness of performance. The body itself was a theater of memory. Second, in the everyday theater of memory on the streets and in dance clubs, memories of past experiences shaped both the individual and the group's movements, and their performance materialized queer lifeworlds. Both these theaters of memory materialized a sense of self to which queerness was central. The theaters of memory performed by participants connected them to the past, to spaces, and to other people. They were a vital way to materialize lifeworlds as heteronormativity dictates public culture in other ways.

In focusing on how both topographical and psychological space changes over time to make meaning in a queer lifeworld, I am influenced by the argument of social geographer Edward Soja that the materialization of lifeworlds not only be studied historically, but also in "a triple dialectic of space, time, and social being," which "re-entwines the making of history with the social production of space" (Soja 1989, 12). This space of queer lifeworlds is produced through movement—walking, stopping, turning, and crossing—and is produced socially through the relationships between bodies expressed through movement—closeness, distance, movement toward and away, and focus directed onto another and avoided. I hope that this focus on movement will reveal the agency of sometimes compatible and sometimes contesting forces to form lifeworlds, to undermine them, and to re-form them. In so doing, I aim to show how the tensions produced between the elements of space, time, and social being may be a part of the engine that gives queer lifeworlds their force and fluidity—in short, their movement. The movements both on and off the dance floor that constituted queer worldmaking were indicative of these tensions. In addition to the fact that people moved through a city, this chapter looks at some of the ways in which people moved in the city and how individuals and groups used these ways of moving to negotiate space, time, and social being to produce queer lifeworlds.

The ways informants performed their memories located them both in the theater of ethnography and in the theater of the everyday that contingently constituted and responded to queer lifeworlds. Through these performances, I assert that a queer lifeworld is not a superorganic form. It is not a given, but rather, queer world-making is a conscious, active way of fashioning the self and the environment, cognitively and physically, through embodied social practices moving through and clustered in the city. In the matrices of the tensions, opposition, unity, excitations, and contradictions throughout New York City, inhabitants of changing historical and spatial conditions used strategies and tactics of performance to construct affirming environments of existence.[1] The tactics of queer world-making may resist what Michael Warner (1993, xiii) terms "heteronormativity." Simultaneously, strategies of queer world-making produced spaces where people could exist as queer and make pleasure. The city, neighborhoods, and dance clubs were host spaces for queer recreational lifeworlds in which queer subjectivities and intersubjectivities were made possible. In order to explicate how these lifeworlds were produced, I focus on the role theaters of memory played in their materialization over time and space.

As a theoretical introduction to his work on national memory, Pierre Nora draws a useful distinction between "real memory—social and unviolated," and "history," "which is how our hopelessly forgetful modern societies, propelled by change, organize the past":

> History [. . .] is the reconstruction, always problematic and incomplete, of what is no longer. Memory is a perpetually actual phenomenon, a bond tying us to the eternal present: history is a representation of the past. Memory, insofar as it is affective and magical, only accommodates those facts that suit it; it nourishes recollections that may be out of focus or telescopic, global or detached, particular or symbolic. [. . .] Memory is by nature multiple and yet specific; collective, plural, and yet individual. History, on the other hand, belongs to everyone and to no one. [. . .] Memory takes root in the concrete, in spaces, gestures, images, and objects; history binds itself strictly to temporal continuities, to progressions and to relations between things. Memory is absolute, while history can only conceive the relative. (Nora 1989, 8–9)

The disparity between history, as it is discursively inscribed, and memory, as the bodies that bear the consequences both of its inscription and its remembrance embody and perform it, has tremendous implications for the cognitive and physical construction of queer lifeworlds. The inscription of gay and lesbian history in New York City, which reifies the Stonewall riots of 1969 as the defining myth of origin and the paradigm of gay activism, models this history as only visible or political in opposition to dominant social forces. This inscription depends upon the forgetting, displacement, and erasure of the diverse experiences that constitute queer lifeworlds in the city. The history of queer culture in the city becomes fixed before and after a mythic point of origin that pivots on the riot's status as documented historical fact. As images and interpretations of the past commonly legitimate a present social order, what disparities might there be in the social orders legitimated by the official history of Stonewall in comparison with the unofficial memories of queer experience performed in narrative and movement?

Nora draws a distinction between "places of memory," the artificial sites of the modern production of national and ethnic memory, and "environments of memory," the mostly oral and embodied retentions of cultures (Nora 1989, 12–13). These retentions are not fixed and static, but dynamic and responsive to the changing demands of the present to reinterpret and restore the past through acts and performances. I would like to be more specific about these environments. They are theaters of memory in which the past is performed—reinterpreted and restored through being retold by narrative and by movement. Through the production of environments of memory queer lifeworlds are produced. Environments of memory have been replaced by places of memory, such as archives and monuments, as Nora evocatively states: "moments of history torn away from the movement of history, then returned; no longer quite life, not yet death, like shells on the shore when the sea of living memory has receded" (Nora 1989, 12). The historical moment of Stonewall is recorded in—among other places—the New York Gay and Lesbian History Archive (where, at the time of writing, there was no archive of queer club experience) and in a plaque in Sheridan Square in the West Village where the riots took place. The plaque is an example of a place of memory, in comparison with a dance club, which, I assert, is a theatrical environment of memory, as are the practices of improvised social dancing, which embody its movement. The first consequence of the establishment and reification of these places of memory is a forgetting of the "affective and magical" practices that construct lifeworlds, in favor of a history in which gay presence only publicly performs itself in opposition to oppression. The second consequence of the displacement of environments of memory by places of memory is that these places enter into a capitalist exchange economy as commodities. The souvenirs of Stonewall that include rainbow badges and T-shirts are also places of memory. These commodities of memory are mass-produced rather than experienced, and are marketed to be purchased and worn by a niche market rather than embodied by individuals and groups.

How did embodied environments and movements of memory persist in the face of official gay history and the market that regulated, distributed, and valued it? Embodied memory remained variously resistant to forgetting and commodification through the transmission of gestures and habits in both narrated experience and in movement to and within queer spaces in the city, including dance clubs. Both these modes resisted reproduction and repetition not only by virtue of being live performance and therefore unrepeatable, but also because they both relied on improvisation. In improvisation, the performer him or herself had agency to play with the story or movement repertoire. In the performance of memory, these storytellers participated in acts of "queer archaeology." Akin to what Foucault (1977) called "a history of the present," queer archaeology is an excavation through layers of past experience to account for the present, which is useful for conceiving alternatives to our present condition. This archaeology applies to the construction of the body, as Foucault suggests, and also to bodies, "to the reciprocal reflections they make on one another's surfaces as they foreground their capacities for interaction" (Roach 1996, 25). However, by understanding storytelling and movement in the theater of ethnography and the theater of everyday life as performances, the source of affective power on performer and audience lay not in the content of queer archaeologies, but in the retelling. The urgency and pleasure of acts of retelling and of the experiences themselves manifested themselves as they are retold. Their affect and their magic were inherent in their manifestation as performance.

To render some particulars of embodied theaters of memory visible, I asked some informants to remember how they moved around New York City when they first wanted to find and create queer lifeworlds. Where did they go and how did they meet others like themselves? What happened at these places? How did they constitute queer cognitive maps of the city? Informants drew maps of the city, labeling and describing the sites they frequented when they first arrived or started going out into queer life in the city, including dance clubs. No one drew his or her map in silence. Informants told their stories narratively, physically, and figuratively on the paper. The stories recounted in this chapter sprung from these acts of map-making; the maps themselves are the traces of these experiences. I asked them to compare the maps they drew with contemporary sites and experiences. I chose these performances of history- and space-making to analyze what queer lifeworlds might be and how they might be constituted and valued through the interplay of the quotidian, play, and theater.

In asking informants to draw cognitive maps of the city, I aimed to discover some of the ways in which a knowledge of the city incorporated dialectical relationships in the body between history, memory, and space. I gave several informants a piece of paper with a rough, hand-drawn outline of Manhattan, asking them to mark the places they went when they first got to the city in order to find other queers and their movements or routes between them. Each map illustrated a rich memory-mapping. When he first came to New York City, Tito lived on the Upper West Side. He first discovered a gay lifeworld in public spaces such as Central Park, where he lost his virginity. Public places were coopted for sexual activity, the landscape was taken advantage of, and long grass afforded some privacy: "In the West Side park, you'd walk down by the wall, in the long grass and everyone was sunbathing nude and fucking" (Tito). Paradoxically, at other times, an open landscape offered safety:

> TITO: I'd go to the Central Park and cruise and pick someone up. Then you'd go right in the center of the meadow . . . you know, the open area, and fuck all night. And it was safe because you were out in the open and could see if anyone's coming from a long way off. No one could sneak up on you.
>
> FB: Who might sneak up on you?
>
> T: You name it, undercover cops, muggers, fag-bashers. You got some privacy in the open.

In interviews with informants, memory always unfolded in relation to sites in the city and to other people. Influential historian of sociology and cultural memory Maurice Halbwachs (1925; 1992) suggests that groups provide individuals with frameworks within which their memories are localized, including the spaces and activities shared by that group. He claims that memory is essentially social: "a man who remembers alone what others do not remember resembles somebody who sees what others do not see. It is as if he suffers from hallucinations" (1992,

167). That these spaces and their use were real—as Tito said, "that they existed"—was confirmed in the maps drawn by others. Collective memory—not just sites and people, but common experiences—materialized collective reality and constituted queer lifeworlds, suggesting the constructive power of pleasure to transform the grid of New York City into personal and communal theaters of memory.

Tito's map did not assume a God's-eye view above the city, flattening out the spaces from one perspective of use as is the norm with official maps, such as printed gay maps of Chelsea. He attached emotional and political meanings in layers of different thicknesses on his map. Parts of the city split open and profiles popped out. For instance, on the right-hand side of the page, he drew a streetscape of the West Side piers. The old City Council salt depot explodes out of his map. It was there that men would go to have sex in valleys of rock salt used for de-icing the streets in winter. Its prominence on the map reflected its importance to Tito. He underscored it symbolically: a big cross through the depot signified the fence that men would climb to enter it, but also its removal from the contemporary physical landscape, if not the cognitive one. The Chelsea Piers leisure complex now stands where it once was. He also marked where the dance club 12 West once stood, and below that, sketched a map of its interior. His perspective opened up interiors and revealed practices inside. So some spaces were co-opted and some not. Tito included them on his map because he used them. The city was a host space, rather than an accumulation of property, and claims of ownership were based on use, rather than capital.

Alex's cognitive map contrasted with Tito's both in content and presentation. Rather than exploding out beyond the bounds of the outline of Manhattan, his map was contained. He marked mainly downtown queer club spaces such as Boy Bar (St. Marks between Second and Third Avenue) and Pyramid (Avenue A between Sixth and Seventh Streets). He also outlined important streets as both connecting thoroughfares and as important places to meet others—for example, the avenues of Alphabet City in the East Village and Fourteenth and Thirteenth Streets. He made connections between these spaces and *queerness* in contrast to *gayness,* which he identified with the spaces of Chelsea and the West Village. Much of this was an identification with particular types of music, namely, alternative and punk. In making pleasure for himself, Alex had to find places where he could meet people who were into the same things that meant so much to him. This was a process of selection, of focusing on to the desired scene and contacts.

As he drew, he described his personal journey from his childhood in California and New Jersey to Manhattan, and from scene-setting downtown nightclubs such as Danceteria and Area to contemporary queer spaces such as Squeezebox, which he was instrumental in setting up and operating. By the time Alex came to the East Coast from California with his family, he already knew he was gay. New York City had a certain pull for him. His theater of memory blended the fantasy of a boy on the brink of owning his queer adulthood with the representation of glamour that was New York City in the late 1970s. He desired to be a part of something he could not name as a teenager, but was something other than the life he knew in suburban New Jersey.

> ALEX: At that time Studio 54 was about to happen, so there was all this press on the east coast about Studio 54 and that was in the news big time, and *Saturday Night Live* was starting to be on TV and that was in New York, and so there was all this pop entertainment press about NY and it was a very happening sort of thing. You know, there's this kid living in Jersey interested in celebrity and interested in music and rock 'n' roll and the punk thing was happening and Patti Smith and the Ramones, and I can go to a certain point in my town and see the top of the Empire State building. And me and my friend John would go to a certain hill and on a clear day, we could see Manhattan. Or it least the top of the Empire State building. On a really clear day. We'd say, "Oh, let's go to the top of the hill," and we'd go.
>
> FB: And what would you talk about?
>
> A: We'd just kind of sigh, and "Oh, we can really see the Empire State building, wow, it's not that far away, it's just a bus ride away." But there it was, this little bit of an icon, off in the distance, it was, "Oh we really want to go there."

He both vibrantly imagined the city from the outside and appreciated its real capacity to supply him with what he could not obtain in his own Jersey neighborhood. This story also demonstrated how Alex actively used mass and underground music media to construct a place in which he desired to be—a psychogeography of fantasy and desire. He imagined himself in the spaces he read about and fantasized about meeting other queers in them. He fantasized the memories he wanted.

From his first family visit to Times Square, he sensed the city had something to offer him and used theatrical conventions of memory to perform the drama of this realization. He seamlessly ventriloquized his father's attempts to perform authority over a space in which he had little. He switched from the present moment of narration to the past moment of experience, restaging and reexperiencing it in the present tense, and he commented upon his frame of reference:

> I don't think I was that conscious then. I'm able to say all these things with hindsight. But at that time I started buying the *Village Voice* in my town. And I started finding things out about the city, and what goes on there and reading the *New York Times* and this whole other world opened up. Here's this secondary socialization thing happening. All of a sudden I can have some of this, and I can get some of these things from here—something I want, and maybe we walked past a gay porno house, maybe we walked past the Gaiety [a gay male burlesque venue]. Maybe I saw those things and I didn't really recognize them but I saw them.

He was attracted by the danger of this world to the safety of his family unit. He performed the drama of his father anxiously pulling his wife and children close to him to protect them against perceived dangers— the very people and places that attracted young Alex. He imagined that this was the place in which a queer lifeworld existed and in which he could use the sleazy elements of the city—the elements that repulsed his family—to construct a queer lifeworld for himself. His eventual move to the city was a way he could break away from his family and establish his difference from them. After a few years in the club scene in New York, he worked on building up Squeezebox as a place of queer sleaze and punk to create a space for himself based on his memories of defunct clubs such as Danceteria and on his fantasies of what a club should be, which other queers incorporated into their lifeworlds.

Tito's and Alex's maps were not reproducible; they resisted commodification, and yet had currency in queer lifeworlds based on socially shared theaters of memory that contextualized the movement on the dance floor. These theaters of memory staged in and by the body as it moved across the urban space offered a compelling framework of interpretation on the relations between space, memory, and the body in the city and in the club. They were more than just the context for social improvised dancing in a queer nightclub. They were the source materials of this movement. The dance floor was a hot space onto which cultural meanings and values informed by everyday urban experiences were poured and worked into creative and expressive form and then turned back out onto the street. It too was a place of storytelling.

Literary critic and philosopher Walter Benjamin draws a useful comparison between "information-giving" and "storytelling" that clarifies the value of understanding informants' performances as storytelling and sheds light on what is at stake:

> The value of information does not survive the moment in which it was new. It lives only at that moment; it has to surrender to it completely and explain itself to it without losing any time. A story is different. It does not expend itself. It preserves and concentrates its strength and is capable of releasing it even after a long time (Benjamin 1968, 90).

The meanings of the memories of informants were not given "data" I must uncover; rather, they were socially constituted and hence contestable representations of history produced by a dialogue of performance, in which the storyteller was the active producer of meaning, rather than the object of the projected meanings of the researcher. The power all these stories held for informants—even after years had passed—was performed in their reliving and reembodying of the experience. As Tito retold, "I go to the nearest trash can, find a bottle, smash it, turn, and I'm standing there, threatening them to try to hurt me." He collapsed the time in between the moment of experiencing and the moment of retelling. He was both director and actor, simultaneously choreographing and performing gestures of frozen shock for maximum effect on me—his audience. At the moment of the experience, he also performed for his assailants/audience, risking his safety on the ability of his performance to convince them that he would carry out his threat of violence. In front of me, he exaggerated his gesture, fully cognizant of his own performance. He twisted his body, mimed grabbing the bottle, smashed it against the breakfast bar at which we sat, and thrust it at me as if I was his assailant, crying, "I will fucking cut you!" In returning again to the moment, and using the center space of the room as his performance area, and the conventions of exaggeration and stylization, Tito was both inside and outside it, simultaneously performing and interpreting it for me. He tucked his leather cap into his jacket as he told me what he did; he grabbed the bottle and smashed it with tension in his wrist and arm; he turned to me. His body reentered the long-past moment. This was also performed in his language. The storyteller entered into the present tense grammatically at the same moments that his body did physically: "They are so surprised." His story released its strength even after a long time. Through paying attention to the performance of that story, an audience—myself and now you—can understand the quality of these interviews as performed stories, rather than as information bulletins.

Tito aimed to produce the effect of deterring his attackers by producing a drama that he hoped would afford him safe passage to his destination. By displaying a conventional gesture of aggression, he created a space for this performance. His assailants were both audience and co-performers. His performance was for their benefit, and yet their role was active: they provoked it and could have changed the outcome. If these everyday experiences and their performance in theaters of memory were to contribute to the constitution of queer lifeworlds, then they could not be understood as mundane by their participants. The everyday must somehow be transformed into performance in the consciousness of the participant, so that it holds vital meaning. In performing this drama for me in the form of a memory, the storyteller restaged the drama. He transformed the everyday again. The theater of memory represents experience and presents us with the conventionalities by which the representation can be interpreted. These conventionalities of memory theater revealed the conventionalities of queer lifeworlds. A queer lifeworld was theater. Its construction relied upon the transformation of the everyday into theatrical acts to produce effects on others and to create a space for performance through movements and gestures recognized by participants and audience as performance. This transformation was achieved by a self-fashioning and self-awareness that constituted performance consciousness.

The theaters of memory constructed by participants in retelling stories verbally and physically used memories of embodied experience—of being and moving—as material. They were long, as in a story, or short, as in a gesture. These strips of restored behavior were the main characteristic of these performances. Performance theorist Richard Schechner characterizes performance as meaning "never for the first time. It means for the second to the nth time. Performance is 'twice-behaved behavior'" (Schechner 1985, 36). But why repeat and restage an experience? How might this "twice-behaved behavior" contribute to queer world-making? In performance, the project-to-be governs what is selected and invented from the past: the future determines the past, and the remembered determines the imagined. Making history involves less doing something than doing something with what is done. In constructing environments of memory as queer lifeworlds through restoring behavior, rather than fixing a plaque to a wall, storytellers/dancers preserved what Schechner calls a "varied culture pool" as a strategy that "fits into, and yet opposes, world monoculture" (Schechner 1985, 114). The performances that created and expressed queer lifeworlds strategically constructed them as theater and as acts of storytelling and dancing. They also established the performance of queerness as theatrical acts in the quotidian.

To summarize, storytellers constituted queer lifeworlds in several ways. First, they retold and released the power of events and experiences years after they occurred. In addition, through acts of poesis in which the everyday harbors transformative and creative acts, and through producing dramas, these properties of storytelling—whether narrated verbally or performed physically—were integral to the historical materialization of queer lifeworlds. The theatricality and transformative potential of these experiences had agency to construct self-knowledge years after the events. These memories even had agency to produce theater and transformation through the act of remembering and reenacting years later. Their performance embodied, by repeating and restaging, knowledge and values that constructed queer lifeworlds.

To implicate space into this dialectic, I want to throw some storytellers' theaters of memory against other gay maps of the city. Informants deliberately constituted queer lifeworlds that overlaid, complemented, and contradicted the official maps and articulated a psychogeography of queerness situated in other places with different routes between them. Notions of queerness were predicated on difference from not only hetero-, but also homonormativity.[2] Each year in major cities in North America, the Gay Pride parade commemorates the historical moment in 1969 when a police raid on the Stonewall bar resulted in rioting by gays in the West Village. The route of the parade in New York City proceeds down the main thoroughfare of Fifth Avenue in the brilliant light of a summer's day. For a few hours, it appears to queer the preeminent avenue of consumption of the Western world. In its turn at Washington Square into the West Village, it legitimizes that neighborhood's status as a place of gay consumption: of bodies, signs (for instance, assorted rainbow paraphernalia), and souvenirs. At the time of writing, the parade ends at the far west side of the West Village near the Hudson River. Parade marshals direct participants away from the piers that have been a center of gay erotic life for decades, and that were subject to redevelopment into a more "family-oriented" site during the period of researching and writing this book. Redevelopment plans included a park complete with shops, leisure facilities, and a curfew to deter youth from hanging out—most particularly queer youth of color who were among the areas' users. This redevelopment valued some leisure activities rather than others, imagining a "good" consumer as citizen and a U.S. public made up of heterosexual nuclear families lining up from coast to coast with their disposable incomes, ready to come and spend them in the Big Apple. This reimagining and redevelopment of queer sites into "family" environments was a prevalent trend in the city during the 1990s, encouraged by the collaboration of the local administration and big business.[3] The parade route does not take in these sites. It moves down Fifth Avenue, into the village, past the site of the riot, and down Christopher Street with its gay-oriented businesses. The direction of the parade down Fifth Avenue into the West Village performs a dominant linear history from public space to the gay ghetto. The direction of the parade funnels queers from mainstream (Main Street) America into the gay ghetto, where they can be identified and contained. The official history of Stonewall and of the parade that commemorates it is rooted in identity politics, which, as Lisa Duggan suggests, "only replaces closets with ghettoes" (Duggan 1994, 5). She calls for the deghettoization of sexual identity in her influential essay "Queering the State," an argument that is cited by the New York-based activist group Sex Panic! as a strategy for destabilizing hetero- and homonormativity and preserving a varied and vital public sex culture (Duggan 1994, 6).

The theaters of memory performed by the storytellers in their cognitive maps and the stories producing them queered this official history. They produced lifeworlds whose politics were not dependent on unitary sexual identity or on a community of sameness. The production of these lifeworlds did not create a bounded, fixed history that could be expressed as performance in a parade, but rather they produced a dialectic of experience, time, and self-knowledge that expressed tensions, excitations, and contestations fluidly and contingently, more like improvised social dancing on the dance floor, perhaps. Both theaters of memory and drawn cognitive maps of these lifeworlds suggested other nodes, routes, bridges, and layers, which created multiple fragmented, layered, compatible, and contesting maps. Their fragments were the material from which Benjamin felt alternative histories could be forged: random historical objects from the past such as the debris to be found in flea markets or discrete historical events that must be allowed to violently collide with others, so that the present may achieve insight and critical awareness into what had once been (Jennings 1987). The dialectic of such memories did not produce a smooth, all encompassing master narrative from the closet to the ghetto to street parade any more than it produced a unitary identity, and a single homogenous community. It evoked diversity and tension. The archaeologies that these theaters of memory produced did not operate on the high "event" status. Rather, they indicated that queer world-making happened at the level of the quotidian: the walk through the city, rather than the riot in the square. The critique of everyday life discards canonical events and individuals and resists reestablishing its scenario within an interpretive frame of "institutional codes and systems or to the private perceptions of a monadic subject" (Kaplan and Ross 1987, 3). To understand Tito's story of an encounter with would-be assailants, I need to map a complex realm of social practice, not a network of streets, or even an historical moment, but a "conjunction of habit, desire, and accident" (Kaplan and Ross 1987, 3). Walking to the leather bars was a habitual practice that interacted with other habitual practices to constitute Chelsea as a gay neighborhood over time. But, at the same time, the fact that gay men were able to move into the neighborhood was also due to the largely successful efforts of landlords to displace Latino families in order to break up family apartments into smaller units and rent them out at a massively increased rate.

If the parade reifies and produces a master narrative of gay progress, then other official gay maps of New York City assumed an audience of a unitary identity and a homogenous community for the purpose of marketing products and sites to a desirable demographic. A full-color gatefold map I picked up during Gay Pride week in 1997, paid for by advertisements aimed toward a primarily gay male audience, imagined audiences distinguished by disposable income: the so-called PINK economy (Professional Income, No Kids). This disposable income is spent in leisure: eating out and vacationing. The sites marked on these maps include restaurants, adult entertainment and video, art galleries and antiques, body piercing, bookstores, clothing, erotica, gifts and cards, gyms, hair stylists, health clubs and saunas, jewelry and leather goods stores, lodgings, pharmacies, publications, boutiques for the urban gay man, tanning salons, theater, and travel services. By assuming an audience of a certain demographic profile, and with particular interests, these maps perform the erasure of other constituencies, namely those who cannot afford or do not want these products and services.

These maps erase the histories of tension in these sites. A disclaimer announces: "A listing or ad in this guide should not be construed as a statement of the sexual orientation of the ownership, management, or staff of the businesses included; only that they welcome lesbian and gay customers." Many gay businesses are not gay-owned. Jermaine, a 35-year-old African-American informant who has lived in the New York City boroughs of Queens and Brooklyn for his adult life and who has frequently traveled into Manhattan for recreation over the last twenty years, described what he perceived as a straight land grab in which gay-owned businesses ceded to straights, especially in the event of AIDS deaths. He cited the Saint Mark's Baths, owned and operated by Bruce Mailman, a gay man running gay businesses, including the Saint dance club,[4] which was closed down under local health ordinances during the city's AIDS panic. It is now a video and music store. Jermaine sighed as we walked down Second Avenue together and recalled another story about the owners of one of his favorite haunts of the 1980s, the Second Avenue Sauna:

> One found that the other was cheating on him with someone, and killed him. I don't know what happened to him, I guess he went to jail, but then the place was closed and bought by straights. It's a Chinese restaurant now.

If this story is not typical in detail and not necessarily accurate, Jermaine told it because for him, the results of a closure of a gay-owned business were typical. The retelling of the story constructed meaning. In the theater of memory, he did not reproduce a fact, but re-dressed it and presented it in the conventionalities by which he wanted to understand it—as a melodrama that resulted in the loss of a site of queer pleasure. I suggest that the importance of this story is not that it was fact, but that it was told to construct a meaning of a queer lifeworld. For Jermaine, this story articulated that gay ownership of businesses is contingent. This story contributes to a cognitive map of the city in which queer lifeworlds are always so.

As this story demonstrates, sites that once were queer spaces, such as the salt depot and now defunct clubs, were not redundant and had great world-making value to storytellers. They were still included in their theaters of memory and still exerted profound force in constructing queer lifeworlds. These memories were full with the presence of absences, which in itself made meaning, because they were deeply missed. Alex looked wistfully at the map he had drawn "Nearly all these places aren't around anymore," he said. He was referring to clubs he would go to when he first came to the city in 1983, as an excited queer teenager living in New Jersey attracted by the glamour and sleaze of New York. Tito explained the importance of remembering these long defunct clubs.

> TITO: We know that this is true, we lived it, and we were part of it. But this epidemic is taking everything away. I see kids, twenty-five years old, and they say, "What's the Saint?" And it's like someone doesn't know who

George Washington is. This existed, at one time, this existed. I was part of
that. Maybe you're here today because I was there then. You are what you
are today because of all that we went through.

The epidemic of which he speaks is AIDS. But it is also an epidemic of
amnesia as people die, deny, or forget. The Saint dance club was an important landmark in a cultural inheritance that all queers should know,
according to the storyteller. A queer archaeology—that "history of the
present"—was a vital part of queer education and socialization for Tito.
The drawing of these maps was thus an act of political activism.

Our past is an important source of our own conception of ourselves.
Our self-knowledge and our conception of our own character and po-
tentialities are to a large extent determined by the way in which we view
our own past actions. A walk through the environments in which individuals shared experiences with others that helped define themselves as
queer reactivated self-knowledge: the walker knew himself or herself
again. Memory affirmed self-knowledge, tied, as Nora and Halbwachs
claim, to environments and to others. Indeed, memory is an experience
in and of itself as well as a way of reexperiencing. The relationship
between the past experience and the present was implicit in the interviews. Each interview performance enacted a doubling: the I who remembered and the I who experienced. Individuals brought these modes
of being, of bearing oneself through the world to the dance floor. In this
place, they recalled and retold their knowledge of bearing themselves
with other queers in this moment and in previous times.

Most studies of memory as a cultural faculty focus on written or inscribed transmissions of memories. In his innovative book, *How Societies
Remember,* Paul Connerton (1989) concentrates on embodied practices,
and argues that images of the past and recollected knowledge of the past
are conveyed and sustained by ritual performances. We frequently do
not recall how or when or where we have acquired this knowledge; often
it is only by the fact of the performance that we are able to recognize and
demonstrate to others that we do in fact remember. According to Connerton, this memory is produced and "sedimented in the body" (page
79). Dancing in a club was an important practice sedimented in Tito's
body. As he told stories of the Saint, Tito started to dance, making gestures, planting his feet on the floor, and gently stamping out a beat in
show and tell. He performed the memory sedimented in his body as self-
knowledge to inform others of the cultural memories that have manifested both his and their own lifeworlds and to share them.

From the theater of memory on the street, I want to move to theater of memory on the dance floor, where participants retold their stories and felt their power released anew. Embodying memory was a powerful method by which people were conscious of their own evolution over time. So, for instance, Ariel, aged twenty-six at the time of interview, regularly visited clubs on the West Coast before moving to New York City two years ago and knew how his past experiences contributed to his present through movement. The dance floor was a stage on which he revisited, restored, and reinterpreted himself in the present through improvised social dancing.

> ARIEL: My dance style is something that evolves. When I was dancing as a little Goth teenybopper, it was a very different thing from what I'm doing now, or even two years ago. I went from Goth spaces to queer and primarily gay clubs, and now my dance is a little bit of everything I did in those places.
> FB: How do you find your movement?
> A: When I was a Goth I loved my black floor length skirt. I can't throw it away now. The costume affected how I moved. So therefore I do this twist thing—where I'll twist in a circle for example—that I know I'll never lose. I recognize it now when I dance. But that came out because I wore a skirt and I loved to have it flare out. It's that simple, a flip back in time. I was moving, not only in relation to my body, but in relation to the clothes that were on my body. I was connecting with what was with me. I would love to see how the lines and curves on my body would change depending on that. So I think that's where it all started from in terms of movement.

He also juxtaposed his performance of embodied memory with new ways of dancing that gave his movement a rich variety of style and content. He used this juxtaposition to create a dramatic dynamic between at least two styles of movement and at least two periods in his life:

> So it started with that Goth scene, and then, when I started to get into the gay scene, that was a different form altogether. I don't know how to describe it, but it's much more poppy, much more fun . . . and I took these movements and obviously I could just fit them into this music, but it doesn't work. But yet at the same time, pieces of it did, and when it would slow down or whatever. I was the dancer who wouldn't stop dancing—as many people do. That's where I completely get into my grind. So that's where I'll start doing something [he moves, extending his arms out and

articulating his torso] like a slow drag that completely came out of my Goth phase, and nothing else. I could take that time to feel out that moment to its entire extension—and I love that, and then as the music speeds up, I can slip back into my gay bounciness of it all.

Whatever new experiences contributed to his movement repertoire, they did not erase other memories and movement elements, but added to his repertoire, making it richer. His memory was also part of a collective memory embodied and performed in the commonalities of how people danced:

> Goth dancing is very slow and meticulous, everything's very precise. Everybody tries to get their own style. There's a sense of care of people in that scene—how they move their bodies. It's practiced, in a way it's practiced on the dance floor and you can see them build what their style is going to be. I don't think I was conscious at the time, but I did it. I watched other people—how they moved and what I liked and what I didn't like and how I liked to move.

Ariel selectively picked up on, interpreted, and used other people's movement, incorporating his interpretations into his repertoire. This was perhaps one of the reasons why memories of being in other queer spaces in the city were almost always remembered in relation to others. For, if, as Connerton suggests, what is most important to a group is committed to the body, then a dance floor would seem to be a powerful space and improvised social dancing an affective practice in which this incorporation and embodiment occurred (Connerton 1989, 72–104). These stories and maps again articulated truths of the experience of the contingency, affectiveness, and embodiment of queer lifeworlds, emphasizing the role of movement in quotidian and social processes. Participants on the dance floor used their experiences of dancing with others to understand, embody, and perform themselves as queer, balancing individuality and commonality.

What was the connection between theaters of memory and improvised social dancing? The nature of improvisation was both an act of fresh creation and a performance of memory. In improvising on the dance floor, participants did not move in an empty space. Improvised movement in performance revealed layered patterns of cultural history, which were textured in meaning for the improviser. In his highly useful examination of jazz improvisation, musicologist Paul Berliner claims that "improvisers draw strength from a symbolic link to the past, as if becoming joined to a long chain of expressive human history" (Berliner 1994, 491). I suggest that what Berliner notes among musicians playing together also occurred among dancers together on a dance floor in this sense. Improvisation on the dance floor may thus be seen as a conversation, not only with the other participants, but also with the past. I would also argue that improvisation was always a conversation with the future, an articulation between what had been and what had not yet come into existence and was performed in the moment to moment production of movement.

As participants conversed with each other using their bodies, they evolved a storehouse of embodied knowledge that built into a recognizable repertoire. On the dance floor, interaction between people took place on this shared basis of repertoire: it was a tangible, culturally meaningful level of ideas that was exchanged during dance. New ideas reached infinity when they were exposed and explored in relation to one another, and thus improvisation was important, not only as an individual practice, but between people and as political imagination. In the following chapters, I enter the clubs themselves to suggest that improvised social dancing in queer clubs rehearsed relationships of generating, applying and sharing ideas by which the dance becomes stronger and richer. I show how in improvised social dancing, participants transmitted movement explicitly, as teachers showed others how to move, and implicitly, as people embodied others' movements through mimesis. I also suggest how, from my observations, participants adapted these copied movements into their own movement style, which was again picked up on by other dancers and adapted. I contend that the rich diversity of movement on the dance floor was akin to conversations occurring across the dance floor, across time, and across experiences. Improvised social dancing negotiates social interactions and this expresses the tensions of queer lifeworlds that mark them not as limited or limiting, fixed forms of world-making, but rich with multiple possibilities.

⫝⫝⫝ 2

THE CURRENCY OF FABULOUSNESS
Fashioning the Self, Fashioning the Lifeworld

Nobody ever saw anything like that in this part of town. When you came out of the Saint— eight in the morning, nine o'clock, every single one of us brought sunglasses, because, girl, when you came out you were so high that you never thought the night would end. This was the emerald city, this was fantasyland, and this was the dream of every gay man. Every weekend, there was something new to amuse you. I remember there were a lot of crazy things before the Saint, and the Saint had to top that. Once at 12 West, they got a huge pig—about four hundred pounds—and they gave the pig acid and they threw him into the crowd, and you have this huge monster pig going wild through the crowd. Now, you have to top that in the Saint. You're dancing and there was this pig, this cute thing, can you imagine?

(Tito)

These are people [going to dance clubs] who don't march, who go to these fabulous, wonderful spaces and expect to see this elsewhere, and it's a different gay movement, stodgy, politicized in some way that is narrow, and they forget the fun part. It's meetings. It's disappointing. I want that other really powerful thing. I go back to my disco dancing. I get my gayness. I get my empowerment, once a week, for the week. And I can look at anybody in the face in my job and my family, and I know for a fact, it's good to be gay, it's fabulous, and sometimes, it's better than you. (Stephen, age 33)

≋ DANCE CLUBS—MOST ESPECIALLY queer dance clubs—were spaces to be fabulous. In these spaces, participants felt encouraged to fashion themselves and to realize their imaginative possibilities through dress, bearing, social interactions, and dance. Why queer dance clubs especially? Because in a queer lifeworld, being fabulous was hard currency. It was exchanged for belonging to a peer group, for being loved and desired, and for self-esteem. It was—in the words of Stephen, an African-American queer man who has lived and danced in New York City since 1991—a way to "get my empowerment," both within his queer lifeworld and outside it. This fun aspect of his life was anything but trivial. It was in fact more empowering for him than going to a march or political meeting for gay and lesbian rights. A space in which to be fabulous produced him as a gay subject: "I get my gayness." It also produced the meaning of "gayness" for him through the pleasure of the grind on the dance floor, rather than the grind of going to meetings and talking about oppression. This identification was based on pleasure and self-knowledge rather than queer resistance, but the spaces he chose to go to and the way he spoke about them and the practices within indicate that the gayness he got was not a one size fits all model. He sought out particular spaces and particular relations and rejected others. He chose the public sphere of embodied relations rather than discursive ones. The pleasure he made for himself dancing in these spaces produced self-knowledge: "I know for a fact it's good to be gay." Making pleasure *worked*. Being fabulous *worked*. But what were the forms, structures, and systems of practices that produced, sustained, and acted as forums for the operation, circulation, and exchange of being fabulous?

As Stephen suggested, the spaces in which he made pleasure—queer clubs—were also "wonderful, fabulous spaces." That fabulousness was a process of storytelling—a fabrication, a place where many different stories were performed through self-fashioning and celebrated for the richness of their diversity and the power of their commonalities. These spaces were fabulous in themselves and simultaneously through his participation enabled him to be fabulous. The space produced him and he produced the space. He was aware that he was one of the elements in a club that made it fabulous—not least because he was a fine dancer with that combination of playfulness, confidence, and enjoyment of his body that made him "fierce." In queer clubspeak, this term was the highest compliment anyone could give another. It was a social legitimation, a mark of high regard. But how did people prepare themselves to move into the third body of recreation—the self that could tell its story publicly and be fierce? In this chapter, I lead you through the preparation for going to a club, arriving at it, and journeying through it to the dance floor. By going through these stages, I am identifying stages of queer world-making. I want to look at the club space itself to understand the practices that enabled a space, a group of people, and an individual to be fabulous.

Many queers are worldless, cut off in many instances from family, church, and other institutions of community-building. They have to fashion their worlds from their own bodies out. Stephen "gets his gayness" from dancing in a queer club. It was a space of self-fashioning. This fashioning started before people arrived at the club: in deciding what to wear, calling friends, listening to music, perhaps even dancing around your own or a friend's room, and packing your "accessories," as I witnessed on several occasions at the homes of participants, all part of a queer lifeworld. In many cases I have experienced, people gathered together at one person's home to get ready and preparation became an integral part of the whole social event. Tito lived around the corner from where in the 1980s the Saint dance club was located in the East Village. Therefore during that period, his small apartment was the meeting place for his friends before they went to the club: "It was a ritual. Everybody would come over, and we'd all watch *Saturday Night Live,* and get ready." This was a typical scene as clubbers prepared for their night out with implications of queer world-making. As participants prepared themselves, they prepared for show—for publicly performing queerness and for dancing. Clothes were thrown on the floor in disgust and whether the reasons for rejection were practical or aesthetic, they were always detailed-oriented: "When I get hot it sticks to me in all the wrong places and stinks"; "Wore it last week"; "It makes my shoulders look round"; "These pants have no pockets. Where am I going to put my cash and my gum? Could you keep them for me?" Alex called it "pulling a look": taking care over appearance, putting a unique outfit together, which for some clubgoers meant not in a designer package, but rather by acts of bricolage—putting things together to form more than the sum of their parts, sometimes working in striking juxtapositions, and preferably for as little cash as possible. For some, this style of dressing was queer. A smart designer outfit was sometimes mocked as too straight. Stephen also testified to the process of pulling a look and the queer pleasure it generated for both participant and audience:

> I loved the way people dressed. And that was also part of the space. They'd wear their T-shirts, but honey, they'd also wear fabulous shit. Looking cute. They weren't designers, graphic designers, they were just artistic types, and they'd still work it out. It wasn't about labels. It was about looking good for the fun of it (Stephen).

Generally, fabulous clubgoers fell into two categories: those pulling a look—trying to look individual, unique, and special, and those dressing for "serious" dancing in clothes that caused as little restriction as possible. These categories overlapped. In both categories, participants also dressed to display their bodies: whether in high bondage heels, tight jeans, or a tight white muscle T-shirt ("muscle-T") to show off the results of all those hours in the gym, for instance. This use of costuming was inherently theatrical. It aimed to produce a glorious character and to attract the attention of an appreciative audience. It also produced status, which in a queer club was broadly bifurcated between those who made the scene and those who came to admire them. Barrel, a white Jewish gay man in his early thirties, recalled the moment several years earlier, when he realized the role his self-fashioning played in other people's responses to him and his status in the club on arrival at Love Machine, an early 1990s gay club on Union Square:

> It was the most dressed up I ever got. Big boots up to my knees, tight leather shorts with a big buckle and a cowboy hat. And a teeny weenie T-shirt and a vest. And leather wrist cuffs. And I remember walking in and people were taking my picture.

Daniel Harris emphasizes the role self-fashioning plays in a queer lifeworld in his recent portrayal of contemporary North American urban gay culture, *The Rise and Fall of Gay Culture*. He suggests that sexual minorities differ from other minorities because they have neither a geographical place of origin (along with the shared cultural traditions that a common national heritage produces) nor physical characteristics:

> Because we are the only invisible minority, we must invent from scratch those missing physical features that enable us to spot our imperceptible compatriots, who would remain unseen and anonymous if they did not prominently display on their bodies, in their sibilant voices and shuffling gaits, their immaculate grooming and debonair style of deportment, the caste mark that constitutes the essence of the gay sensibility. (Harris 1997, 35)

Participants dressed "queer" to create themselves and to be read by a target audience of other queers, which, in a gay, lesbian, or queer club, can be exploited to the utmost. No longer a secret code on the street, in a club people wore and carried themselves without censorship—external or internal.

As I sat around a table in the East Village with a few other clubbers, Jermaine conjured up a terrific image of his younger self as he dressed to express and impress in a club in the 1980s in a truly fabulous piece of storytelling in which all of us present participated. The permission to be outrageous explicit in some clubs offered him power not available in other spaces. The awkward, chubby black kid from Queens transformed himself into a glorious creature of the queer demimonde.

> I wasn't attractive, so I made up for it by being outrageous. This was the time when African hair was back in. So you saw a lot of flat-tops. I had one that went up and slanted to one side—oh my God, what must I have looked like! I had a snake skin suit from the Salvation Army, 'cos that's where you could find stuff that was cheap. And it was OK. But it wasn't *enough*. So remember those gladiator sandals Capezio did? [Much groaning and laughing.] Well . . . I put those on too. So I have the slant top [he mimes hair with movement of hands], the snake skin suit [he runs hands down body as if showing off the suit] with the gladiator sandals [his fingers pick at straps, cueing us to visualize them.] But it wasn't *enough*. After all it was the '80s, all about excess right? Well, this was also the time of those backless shirts for men. Now who did those? ["Gaultier!" someone cries.] Well, I got a cheap copy and it had blue paisley amoebas on the chest. [Howls of laughter.] So I've got the slant top, the snake skin suit, the gladiator sandals, the blue backless shirt [he repeats his mime and some of us join in]. But, I'm still thinking . . .["It's not *enough*!!" we scream.] Exactly. So I get some body glitter . . . and [we scream with mirth as we all spontaneously complete his story by miming throwing it down our own backs]. So now I'm thinking, I'm *ready*.
>
> DANNY: Oh yes, y'all ready for the R train now, baby!
> KEVIN: You sure you didn't need a belt, honey?

The joy we shared at hearing this story was an integral part of its performance. We became its fellow participants, chorus, and audience, supporting and commenting on it. One story became the opportunity for sharing many more stories of going to clubs, often opened with "Do you remember this club, or that period, or that song, or that feeling," calling upon all of us present to participate in the theater of memory. The particularities of Jermaine's story revealed two important truths about "being fabulous." One, it could be a form of compensation. In this case, Jermaine did not feel himself to be attractive within the queer lifeworld and so compensated by fashioning himself into a fabulous creature. Stephen's story also revealed how being fabulous compensated for homophobic responses and the dullness of hetero-orthodoxy or homo-orthodoxy outside of his queer community. Also, being fabulous was something about a unique style, often pivoting—in the realm of dressing up, at least—around excess: "It wasn't *enough*." Excess worked both ways, not only extending out from the body, but clinging to it as tightly as a second skin.

Clubgoers executed this self-fashioning for potentially critical (queer) audiences, one of which had a very practical role to play as gatekeeper of the club itself. Door people did not only have to monitor the ages of the patrons (the legal drinking age in New York State was twenty-one), but they also selected the type of people they wanted in a club. The way people dressed was one way of deciding this. As a doorman at Foxy, a queer party at an East Village bar called Velvet (Avenue A and 10th Street) that ran from 1996 to 1998, Alex paid attention to how people dressed when he decided who got in: "If you're going to wear a T-shirt, it'd better be really tight, your jeans better be really tight. And you better not have underwear on." He expressed disdain at what he saw as the asexual sartorial style of frat-boy grunge (baggy flannel shirts and jeans) and designer label clones. On several occasions, I stood with him at the door while he did his job. I watched him shine his Maglite onto the shoes of people in the line: "You can tell a lot about people from their shoes," he informed me. If a person was not "pulling a look" or looking "fabulous" he or she was sometimes met with a comment like, "You know it's queer night?" As I was wearing unremarkable boots one time, I asked him if he would let me in if he didn't know me. He smiled. "Combat boots with laminated hipster drainpipes and a fake fox-fur jacket?" I took this as a positive response. The items of clothing themselves may not have been fabulous, but unusual or anti-fashion-clone combinations were.

As well as deciding what to wear, participants also took care to decide what to take. One clubgoer, Catherine, referred to this as packing your "club survival kit." In a clubgoer's apartment at 2:30 A.M., after the outfit was finished, the participants assembled and checklisted their kits like Navy Seals readying for a mission. Everything we loaded into pockets and minibackpacks had to be portable, useful, and able to be carried without causing unsightly bulges in clothing. Barrel recalled his kit checklist, relating each item to its usability:

> Gum and candy for the sugar, sunglasses for when I leave the club in the morning, breath spray—I had this thing for breath spray, in case I got lucky at the end of the night. Cigarettes, lighter, money, bankcard. I figured out I

would need twenty-eight dollars 'cos I would always drink the same number of drinks, always the same thing.

Some participants considered gum essential for anyone taking club drugs,
such as ecstasy ("E" or "X") and ketamine ("Special K"), most especially as
they produced a tenseness in the jaw that chewing alleviated. These drugs
also left the inside of the mouth feeling somewhat coated. Chewing gum
relieved this as well as acting as a breath-freshener and as an immediate
source of dietary energy in the form of sugar. Often clubs were so loud
and busy that it was difficult at times to have a conversation. Gum literally
occupied the mouth. It was also a medium of friendship, along with water
and cigarettes, as it was often offered and passed between people. When it
was offered to someone outside of the circle of friends, it was a social ice-
breaker, which was also used in cruising. Clubgoers rarely put water in
their kit, although every seasoned clubgoer knew how important it was to
drink water when dancing for hours. Most clubs (Vinyl, Twilo, and Tunnel
among them) did not allow people to take in their own bottled water as it
could have contained drugs and because the bars charged around four
dollars for a small bottle, thus increasing profits. At some doors there was
a garbage can full of confiscated bottles of water.

Preparing the body for the party also took other forms, as Barrel
recalled:

> It would start with plans a few days before and that would include when are
> you taking your disco nap. I was going to school so if it was a school night I
> would get home from class around six or eight and sleep until twelve—and
> that was the disco nap. Then I'd get up and eat something, so I had some-
> thing in my stomach.

Barrel knew how important care of his body was in his preparation for
going to a club. In one of his early forays into the demimonde he ended
up passing out due to the rapidity with which his empty digestive system
absorbed the drugs and alcohol he imbibed and the exhaustion he suffered from dancing on empty. He learned his lesson. His comments
show how he consciously made sleeping and eating forms of self-care
and preparation.

The ritual of drug taking had both a social and a personal importance. The ways drugs were taken cemented social relations. Several storytellers, like Ariel, below, recalled meeting with people before going to
a club to take drugs as part of a "ritual."

When I went out before, it was with friends, and it was a whole ritualistic process. You'd start as early as six and we wouldn't even go to the club until about midnight. Our dressing up, our cocaine habits . . . it's an elaborate thing.

Some participants discussed what drugs they would be taking and shared them with each other, passing around a joint, or a small paper or plastic sachet of white powder or pills. In preparing the body, the clubber began to enter "club time": that temporal space with no clocks, measured by and through the body. It began with looking forward and planning (unless going out was a spontaneous event). This anticipation might reach its zenith waiting to get into the club itself.

Participants used drugs to enable them to stay awake during the antisocial hours of the club (usually midnight to as late as midday and beyond, although many participants felt it was more hip to arrive between the hours of three and five A.M). The effects of club drugs such as E and Special K further separated the body of the home and the workplace from the club body. The former narcotic made the body feel looser and more fluid as if warm water was gently pumping through the muscles and central nervous system, as well as producing increased sociability, a warm feeling toward fellow clubbers, and an increase in touch. The latter produced what one informant described as the sensation of walking on platform shoes made of marshmallows and a looser body sense. Unlike E, Special K had to be more frequently ingested—usually snorted as a white powder—as its effects were shorter in duration. Drugs enabled participants to stay awake and dance for long periods of time, and to achieve a separation from an everyday state of mind. Drugs distorted time: it seemed to slow down and suspend or speed up. There were no clocks or windows in a club, nothing to indicate the passing of time. Time was measured instead in the body.

Many people testified that in clubs they felt more "real"—more true to themselves than at other times in other places. The practices of play were recreational and separate from mundane self-maintenance and working and were played out within certain limits of time and space. The club time frame was usually out of the nine to five period; in fact, its peak hours of one A.M. to as late as midday the following day marked it as antisocial in the normative sense. It was a separate time period from that in which the rest of the world operated. Clubs offered a separate reality for many participants. As a third space, the club world did not only offer different physical experiences from home and work, for which participants fashioned themselves sartorially, psychologically, and psychopharmaco-logically—the club world was sometimes also socially separate from the other lifeworlds of participants. This was demonstrated in a poignant narrative that a now forty-year-old ex-clubgoer told me. In the period in the 1980s when Iain had been a regular clubber, he had attended the fu-neral of a friend he had known for several years, although he had only seen him in clubs. However, in the church, the separation between this queer club lifeworld and other spheres of his life was strikingly apparent:

> There were two separate sides of the church and we were shocked, we thought everyone would know him as we did. But he had a wife, and chil-dren and straight work colleagues and they all sat on one side and all the flaming queens sat on the other and we all just kind of stared at each other.

As this story indicated, clubbers sometimes separated their social worlds of play, home, and work. This may seem unremarkable except in the light that many queers already had a heightened sense of living separate realities. A club was a separate space in which several informants ex-pressed that they could be themselves, fully able to articulate their sexu-alities and their desires.

After preparing and dressing, the queer clubgoer could attract a great deal of attention traveling to his or her destination on the street or on public transportation. While such visibility could be a proud proclama-tion of queerness, it could also attract unwelcome attention. Members of Harris' "invisible minority" marked themselves with dress and traveled through potentially dangerous territory before arriving at their destina-tion. As clubs were rarely in residential neighborhoods, clubgoers often had to consider their safety when they traveled to them. Even in gay areas such as the West Village and Chelsea, the Anti-Violence Project re-ported a 100% increase in attacks on gay men and lesbians in 1997. Mar-ginal spaces in the city, the location of many clubs, were often badly lit and had few places of refuge for a person under attack—no stores and few bars. Participants going to clubs at late hours of the night often bud-geted for a taxi, rather than risk walking alone. Typically, they met at a safe space like someone's apartment or a queer bar and traveled to-gether to a club, often splitting a cab fare. Others decided to walk to-gether. They avoided particular bus or subway routes they identified as potentially hazardous. People sometimes concealed their club outfits or gay signs with a zipped up jacket or coat for fear of being read as "gay" and verbally or physically attacked. Even the routes to the clubs were fashioned by a consciousness of queerness that shaped participants' psychogeographies of the city.

Many New York City clubs were located in nonresidential areas, such as in the industrial zone near the West Side Highway in Manhattan where megaclubs Twilo (530 West 27th Street) and Tunnel (12th Avenue and 27th Street) were located at the time of writing. Clubs were often converted from industrial spaces such as warehouses and garages. However, sometimes they were in residential areas, such as the East Village and Chelsea in Manhattan, although these tended to be smaller because less space was available. One exception was the Saint, a huge multilevel, planetarium-domed dance club on Fifth Street between Second and Third Avenues in the East Village. The Saint was converted from the old Commodore, a one-time movie house that was reincarnated as the legendary rock concert hall the Fillmore East (1968 to 1971). Its spectacular refurbishment cost four million dollars. Tito spoke about how, at the time it opened in September 1980, the East Village was mainly a patchwork of East European and Latino neighborhoods:

> Oh, at that time the white people didn't pass First Avenue. They could get stones thrown at their cars by locals along St. Marks by the Electric Circus [a black and Latino dance club]. The area was very Spanish, very traditional, Polish, Ukrainian. And to the people in the East Village, gay was like hustling in Christopher Street, we were all prostitutes. Every Friday, Saturday, and Sunday you used to go with your lover to Christopher Street and the piers and everybody saw everybody, and that was the way to meet people until the Saint opened. When the Saint opened, all that crowd moved to this neighborhood.

The East Village was not a known gay part of town in the 1980s—that honor went to Christopher Street in the West Village, nor was it then the nightlife mecca it has since become for clubbers.

When a participant arrived at a club, he or she often had to wait in a line while security checked each person entering, unless he or she was on the guest list. Several informants told stories that illustrated how, in such moments outside the club, the lifeworlds of the clubber and the local resident collided:

> Now at one point, the church opposite the Saint started exerting pressure because all these parishioners were attending mass while all these people

were leaving the Saint with no shirts, wearing jockstraps, and grabbing taxis while wearing leather chaps with a slave hanging off their arm by a collar. All these Polish ladies were saying, "What the heck is going on?" These people never saw anything like that. I remember being in line and people eating pierogis were watching us through the glass of Kiev's like, "Whoa, where am I? Another planet?" We don't care, we don't give a shit, 'cos this was our land, this was the only time that we had something for us.

Although queers may have courted danger by traveling to a club, Tito's story, above, suggested that the line outside gave participants confidence. Another informant, Catherine, alluded to this. When she first tested the waters of a queer sexuality, she experienced a profound moment when she saw the line outside of the first dance event she went to soon after she arrived in the city:

I was still in the cab and we drove past, 'cos I wasn't sure of the address. And through the window, I remember seeing all these people. The cab was still moving, so I was tracking along this line, and I couldn't believe how many people there were. It just went on around the block. I felt exhilarated and terrified, and . . . turned on. 'Cos all these people were gay, or wanted to be in a queer space. I knew there were lots of queers, but I'd never seen them before in these numbers. What a trip. Even now, I get a little of that excitement when I see a big line. If I don't . . . well, I guess I get a bit anxious and hope I've come to the right place.

Stephen recalled that at Crowbar (10th Street between Avenues A and B), a small East Village dance club that ran from the early 1990s to 1997, the scene outside the door was a good place for a participant to surmise what might be happening inside and if he or she wanted to be a part of it:

There was always a door person, but not like a doorman like some of these other spaces where they were intimidating. Just some young little kid, someone who went to Crowbar, just somebody at the door to say hello. We'd go upstairs outside to have a cigarette, rest, and chat. We'd get people from the outside to come in, 'cos they'd see people there, and you could always go to the door and hear and feel critical mass inside.

When he saw the line of cabs in front of the Saint, Tito connected this site to a local and global constellation of gay pleasure palaces, which he describes in terms other than secular:

From Sixth Street, at least to Seventeenth Street, lines and lines, bumper to bumper of taxis, we never fucking saw anything like that in New York. This is when we realized that this club was the fucking club of the world. Saint Marks Baths, the Saint next to us, and then Heaven in London. That was the trilogy, the Father, the Son, and the Holy Spirit. We had everything, but we never realized it was so big until we saw the lines.

For all these storytellers, the sight of the line had the force of revelation from which they constructed themselves as queer subjects connected to a larger queer lifeworld than previously experienced. Queer world-making often started with an informant's attraction to connecting with other queers, not only in the same space, but also through imagining a wider connection through a global, national, regional, or local constellation of spaces. This established what Benedict Anderson calls an "imagined community": community as an imagined, but affective reality in which "members of even the smallest nation will never know their fellow members, meet them, or even hear of them, yet in the minds of each they carry the image of communion" (Anderson 1983, 15). While participants may not have physically seen all of their peer clubbers in the club, the city, or across the nation and beyond, they imaginatively experienced and shared a vision of being a part of a larger lifeworld. Although the realities of community within a club were occasionally dystopic, this articulated vision expressed a desire for community and the celebration of belonging.

The door of a club was a theater of anxiety around belonging. Informants often expressed a desire for community that was sometimes vague and fuzzily utopian, but in the field, I experienced several instances in which that desired-for community was very sharply delimited. My observations seem to support a view, occasionally articulated by more reflective informants, that the door of a club was less a gateway to a utopian community, than an entrance into a particular market economy that might not be so alternative to other public economies based on who you know, what you look like, and ultimately, if you can afford the fee. Queerness itself did not always guarantee status or even belonging. My fieldnotes of a gay Pride party, Clubzilla, at the Limelight (Sixth Avenue and 20th Street), which I attended with a group of regular club attendees on June 28th, 1998, demonstrated how the anxieties of belonging, which I assert were anxieties about community, manifested one night.

The line stretched around the block and the drag queens at the door informed us that despite being on the promoter's guest list, we still had to stand in line. The regulars were incensed. During Gay Pride weekend a lot of "out-of-towners" and straights come to gay spaces. Regulars called them "tourists." Some I overheard said that they only bothered coming out this evening because they were on the guest list and thought they wouldn't have to stand in line with "everyone else." Regulars felt humiliated and annoyed at the failure of the door people to recognize queer or fabulous status as superseding straight, in addition to their failure to reward their loyalty to the club. They pointed out well-known figures on the scene, one of whom was the mother of a gay house, expressing shock and shame that she would have to stand in a line with a bunch of curious straights from "out-of-town."[1] As a group of straight-looking folk (identified by informants by their dress and demeanor) were let in by their straight-looking doorman friend, consternation rumbled among those waiting. "Excuse me," grumbled one, "is anyone here tonight actually gay?" People were pissed that Gay Pride offered an opportunity for straights to play "tourist" in a gay territory. It was not that different from usual, but tonight was extrasensitive, especially as queers on the guest list were being asked to wait.

Eventually, someone got word to promoter Kevin Aviance that his friends were waiting outside and needed help getting into the club. Resplendently fabulous in a green spandex body suit, six–inch platforms, shaved head, and glamorous make-up that made him into a cross between Patti LaBelle and Godzilla, he came out of the club and pulled us in. He led my companion David and me through the crowd by the hand. We proceeded in a little train through the labyrinthine passageways packed with people. Several times we were almost separated by the sheer force of people pushing against us. It was slow going as Kevin was stopped and greeted every two steps. "Kevin, come and talk with me," implored one clubber. "Not now honey, I'm running a party," he snapped back gently and kept moving.

Clubs had to be self-policing, queer clubs even more so as they were more contested spaces than straight clubs. This tension was not just driven by those who sought to control clubs and close them down, but by those who wanted to get into them. Promoters and door people needed to preserve a critical mass of queer bodies to attract queer partygoers.[2] The presence of too many straights could rupture the safety or dilute the fabulousness and queerness of the club. Door people decide who they don't want in a club and decide who they do want. Back in the 1970s and 1980s, at clubs like Studio 54, door people became local late-night celebrities with a notorious penchant for picking and choosing people from a huge throng of would-be party-people eager to mix with celebrities.[3] As a young hip clubgoer in the 1980s with a "look," who was therefore often admitted free by doorpeople with whom he was on a first-name basis, Alex remembered those times and offered suggestions as to why they seem to have passed:

> ALEX: You always wanted young, cute people in a club. It's always good to
> be a part of that crowd, to be around cute people. And I got for a while to
> be one of those kids, just because I went out all the time and I worked in
> the Boy Bar and some of these people would come in there and I was eigh-
> teen years old and looked a little funky, a little trendy. So you could go to
> these places for free and got VIP passes and hung out in the back. 'Cos you
> made your own outfits and hats and looked hip, and sometimes you wore
> make-up. You want kids like that at a party, it makes it fun. Area opened
> around '84/85. For me, it was the last of the really great clubs—places that
> created a scene. It was the first place I saw A-list celebrities, Nicholson,
> Cher, Andy Warhol, with Debbie Harry. It was hot, like Studio 54 hot. And
> the door [people] could pick and choose, and now they can't because
> there aren't that many people who go out anymore. Back then, you'd have
> a full club and three thousand people waiting outside to get in, crying,
> "Pick me, I'm on an invite, look at how I'm dressed." And now, what club
> opens up and there are three thousand people waiting outside? So every-
> one gets let in.
>
> FB: Why do you think it's changed?
>
> A: A lot of people died. AIDS really changed people's idea about going
> out, about their behavior. The Palladium (14th Street between Broadway
> and Sixth Avenue) was the last of those clubs that had a scene outside
> when it opened. The crowd rushed the door to get inside, and they had to
> bring down the gates. That was in 85/86. And I think New Yorkers got a lit-
> tle more jaded. Life opened recently on Bleecker and it wasn't even in the
> press. And there certainly weren't three thousand people outside.

Promoters had guest lists of people they wanted inside the club. Someone on a guest list expected certain privileges, for instance, not having to wait in line with people not on the list, free or reduced admission, and access to the VIP room, if there was one. A bad door policy, such as evaluated by the regulars at Limelight that night, failed to fulfill these expectations. The dissatisfaction of participants betrayed the elitism inherent in the guest list system and in door policy as a whole. The door of a club was a theater of anxiety revolving around belonging and status. At a gay club, these two issues were particularly sensitive. Generally, queer clubs admitted heterosexuals (although people's sexual orientation might not always be readable, door people read people as queer or straight through clothes, attitude, and behavior—through self-fashioning) and generally most queer patrons accepted them, "as long as they don't gawp and take photos like we're creatures in a zoo" (Tito). But all informants expected a reverse discrimination from everyday life situations that excluded or stigmatized queers. For most club patrons, a queer club was a safe space, free of the external and internal restrictions and oppressions they lived under outside. Some clubs negotiated the need of queer clubgoers to have a space populated with queers and a queer club experience with their needs to turn a profit by having two doors—one for queers and one for everybody else—and spaces within the club earmarked for queers. This could only happen in large clubs like Tunnel and Limelight where there was the space to offer places such as the Kenny Scharf Room at Tunnel.

Queer clubgoers invested door people with the responsibility of protecting their space. The club was fiercely territorialized. It was a special space, separated off, a "sanctuary." This need for a "safe space" was expressed even more strongly by women I interviewed. Some were very aware of men entering clubs and watching or interacting with them as desire-objects. Antidiscrimination legislation safeguarded the right of men to enter these spaces, but that did not mean that door people could not offer subversive tactics. Edie, in her midtwenties, was a door person at a women's bar and dance space, Meow Mix on East Houston and Suffolk, and chuckled as she recalled some of her special tricks to exclude undesirables:

> My favorite is we can't tell a guy he can't come in, so we say, you have to be on the guest list. But to do that you have to produce a guest list and you can't be charging money. So we pretend that the cash box is where we keep the guest list. We ask them their names and they make something up and they're fucking with us, and we're laughing our asses off 'cos we're fucking with them too. We get a big kick out of making them spell their names five times.

Negotiating entry into a club was a rite of passage. At the time of writing, club security was even more stringent about asking for proof of age, under the watchful eye of the New York Police Department. When they raided a bar or club, police officers asked for everyone's identification.

Alternatively, a young (under 21-years-old) officer acted as an under-cover agent provocateur. If this person was served alcohol without being asked for identification, other undercover officers observing this in-fringement slapped the bar person or owners with a citation. Each viola-tion resulted in a $1000–$2000 penalty and threatened the renewal of a liquor license. For smaller spaces with a low profit margin, too many of these fines sometimes resulted in closure. As spaces for women and queers of color were often small, profit margins were tighter, thus fines had a greater effect. Participants often expressed the sentiment that queer establishments and those for people of color were more fre-quently monitored and cited for violations than other spaces. My experi-ence in the line outside Escuelita, a queer Latino club on 39th Street on the West Side, supported this sentiment, as well as demonstrating that door people occasionally ignored these tight regulations:

> A police wagon is parked outside this Latino gay club. "Haven't they got anything better to do?" grumbles someone in the line. "Yeah, I bet they ain't hanging around outside straight, white clubs," intones another. At the door they are insisting on seeing ID. A moment of anxiety. I don't have any. "So what happens if you're murdered down stairs? Who we gonna know who to send the body back to?" quips the drag queen on the door. My friend explains I am foreign. "Huh!" says the drag queen, "You're just lucky this ain't communist Cuba, they'd throw your ass in jail for walking around without an ID. Now get your butt in there!" She laughs and we enter (Fieldnote: Escuelita 6/1/98).

Once inside the door, the initiation continued. One regular clubgoer interviewed by Sally Sommer for her article on New York City's under-ground dance clubs, "Check Your Body At the Door," saw frisking as a rite of passage, as a way of saying, "I come in peace" (Brahms LaFortune in Sommer 1994/5, 7). Although that night at Escuelita, door people played with the regulations, I have noticed that at black and Latino clubs, security tended to conduct searches more thoroughly than other clubs. At Flava at Club Farenheit on Leonard Street in Tribeca, security personnel waved a hand-held metal detector over me, looking for weap-ons or drugs paraphernalia. At Krash in Queens, the security person asked me to open my cigarette pack, shone a flashlight into its cardboard depths, and then frisked me thoroughly. At Escuelita I lingered a little too long as I stood being frisked by the security person, prompting his re-sponse, "Hey, that's it. Any more and I'll have to charge you." Security people were aware that they were under close surveillance by the police department, especially at clubs for people of color. They had to be seen as thorough by a tough audience. During the period of research, there were incidents of weapons in clubs and two shootings in 1997 in a downtown Manhattan club known for its predominantly African-American clientele.[4] Owners needed to reassure the police, neighborhood groups, and their patrons that their space was safe.

Entering the Saint in the early 1980s was a very different experience. Clubbers had to be members, which entailed visiting Bruce Mailman's (the club owner's) offices and paying a fee in return for a much-prized membership card guaranteeing entry for the member and two guests. Door people excluded anyone without a card or without a companion with one. But in return, the club offered a VIP standard of care that its patrons eagerly anticipated:

> TITO: You walked in between the marble of this old theater [Fillmore East]. All the fixtures were there, they left the entrance the same way. The people who received you and took care of you were in tuxedos. One checked your card, a second person sent you to the box office to check your name and your guest's in a computer. This was something, because this was a time before computers were everywhere. They checked you like they check a credit card and then you get a receipt back. No clubs at that time were giving you a receipt. For taxes, or whatever.
>
> FB: Did they search you?
>
> T: Nooo, hello! Only three years after it opened did they begin to send police. It's funny because I had a girlfriend who was in the police department and she said two of the bouncers in the Saint were regular police officers, which I don't think is allowed.

In the lifeworlds of queer clubs, the participant was special. He or she expected welcome and entry, compared with the exclusion queers felt in other spaces such as the family home or workplace. In a lifeworld, the queer was glad to be special; in other spaces, being special or different was potentially a dangerous and uncomfortable position.

The role of one particular club as a node in a queer lifeworld was contingent and often fleeting. Queer lifeworlds were negotiated on this contingency and produced it. Door policies often changed over time, sometimes prompted by changes within the lifeworld and sometimes from pressure from external agencies. Sometimes when participants had been to a place several times, they expressed increasing dissatisfaction and boredom. A club sometimes seemed to offer decreasing returns, especially if the space became too diluted with straights or failed to offer new excitements on repeated visits. A queer club as lifeworld required periodic infusions of novelty and new blood, in terms of both spaces and people. Alex suggested, "Clubs are like a show and like a Broadway show it has a good run and everybody's seen it, and it needs to close." When a club lost its usual crowd because they moved on to the next big thing, were scared of AIDS, died, suffered drug exhaustion, or because of repeated raids by the police or fire department; people who were previously excluded were let in to keep the club profitable, and the queer fabulousness of the club was diluted. At a certain point, regular queer clubgoers sensed that the party had passed its use-by date. Tito remembered the demise of gay clubs in these terms:

> By the end of '84, beginning of '85 you start seeing straight couples from Jersey. They were amused to see these faggots. It seemed like they had a good time, but they didn't understand what this place and these people meant. One night, the whole of Studio 54 was designed as if there was an airplane inside. Sylvester [the famous gay disco star] was singing dressed as Marilyn Monroe with this white dress on top of this plane. This couple was so amused, and said, "Excuse me, is that a real woman?" This kind of people were now going to the Saint. Honestly, it was like rape. This was our sanctuary and it's like someone without respect was walking in the tombs of your dear friends who died. And you see these kids rolling and crawling and going everywhere, and you think, my God, this was not like this before, something tragic's going on. And in 1987 I stopped going.

It was not enough to be in the same space at the same time. Participants needed to demonstrate that they shared a sense of its importance, codes, conventions, and values. One of the ways they did this was through movement. Participants claimed the space as their own, proving that they knew its codes and conventions through their entrance and circulation before they even reached the dance floor.

A queer club did not become fabulous, or even queer until it was claimed or activated. Most clubs in New York City that I visited were not purpose-built, but spaces converted from disused factories and warehouses. Very few were queer spaces every night. Many queer events took over a club for one night a week. Participants might not be able to explicitly perform their queerness throughout the week and across all spaces. Therefore it was even more important to look for examples of how people used the space to claim it and themselves as queer. Movement transformed the space: by the circulation of people within it, from preparation, to entry, to walking, to dance. Both the subject and the environment were transformed through the act of walking through the club. In "Practices of Space," Michel de Certeau suggests that the walkers in a city write an urban text they cannot read: "These practitioners employ spaces that are not self-aware, their knowledge of them is as blind as that of one body for another, beloved, body" (Certeau 1985, 124). But by looking at how people posed themselves in front of others and at certain points in the club, how they deliberately did a circuit of the club, how they expressed desires to connect with people and a desire to see a mass of queer people, a vision began to emerge of the queer club and a queer body as a very self-aware space, one that practitioners both read and *wrote*. Participants read and wrote their own histories, presents, and possible futures and, as they did this through moving in a club, these texts held potential to resist and evade discipline and commodification. Queer world-making required laying claim to space and to one's own body as queer. In these ways, participants established not only a space and a body, but a way to communicate with each other through proximity (they experienced each other through sight, sound, touch, and the physical sensation of closeness), style, and such activities as entering, moving around, and dancing in the space.

From my observations and experiences, patrons claimed the territory of the club space in a number of ways. At the Body Positive T-Dance at Webster Hall in the East Village, I observed how people re-territorialized the space from the time the club opened to its zenith of occupancy. First, on crossing through the doorway from the hall to the party area itself, people usually stood just on the inside of the lintel and surveyed the room from this vantage point. This was also a position from which to be observed by others in the club. Second, participants walked a circuit of the club in a variety of ways, but all, I suggest, with the same function of claiming the space. An individual or small group walked across to the bar to get a drink, or around the sides of the dance floor, pausing occasionally. Although in these pauses circulation of the individual in the space seemed to have stopped, in fact they were still very much in circulation as their eyes scanned the space and as they were scanned and picked up by the circulation and self-orientation of others. Third, people claimed a meeting place, usually by arranging a group of moveable chairs and a table, if available, in what Edward Hall calls a "sociopetal" arrangement of furniture which brings people together (Hall 1996, 101). One of the functions of moveable chairs in a social setting was to enlarge choice about where to sit, with whom and how close. Most people I noticed moved chairs around, drawing them together. But by moving the chairs, the would-be sitter also made a stake on the space of the chair as well as on the larger environment as the space was carved and shaped by the clustering together.

Participants used the space's entrance features to make an impression. The clubgoer expected to be noticed and judged on his or her first entrance. Being special or fabulous was a way to enjoy the attention of peers. Entrance was the opening line of nonverbal communication. Walking into a club was the opening gambit of speaking queer; a way of expressing, "I'm here, I'm queer, I'm fabulous." It was world-making in two senses: the participant claimed the space and the self. The act of moving through and in a club was both appropriation and transformation. De Certeau compares the act of walking through the city to an act of speaking:

> The act of walking is to the urban system what enunciation (the speech act) is to language or to the system of available utterances. At the most elementary level it has a triple "enunciative" function: it is a process of *appropriation* of the topographical system by the pedestrian (in the same way that the speaker appropriates language for himself); it is a spatial *realization* of place (as the speech act is sonorous realization of language); and finally it implies certain *relations* between differentiated positions, that is certain pragmatic "contracts" in the form of movements (in the same way as verbal enunciation is an "allocation," a "positioning of the other" in relation to the speaker, and establishes a contract between speakers). Walking would therefore find its primary definition as a site of enunciation [. . .] Walking [. . .] creates a mobile organicity of the environment. (Certeau 1980, 180)

The individual moving in a club *appropriated* the space that existed prior to entering the club. He or she *realized* it as a queer space, both by the presence of his or her queer body, and also by queer acts—kissing, touching, looking with desire, celebrating the presence of other queers, and expressing queerness openly and physically through self-carriage without fear of surveillance or reprisals. The participant enacted a contract that preserved his or her own and others' differences while at the same time affecting a collective within the space, by moving as he or she wished, but without obstructing others. Movement affected a "mobile organicity of the environment" that determined the nature and form of the text—both as written and read. It was a text that could only be understood through movement. These practices were modes of experience that resisted the reduction of movement and gestures to the status of a sign. Participants generated and expressed meaning through their own bodies as they moved in a queer lifeworld, conscious of the performance of queerness of the self and the club. Presence and movement promoted queerness as a state of "fabulousness." Fabulousness was movement as self-fashioning. This context and contention reinvigorates what de Certeau reduces to a walk by concentrating on *ways of moving*. Certain ways of moving with performance consciousness enacted the appropriation, realization, and negotiation of interrelational contracts that constituted particular forms and models of queerness based on pleasurable play. As Stephen reaffirmed, these dance clubs were the places, these movements were the practices from which he "gets his gayness." This *works* outside of the club as well. His movement practices crossed supposed boundaries between the inside of the club and its outside and between improvised social dancing and social relations.

In most clubs I visited, the door was usually not the place from which participants made their entrance either directly onto the dance floor or its surrounding area. After entering a club, I found that many were disorienting spaces within which participants had to orient themselves in order to recognize and make a lifeworld. Before they arrived at the dance floor, participants might have to navigate stairs (up in Limelight, down at Escuelita, Crowbar, and Flava), coat checks, and foyers (for instance in Twilo and the Palladium), bars, juice stops, and chill-out areas, as well as the throng of people circulating throughout them. Sometimes participants had to walk through a curtain or dividing door (as at Sound Factory Bar at 12 West 21st Street and the Clit Club). There was usually a place to pay inside the door. The entrances to these clubs were sometimes like a labyrinth, sometimes illuminated with sweeping, spiraling, and flashing lights that destabilized participants' visual grip on the world around them. Over all this was the soundscape, rich with layers of continuous sound, a pulse that made my internal organs vibrate, samples of noise, sirens, sonic booms, samples, and repetitions. Orientation had a double meaning in a queer club. Participants not only had to exert some kind of comprehensible map over the space with nodes they could locate and orient themselves around so they knew where they were and where they wanted to be, but they also had to orient themselves in a queer club, within a matrix of sexuality different from on the street or in the workplace. Catherine suggested that she had to struggle more to orient herself within the matrix of heterosexuality at work and in her family home. The matrix of queer sexuality in a club therefore felt less like a rupture. It felt, she asserted earnestly, "more real" to her, "more like my reality." Queer world-making could transform and rupture the force of heteronormativity. The spatial, sonic, and effects-oriented disorientation of a club produced an effect akin to the experience of liminality between a queer life-world and other realms of existence, both spaces and states of being.[5]

Shifts of spatial, temporal, and interpersonal orientation took you into the club experience. All-night clubs such as Tunnel, Arena, Limelight, or Twilo (approximately 11 P.M. to anywhere between 8 A.M. and midday or later) tended to have a mix of people until later, when it was overwhelmingly male and gay. "We party harder. That's what being queer was all about when I was younger. We'd laugh at the straights who went home at three A.M. That's when we were thinking of going out!" said Mark, a clubgoer in his early forties who still could be found at some events such as Twilo after over twenty years on the scene in New York City. Temporal appropriations lead to some interesting spatial juxtapositions in the crossover period. At four A.M. in Arena, I stood watching the dance floor as smartly dressed college girls danced next to a group of gay leather men in body harnesses and chaps. They did not interact, but seeing them dancing in the same recreational space, even for a short while, was a striking juxtaposition. You could tell what time it was by reading the critical mass of types of bodies on the dance floor. At Arena at least, if there were too many straights, a queer participant knew he came too early.

In the *Time Out* club listings of November 1995, Tunnel Saturdays (the gay night) was listed twice, once in the general club listings section and again in the Gay and Lesbian Club listings. The differences between these listings revealed both the temporal appropriations in these spaces—what to expect at different times—and the expectations of the pleasures of two audiences:

> Tunnel Saturdays *Tunnel. 11 P.M., $20.* It's officially the largest Saturday night party there is. Junior Vasquez spins for thousands of disciples from his elaborate DJ booth until late Sunday morning (the idea being that you can now stop by after mass). It's dance party music—basically, whatever Junior feels like playing during his twelve-hour stint. Hope you like big parties; Vasquez's first night brought in close to six thousand revelers. Stop by the fruit and juice bar upstairs, where the music is pumped in softly, lest

you miss a beat. The big, comfy booths are up there too, so you can take a break if you're sleepy. And you probably will be, because the club doesn't get going until three or four A.M. Be sure to stop by Martin's Lounge, the VIP balcony lounge guarded by the lovely Connie Girl.[6]

Tunnel Saturdays *Tunnel. 11 P.M.–10 A.M.; $20 before 3:30am, $15 after.* This mixed mega-club, now boasting DJ Junior Vasquez, gets gayer after-hours, as mind-altering substances begin to separate the men from the girls.[7]

The first listing employed the discourse of tourism—"stop by the juice bar [. . .] Be sure to stop by Martin's Lounge," marking the sites of interest in the club, and also marking the general reader as "tourist," as someone unfamiliar with the club. This was also implied in the length of the listing: more description in the first contrasted with the stripped down essentialism of the gay and lesbian entry, which implied familiarity. The tourists were also directed to "big, comfy booths" in which to sleep; the queers will not need to as "the mind-altering substances begin to separate the men from the girls." The gay listing suggested a later arrival time with lower entrance fee (after 3:30 A.M.), and indicated that their party started once the "girls" had gone home to bed. In short, the space was gayer later. The listing described this phenomenon as a form of social Darwinism assisted by drugs, and signified how status was marked generationally and in terms of gender: the men endured longer than the girls. The term "girls" did not only refer to biological females and did not only reveal the heavy gender-bias in the queer ownership of this space. In this context, it disparagingly referred to men who could not stay awake and party until the early hours.

To enter the place or state of a queer lifeworld often seemed to enact a coming out. But even when I entered Tunnel at the gayer hour of 5:30 A.M., the experience felt too disorienting to be an affirmation of any orientation: as Mark, a long-time clubgoer commented, "I can no longer tell the difference between drag queens and girls from Jersey." There was no architectural, scopophilic, sexual, or aural center to the club. The main room extended almost the length of the space. I walked through a lounge area to an emptier space in the middle of which a large bar rose like an island complete with go-go boy and muscular male bar staff. The sound of hard-house music was so omnipresent that it offered few clues as to the direction of the dance floor. I found it at one end of the long main room, not surrounded by any higher levels from which observation could take place. The dance floor was long and narrow, and its boundary was ill-defined. As a result, I found it difficult to get a sense of the mass of movement from the outside, because on the outer margins of the area, dancers were more diffuse in critical mass, density, and energy. People stood around in clusters, and preserved social space between their group and others. Some swayed or bobbed slightly to the beat. I wandered deeper onto the floor in search of dance. With few markers to orient my position, the club neutralized typical reference points. As a result of the initial deliberate disorientation effect produced by darkness, flashing lights, and pounding music, the circulation of bodies in the space became a prominent marker and shaper of not only orientation, but of the nature and energy of the populated club.

It always took me a while to get oriented in a club. I used two strategies. First, I usually went on a reconnaissance mission. Clubs like Tunnel, a converted railway warehouse with a labyrinth of rooms and passages, and Limelight, a converted church, were tricky to orient myself in until I became familiar with the space. On my first visit to Limelight, I stood on a gangway above the dance floor at around seven A.M. pondering whether to leave. I wondered what was holding me there—until I realized that part of the problem lay in the fact that I had no notion of how to get out of the place. My second orientation strategy was to find a high place from which I could see over the dance floor. I was looking for indications of order to emerge from the initial chaos of disorientation. In his discussion of the city, de Certeau (1985, 124) acknowledges that a god's eye view "transforms the city's complexity into readability." From this vantage point I and other partygoers were able to read the energy level of the party, its hot spots, who was on the dance floor, and how fabulous they were. Many clubbers took up positions on gangways, bleachers, podiums, and stages in order to survey the crowd, sometimes in order to look for friends, sometimes to cruise, sometimes to get a sense of the whole event of which they were a part, and sometimes to take a rest from the bustle of the crowd. But this was only a temporary deification. The desire to descend and place oneself with one's peers lead to participation. The surveyor on the gangway or bleachers also circulated his or her gaze around the club, but it was the circulation of the body in that space that defined the next level of participation. A participant in this queer lifeworld transformed the complexity of the environment and the experienced self into a reading and writing of queerness without sacrificing contesting and chaotic elements.

There were two possible other centers by which participants could orient themselves. In all clubs I visited, the DJ booth was separated from

the dance space and areas of public traffic, typically raised and sometimes protected by security. At some points, the crowd acknowledged
Danny Tenaglia, the DJ at Clubzilla at Limelight, by turning and saluting
him on a call-out.[8] The player of the music was less central than the
sound he or she produced. The speakers were positioned so as to form a
saturated center of sound. That gave us a cue for where to head to
dance. Within the club, I and other participants oriented ourselves in
relation to the space itself, the movement, and the soundscape. In the
following discussion, I explore how these three environments oriented
participants.

Tunnel, Limelight, Twilo, and other big clubs had more than one territory and more than one territory of queerness. They held variety in a
way that problematized and resisted models based on community and a
single identity. As big clubs tended to be converted warehouses or factories with different rooms or chambers, they offered contrasting experiences. For instance, in Limelight, in a smaller chapel used as an alternative dance space to the main dance floor, the scene was less crowded and
garage and pop classics were played in contrast to the hard-house soundscape of the main dance floor. In the 1980s, participants at Danceteria
could sample rock music, live bands, disco, and house music on four
floors, as well as the different pleasures of other rooms in which they
could eat and relax. There were always places to explore and things to
do, as Alex described:

> It was our playground. It wasn't just one type of music, it was all kinds of
> music. And on the third floor there would be a gay party and a "Straight to
> Hell" party upstairs for this fanzine. And on the fourth floor was the VIP
> lounge called Congo Bill and it would be really different and really trendy,
> with Boy George and people like that. And it would all filter down on top of
> each other, and you could go in between these parties. So you could go up-
> stairs to the gay party and run downstairs and see the band and "oh, I like
> the music here" and run down to another party, let's go chase this boy up
> the stairs and see where he's going, and look at him, and look at her hair.

Participants could turn a static, fixed space into an infinite number of
combinations and possible experiences by their movement. By choosing
to follow one environment with another, participants could make the
club more than a sum of its zones: they made it a space of play. The
space attained a repertoire when activated by movement. Not just the
zones themselves, but the movement between them shaped experience.

The lifeworld produced by movement was not fixed, but fluidly determined by the moving participant. The participant actively created the club and the experience, rather than being its passive consumer.

U+Me, Octagon's Friday night event for African-American and Latino gay men on West 33rd Street, which started in 1997 and closed 1999, took over two floors: one large space at ground level with house music and a first floor attic with mainly rhythm and blues (r'n'b) and hip-hop music. Colin, an African-American informant of thirty-one who went there twice a month on average, noticed that some folks stayed in one space, rather than moving between the two. Some participants still needed to orient themselves primarily around more stable concepts of identity and community reflected in music, movement, and style. Colin expressed this: "Sometimes I'll move between the two. I enjoy the movement. You feel like you're in a different club actually. Some people never go upstairs and then there are those of us who go between the two." He compared the difference in movement styles between the two floors at Octagon with Suspect, another party for African-American gay men on Sunday nights at a smaller space at Nowbar on Seventh Avenue South in the West Village with one dance floor:

> It has some elements of Octagon, but because the space is smaller, there's more a need to front, [he mimes a posture], more a need to be hard core. It's difficult to distinguish between the posturing and the moving. There's a shift in personas. I think what happens in a smaller space is there's a need to be more hard core, whereas in Octagon you can go to the house level and be more arms in the air. But you'd never do that upstairs.

Participants produced themselves through their style of movement. Colin associated a hard-core, masculine-styled movement with upstairs at Octagon, and a more playful, freer movement with downstairs. He noticed that the upstairs movement style seemed more contained, as participants typically danced with shoulders low, and arms crossing and uncrossing to the beat close and slow in front of their bodies. The mainly black and Latino men in attendance held their energy within their bodies. Their heads nodded to the beat, shoulders hunched, chests downward, knees and weight flexed low and scooped down toward the floor. Colin commented that the dancing style seemed less expansive than in evidence downstairs: few jumps, or arms raised in the air, as if, he noted, that excess was too queen-like. As if, he continued, they were expressing, "We aren't *them* (meaning straights), but we're not *those* (meaning queens)." The movement seemed similar to moves in hip-hop music vid-eos on MTV and Black Entertainment Television. It appeared to be a gay-ness firmly rooted in hip-hop masculinity. Downstairs, dancers moved with gracefully arched spines, twirling and jumping, or raising their arms in the air, with reaching and twisting hand movements. Colin further interpreted this bifurcation:

> Upstairs there's lots more b'boys and posturing. I think the postures peo-ple adopt depends on the music. If you're hearing Biggie [Smalls] or Mase whatever they're saying and even the sound of the music, maybe it's a cue, a clue for adopting a certain posture. Downstairs you're like [he waves hands in the air] "can-you-feel-it!" [he laughs.] And the lights are going . . . 'cos that's also part of it too. Upstairs doesn't have that. It's a room. And I think that's very important that it's just a room. It's darkly lit, and the beats are slower. It's harder to dance downstairs when the beat is faster thump thump thump. It's hard just to be and relax.

Both the movement of others and the musical environment offered cues for distinct body attitudes and movement styles, which were inappropri-ate in other environments. Colin was right. You'd never jump up and down, waving your hands in the air upstairs. In movement styles both up-stairs and downstairs at Octagon, a person and a crowd's self-fashioning within a dance space may be based on sameness and on difference: on what you want to be and on what you don't want to be.

All clubs were stage-managed to some degree by promoters and DJs. A club was a produced event, not only spatially but also temporally. It was a theater prepared for us before we entered, as Alex acknowledged:

> You produce a club. So there are things that need to be performed inside the club. There are people behind the scenes saying we need to have this person doing this inside the club. There's some sort of production going on. On the night there's a lot of stage management. You can manipulate the crowd. "I need you to play this record at this moment, 'cos this is what it's going to do to the room. Or I need this act to go on, 'cos this is what it's going to do to the room. And I need this person to go on, 'cos I want to clear the room." You can change the mood of the room, and a DJ has a lot of power like that and you can change a room of people by one record. You have this idea that works for a while, and then you need to come up with a new idea to change the show a little bit.

As a queer lifeworld, a dance club could produce security and familiarity, but had to balance this with novelty and fantasy. For instance, in the 1980s, the popular dance club Area in Tribeca (1983–87) had a different theme on different nights, sometimes designed by stars of the downtown New York art world such as Jean-Michel Basquiat, Keith Haring, and Nam June Paik. The club itself contained installations and was an installation itself in which people fashioned themselves through costume and movement into pieces of temporary site-specific performance art, as Alex described:

> It had these display cases in the front and they would have live people in them doing things. One month it would be home. And you'd walk inside and the whole club would be like a living room. Or the future. The whole place would be painted silver and they would have gone out and bought all these futuristic furniture pieces.

The theme of the event offered cues to orient participants, from suggesting what to wear to playing certain roles.

The Saint was famous for its theme parties. One such party, recalled by Tito, reproduced the mise-en-scène of *The Wizard of Oz:* "I never saw such a production. You walked in and saw the sign, 'Beware of the witch,' the fields of corn, the yellow brick road." For the fantasy to work, a theme party could not be permanent. It had to be a special event, even for a club. Themed parties drew attention to the fact that going to any club was a special staged event in which clubgoers were invited to cast themselves, whether as futuristic cyberslut, s/m leather boy, Judy Garland on mescaline, or any simply fabulous dramatis personae of the demimonde. This invitation to be fabulous, this acting out of fantasy might have been more "real" than the quotidian reality of everyday life for its participants. They told the story of their experience and their imagination.

I have led you through the streets of New York City, into the apartments of participants as they prepared themselves for the coming night's party. We traveled vicariously to the club, stood in line, were frisked by security, moved through the club, standing on gangways to sense the energy of the crowd, and moved through its zones of décor and movement. Now we stand at the edge of the dance floor. Participants fashioned their worlds from their own bodies out in preparing and moving through a club. This was the experience of world-making through which queer participants moved themselves from a state of worldlessness. They used the practices and the space to produce themselves and their meaning of queer. It was empowering and pleasurable. It was truly fabulous. But these are only parts of the story.

⫩ 3

SLAVES TO THE RHYTHM?
Using Music, Space, Composition, and the Ideas of the Body

In a way it's easier for me to talk about my go-go dancing than dancing on the floor. Maybe because I find something less remarkable, less notable about it. The everydayness of it. For me social dancing is like eating or drinking. Like music. I mean to not have music and dancing in my life, the thought is amazing.   (Colin)

≋ NOW WE ARRIVE at the dance floor—the end of the yellow brick road. The music throbs around us. In front of us all, movement. It seems indecipherable, fearsome, thrilling. We sure ain't in Kansas anymore. How did the sound and movement contribute to the construction, articulation, and expression of queer lifeworlds? How did participants work together music and movement to extend and expand this world-making? Improvised social dancing offered empowerment and a pleasurable form of queer world-making. How do you get your gayness from this? What kinds of gayness do you get? Improvised social dancing involved the incorporation and embodiment of self-knowledge, self-presentation, sociality, and self-transformation. It could embody and rehearse a powerful political imagination, which, while not always utopian or even complete, had agency in queer world-making.

Hedonism can appear to be happy chaos, a rejection of rules and restrictions. But appearances can be deceptive. Queer lifeworlds need a sense of order, which in a dance club was performed through the vehicles of music and dance. The primary function of this order of creativity "was not to be sought in aesthetics, which was a modern invention, but in the effectiveness of its participation in social integration" (Attali 1985, 30). In *Noise: the Political Economy of Music,* Jacques Attali suggests a new theory of creativity in which composition is not the commodified product of privileged endeavor by individuals sanctioned by an elite. Rather, composition is a field and a practice in which composers create and express themselves and their relations with others. The appearance of pleasure for its own sake reveals more about the perceiver than the practice. Where else does this pleasure come from, if not from relation with one's own body and with others?

> In composition, it is no longer, as in representation, a question of marking the body; nor is it a question of producing it, as in repetition. It is a question of taking pleasure in it. That is what relationship tends towards. An exchange between bodies—through work, not through objects. This constitutes the most fundamental subversion [. . .] to stockpile wealth no longer, to transcend it, to play for the other and by the other, to exchange the noises of bodies, to hear the noises of others in exchange for one's own, to create, in common, the code within which communication will take place. [. . .] Any noise, when two people decide to invest their imaginary and their desire in it, becomes a potential relationship, future order (Attali 1985, 143).

The collaboration between dancers and DJs and dancers and other dancers produced pleasure through valuing exchange; this reflected a utopic imagination. In addition, an order that valued working together for pleasure might be, as Attali describes, a manifestation or physicalization of "the most fundamental subversion." In the next chapter, I investigate how dancers worked together to produce a choreographic order. In this chapter I describe how dancers and DJs actually realized this order through sound and movement, which were both the framework and the vehicle of queer world-making.

Every time I walk into a club, I feel a vivid confusion. It's like entering a city in an unknown country. The elements are the same as every other city—people, buildings, roads, vehicles—but the rules that act as interface between me and my environment are unknown. When I walk into a club, the elements are the same as every other club, but what orients me is not bricks and mortar, but the beat and the bodies, both fashioned by producers to produce certain effects. Attali (1985, 143) has even claimed that music is "prophetic" because it creates new orders, unstable and changing. It alters my sense of time. The steady beat provides a solid background against which to appreciate the elements of sound mixed over it. Gradually, I start to detect patterns in the music programmed over both short and longer periods of time. The elements of music set up an order that dance threw itself against, working with it, even as it seemed most contrapuntal.

Garage, hard-house, and Hi-NRG: all of these genres of dance music common in the clubs I visited implied a historical continuity with gay parties of the 1970s. Garage music developed in New York City in the legendary club Paradise Garage (84 King Street, 1976–1987) on the turntables of DJ Larry Levan. Levan, an openly gay African-American, learned his art in the 1970s in clubs such as the Gallery (1972–78)[1] and the Continental Baths, an upscale gay bathhouse in the basement of the Ansonia Hotel on 73rd and Broadway. His musical choices were eclectic in those predisco days, and included rhythm and blues (the progeny of the urban development of blues) and anything danceable; for instance, Aretha Franklin's "Rock Steady," James Brown's "Give It Up or Turn It Loose," and First Choice's "Love and Happiness." In 1976, when Michael Brody opened the members-only Paradise Garage in Soho, Levan went to work there. Paradise Garage, in contrast to its famous contemporary, Studio 54 (254 West 54th Street, 1977–80), had a majority black and Latino clientele. The "garage" style of music he developed there had a strong, heavy beat, with hard percussion, and most important, a soaring lead vocal.

One of his New York DJ peers, Frankie Knuckles, with whom Levan had worked at the Gallery and the Continental Baths, moved to Chicago in 1977 and co-founded the Warehouse dance club. By 1981, he was reconstructing and remixing tracks live with additional percussion effects. House music—as it began to be called after the Warehouse—was more beat heavy than garage, with rhythm as important an element as vocals or other aspects of recording.[2] House went on to become one of the most successful and influential of all dance music sounds. DJs and remixers became its stars, rather than the recording artists. They wove a wide range of samples into the mix from found sounds such as synthesized beeps, movie dialogue, sound effects such as sirens, and vocals, and in the process worked the dance floor into a frenzy. House achieved great popular success, especially in Britain in the mid-1980s, while garage remained largely underground.

But just as house was co-opted by the mainstream and then subjected to the "real music now" backlash, so its progenitor, disco, had walked a similar path several years previously. From 1974 to the end of the seventies, disco was embraced by the entertainment industry, which cashed in even further by spawning movies, mass-produced fashion items, and

bastardized mutant offspring whose genetic inheritance was fatally weak-
ened by the insemination of record companies looking to make a quick
buck (Leif Garrett's "I Was Made for Dancing," anyone?). By the end of
the 1970s, the backlash was beginning with the notorious "disco sucks"
campaign. This reached its zenith in 1979 when Chicago DJ Steve Dahl
urged his listeners to bring disco records to the White Sox baseball game
in Comisky Park so that he could blow them up. But as disco faded in
mainstream America, a new sound was already coursing through New
York gay clubs such as the Saint. Record producers increased the speed
of dance cuts and coupled this with strong vocals and melodies to produce a purposeful sense of joy and excitement. While middle America
was torching vinyl, Amii Stewart's "Knock on Wood" and Patrick
Hernandez's "Born to Be Alive" had already jumped the flames. Gay club
patrons heartily embraced the positive vibe and reaffirming message of
what was later termed Hi-NRG. Its energy matched the often drug-fueled
passion of the dancers in the years before AIDS devastated the scene.
One of the biggest stars of the Hi-NRG scene was underground transvestite star Divine who cut tracks such as "Shoot Your Shot," "Native Love,"
and "You Think You're a Man," much to the delight of many patrons
who celebrated their thinly veiled queer sex references.

By late 1981, the mainstream audience for disco and Hi-NRG had
shrunk. Mainstream America was more concerned about the serious economic recession with its attendant massive unemployment than the
glamour of the dance club scene. Under these circumstances, the core
audience for dance music, a significant segment of whom were urban
gay clubgoers, became an even stronger influence on the artistic direction of the music. Lyrics of tracks such as "Menergy" by Patrick Cowley
and "Cruisin' the Streets" by the Boystown Gang appealed directly to the
gay male audience. The open secret of some mass-marketed, record-
company-produced acts such as the Village People was that their perso-
nas (cop, construction worker, etc.) were gay erotic object types. Tracks
such as "Y.M.C.A." and "Macho Man" were loaded with meaning gay men
could recognize. Although these gay caricatures were popular among
mainstream audiences who saw them as safe, the identification of disco
and Hi-NRG with gay men probably kept a large section of mainstream
audiences away from an interest in dance music. That identification was
so imprinted upon disco music that one man I met declared he doubted
he was gay for many years because he hated it.

The cultural history of dance music and improvised social dancing
developed as people moved into urban centers such as New York and

Chicago. The music and dance African-American and Latin populations brought with them greatly influenced improvised social dancing. The web of social relations and histories that have resulted in such musical and dance style appropriations are fundamentally maps of power. While underground dance music scenes have been more influenced by smaller labels owned by producers of the music itself, the history of the influence of black and Latin music and dance on national popular culture is one in which predominantly white record company owners, producers, agents, and performers benefited from the efforts of African-American and Latino performers and composers. The appropriation of the "difference" of the cultures from which these styles and forms derive historically anointed social improvised dancing as a "transgressive" act and an antidote to a perceived lack of vitality in mainstream white culture (Fusco 1995, 67). This cultural history has implications for queer world-making. In New York City, queer world-making uses the urban texture of the city shaped by its histories of diversity within one relatively small area. In all the clubs I visited, the music and dance were shaped to a lesser or greater extent by African-American and Latin influences. Maps of power were noticeable. The dance floors of the large clubs with the highest entry prices and big name DJs were mainly populated by white men, while many of the people of color with whom I spoke preferred to go to smaller black and Latino or Latina clubs in which salsa or hip-hop was prevalent. In the larger clubs, the beat was maintained, but these influences were somewhat flattened out and whitewashed.

The development of dance music also rode and informed the wave of new technology used in the recording studio and in the DJ booth. The cultural history of dance music and the rapidly advancing technology that enabled it to be recorded, mass-distributed, and played produced particular relationships between the DJ and dancers through the medium of sound. The genealogy of contemporary dance music and DJ technique started in urban, predominantly black clubs, when DJs started to segue tracks into each other to achieve a continuous mix. DJs used two or in some instances three turntables that they operated simultaneously. They played one track on one turntable while listening to another on headphones to cue it up.[3] As technology advanced, DJs used mixing consoles or "mixers" between the turntables to control the relative volume of each, allowing one track to be brought in under another, before it assumed dominance and its predecessor faded away, perhaps to be superimposed later in the new track. The technology assumed the role of a creative instrument, rather than a record "player": as a tool for performance, rather than a copy of one. When DJs themselves were praised by club-bers not just for their technique, but for their artistry in weaving a sound-scape, this neatly captured the shifting role and meaning of recorded music in performance.

But don't think that improvised social dancing evolved in response to changes in DJ technique. More precisely, DJs saw the frustration of danc-ers when they had to stop the flow of movement to allow a record to be changed and therefore sought ways to keep the flow going. This joyful flow of improvisation has order, but is not formally organized as an ob-ject with a beginning, middle, and end. Instead, improvised social danc-ing was an activity, rather than a fixed structural form. Dancers could join in when they wanted and stop when they felt like it. Their flow wasn't halted when a record stopped; their energy wasn't dissipated by a fade-out at the end of a record. Improvised social dancing worked off a continuous flow that encouraged participation by anybody at any mo-ment. The effect was of an ever-present now, as Iain Chambers describes: "Disco music does not come to a halt [. . .] restricted to a three-minute single, the music would be rendered senseless. The power of disco [. . .] lay in saturating dancers and the dance floor in the continual explosion of its presence" (Chambers 1985, 187–88). As technology has ad-vanced, DJs have evolved techniques that have enhanced previous indi-vidual and group responses, such as making associations with lyrics that can now be scratched, sampled, and repeated, to reinforce these associa-tions. Technology's achievement has been to take the collaboration between DJs and dancers to new heights of respect and reciprocity.

The music and dance in clubs I visited was built around a founda-tional pulse beat, typically around 127 beats per minute in the case of house and Hi-NRG, slower in garage, and it was underladen with heavy bass tones so that dancers did not only hear the beat, but felt it. The pulse felt as if it was coming from deep inside your body. This connected the body with the soundscape environment, so that, rather than being acted upon, participants actively engaged and intervened with the soundscape. DJs segued from one record to another between two turn-tables by slip-cueing, cutting, and overlaying. Slip-cueing allowed for the construction of an uninterrupted musical program based on individual records blended together to form one seemingly unending musical land-scape. DJs placed a felt-disc (slipmat) between the record and the turn-table so the record about to be played could be held stationary while the turntable spun underneath it. Thus he or she introduced the track ex-actly on the beat of the record already playing, as if the musicians had changed tune without stopping the beat. DJs fast cut between tracks with rapid, almost instantaneous switching between two turntables, and composed overlays by playing two records at the same time through the speaker system, synchronizing them so the effect was of one piece of music. These techniques not only allowed for the continuousness of the music over an extended period of time, but also for the layering of pieces of different tracks on top of each other.[4] This layering also allowed DJs to mix polyrhythms over the foundational pulse, as well as to strip them away dramatically. Samples and repetitions are the signature elements of much dance music, texturing and varying the soundscape at the same time as the pulse offered security. This order of play encouraged stability and variety simultaneously.

In her useful analysis of social dancing in an African-American community in Philadelphia, dance scholar LeeEllen Friedland identified four musical factors that influenced an individual's dancing performance: tempo, rhythmic structure, phrasing, and lyrics (Friedland 1983, 32). These factors and any combination of them influenced the choices I observed dancers make in incorporating elements of movement repertoire. The tempo of the music affected the likelihood that a dancer would develop rhythmic subdivision or elaboration of the pulse to layer on top of it in syncopation. A slower tempo was more conducive to this. The tempo of the pulse was the primary element to which dancers responded, as Colin indicated:

> As I get older, I don't like to move so quickly. [He laughs.] With that fast house beat I feel compelled to move faster. With r'n'b and hip-hop tempo, there's not so much need to exert as much energy. You can just chill out and relax.

People embraced the music through movement. The beat asserted a tangible control: some dancers moved only on the pounding beat, and others played more with it through syncopating movement rhythms around it. Some embellished it or created variations, and some broke into improvisation, involving themselves completely in composition, transforming the structure and elements of the soundscape through movement. But the parameters of space in the soundscape and on the dance floor also affected to what level a dancer pushed his or her movement. The space within music was a key parameter for improvisation. If there was enough space in between the rhythmical elements, a skilled and confident dancer would extemporaneously compose in between and around it. When the tempo of a piece was too fast, there was less space for the dancer, as Colin described: "It's harder to dance when the beat is faster thump thump thump. It's hard just to be and relax." He distinguished between "just moving" and "dancing." "Dancing" involved some type of artistic invention: it happened when movement became composition in the moment, and that, according to Colin, required relaxation of self-consciousness in order to "be." Rhythmical space could open up or close down those inner spaces.

In the subgenre of "hard-house" often associated with DJs such as Danny Tenaglia, the beat was more than the structural drive; it was often its primary content. Thomas described how lack of rhythmical space could close down the possibilities for creative physical invention:

> There's so much crazy music out in Tunnel or the Sound Factory or now Twilo, where it's not really music anymore, it's just rhythm. Up and down, up and down, it's not real dancing where you really need some space because you're moving a lot more than just dancing up and down.

In a hard-house soundscape I have generally observed less variations in dancing. When I stepped into that soundscape, it wasn't just the speed and power of the beats that restricted my movement. Because it restricted the movement of others, it was difficult to dance as there was little giving or taking of physical space between people, which happened more when people got inventive with movement and used space, rather than occupying it. An order of music with less variety of sound, like the hard-house in Twilo, for instance, seemed to affect less variety in movement. Perhaps not coincidentally in this space, there was also less variety in the bodies present. Keeping this house in order were predominantly white men who worked their bodies in the gym to an Adonis-type template that they worked on the dance floor. They almost all wore tight T-shirts, which they removed and tucked into the back of their pants when things got sweaty on the dance floor. Typically, their range of movement was similar to gym exercises: little flexibility of the spine, with shoulders moving as a yoked unit. Movement was about effort, not fluidity. The mass of movement seemed to be, as Thomas noticed, more up and down, although never leaving the floor. Generally, the men held their arms either close to their body, occasionally raised in the air, or clasped around a friend. More than once, when I was on the dance floor trying to make some space in the music and on the dance floor into which I could insert myself creatively and dance, I felt frustration as I kept banging into more static bodies around me. People who shared this sense of frustration sometimes scolded their more static peers, "If you ain't gonna dance, get off the dance floor." On the dance floor, tensions between dancers were evident not just in comments, but kinesically, as some dancers performed their frustration by audibly huffing, tensing their bodies, or throwing disparaging looks at "nondancers" taking up space. Alternatively, they moved away to find another space.

The rhythmic structures of the beat, rhythmic syncopations, musical and vocal elements, with dropped-in found sounds and noise such as sirens and whooshes, and the force and textures created by their interrelationships in the soundscape mix formed a rhythmic whole, any part of which influenced the choice of rhythmic patterns that different body parts performed and the rhythmic relationships between them. The DJ further played with time by working overlays of samples of sounds such as disjointed, repeated phrases into the rhythmic structure: short samples of a Latin piano lick, for instance, or Madonna incanting, "You're frozen." DJs mixed in several ways. First, successively from record to record. Often a DJ segued in a three-four beat from one record into the two-four beat of its successor to create a few moments of rhythmic disorientation during which dancers sometimes paused for a few seconds with hands on hips quizzically scanning the soundscape for a secure rhythm to ride. The second way in which DJs mixed in tracks was to superimpose them on top of each other relatively seamlessly. Professional turntables have exceptionally powerful motors and a slider, which can increase or decrease the revolution speed of the table by up to eight percent. This feature allowed DJs to accurately synchronize the beat of two different records. Therefore, two tracks with slightly out-of-synch tempos could be played together. The superimposition of one track over another deepened its rhythmic texture, creating polyrhythmic layers dancers played with. DJs sometimes mixed in a sonic boom or prolonged gush to signal a new phase of the program, rupturing the soundscape, opening it out for new interventions of rhythm and noise.

The club, the soundscape, the movement-scape, and the lifeworlds they composed and expressed seemed to be predicated on a balance of stability and novelty. DJs tried to balance new material with better known records to keep the dancers in a familiar but still novel musical environment. Even the best-known tracks were played in unusual relationships or the latest remixed form. Sometimes a rhythm section selected from a more familiar tune was used as a background to extracts from a new one, or was reprised throughout a new piece. Rhythmic patterns pounded relentlessly for hours at a time, while many layers of changing colors and meanings flowed in and out of the matrix. Phrasing or nonmetrical aspects of music affected the nature of rhythmic movement, such as melodic contour, timbre, dynamics, and articulation. It influenced the effort qualities or the character of the energy used in body movement as well as articulation. Participants grouped movements together to form distinct units or phrases. Movement began with an impulse that was carried through to its end, and then either abandoned or transformed as the dancer initiated a new idea or impulse. The flow of movement was generally uninterrupted. Transitions were smooth. The exception to this occurred when a DJ mixed in a new track. At these times I sometimes saw dancers pause until a new secure beat emerged from the crossover between two tracks and they began again. From my own dance floor experience, this was often a good moment to catch your breath and monitor your body's exhaustion. At times I have paused and then realized I needed a break, as I was too hot or too exhausted. DJs programmed and mixed tracks in response to dancers. It was both this element of uncertainty and the need to quickly assess the mood of the audience that DJs seemed to relish in performance and that the audience appreciated in return.

As well as using tempo, rhythmic structure, and phrasing to shape dancing, the lyrical content of tracks often influenced dance in striking ways. Lyrical content and style could prompt dramatic or generally representational gestures, facial expressions, or body attitudes from participants. As a singer implored us to "reach," I saw a dancer respond by bringing his arms up above his head as if aspiring to a higher place. It was as if the dancer brought the lyric into his body, saturated it with his own meanings, and pushed it out through movement back into the world. Historically and contemporaneously, the relationship between marginal lifeworlds and dominant lifeworlds was neither static nor passive: they did not merely coexist, but constantly created and recreated themselves in relation to each other in a dynamic, interactive, and contested process. Making something out of the resources available, seized, or stolen from any context was a practice of queer world-making, which, in appropriating the meanings of these artifacts and loading them with personal or communal meanings, in effect queered them. On many levels, the experience of going to a gay club was one of being immersed in a work-in-progress of *bricolage:* the appropriation, manipulation, and revaluation of signs and practices available to people in their historical parameters.

As individuals and as a group, dancers replaced or accentuated the original meaning of the lyrics with personal and often queer significance. Often the favorite choices for this treatment were tracks that rhythmically and lyrically uplifted the listener with a vision of a world in which unnamed obstacles that could be understood as homophobia, for example, were overcome with the support of a lover and/or a desired-for loving support network. An example was the popular track "Always There":

Always there to please you/ Always there 'cos I need you/ Always there to love you/ Always there thinking of you/ Hey if you wanna, I wanna do it too/ There's nothing better than being here with you/ 'Cos your love is such a precious treasure/ Only you can bring me joy and pleasure/ [. . .]/ I'm gonna be right there when you want me, baby, when you need me baby/ [. . .] / How can I leave you, when you're a part of me?

As the objects of repetitive hearing in clubs, these tracks became the vehicles for a vast range of private and social associations and for individual and social memory. By making these associations, dancers could compose an imagined community in the moment. The original text might assume less significance in itself as more meaning was read into or invested in it and as it became a part of the life of the hearer through repetitive hearings. Although participants forged identifications with lyrics, they did not identify with the singer, but with the expressed experience of overcoming difficulties. But this was only possible if she was allowed to sing her song, as Stephen said:

STEPHEN: And it was about this music, and this vocal house was really important because it was what the lyrics were talking about.
FB: What were they talking about?
S: It was always about, let this black girl sing. She was always singing about hard times and asking us to feel it. And all these songs were about love. And it wasn't just a romantic love, it was a spiritual love of yourself. How to get through the next day. You know? Getting up and dealing with this hard city in terms of the sexual and racial and class politics. It made you feel good. You really came out of there feeling good.

In hard-house, the voices of black female singers who featured heavily in garage and Hi-NRG were cut and sampled in shorter bursts. Then these samples were repeated to such an excess that the meaning became abstract, and the vocal primarily became another element of rhythm rather than the discursive or narrative performance of a subject with whom dancers forged an identification.

But a crowd was not ready to give up their precious reappropriated love on anything the DJ served up. On a dance floor you voted with that most highly valued currency—your feet. At one point in a long continuous tribal rhythm mix of a house track during Junior Vasquez's set at Arena at the Palladium, he broke the flow. Dancers stood disoriented in the pregnant absence of sound and light, which had also stopped flashing. Then a slow, heavy pulse began with a different quality. Powerful bass speakers were lowered from above us, carrying the sound across the dance floor. My organs began to vibrate with the deep pulse that opens "Closer" by Nine Inch Nails. My movement changed. It became slower, as if forced out from deep inside my gut. Suddenly space opened up around me as a few other dancers left the floor. Perhaps they were dismayed or bemused by the new spatial quality of the sound, or the insistent slow grind of the groove, or unable to accept a track from a rock genre more associated with male heterosexuality on a queer dance floor more associated with disco and its legacy. Then again, a few months before at Twilo, Vasquez played an overtly sexy track for what seemed like forty-five minutes. By the time it was over, the floor had lost a few amorous clusters who had perhaps decided to go home to get a private party going. And as it was only 5.30 A.M., they could always come back later.

Typically, a dance club DJ's set lasted from three hours to Vasquez's twelve-hour marathons. Structurally, the performance was endless. Even when DJs cut the sound as in the example mentioned, they used silence plastically as a new sonic experience: an absence so full that it was a vital part of the dynamic texture of the soundscape, rather than bringing it to a full stop. Silence—used strategically by a DJ—had the intensity of sound itself. DJs created a sonic narrative with dramatic dynamics that built toward a cathartic peak. These narratives or programs were both relatively short-term and extended over the entire set. By six o'clock in the morning at an all-night party like Arena at the Palladium, for instance, Vasquez took more risks, mixing in more incongruous sounds. In the hours after eight o'clock in the morning on several occasions at Arena, I heard him mix in alternative rock samples such as the aforementioned "Closer," "Smells Like Teen Spirit" by Nirvana, a maniacally speeded up track from *The Wizard of Oz,* and a Mariah Carey track played backward with its rhythmic integrity intact. At least it sounded that way to me. After several hours in the sonic empire of Vasquez, dancers accepted much more. The drugs also had their strongest grip over the crowd as well at these later times. In addition, by that hour, a hard-core crowd of Vasquez fanatics remained. On a micro scale, DJs programmed several tracks together to form a mini set. At Twilo, I danced to a track that then faded out until several minutes later when it was mixed back over its successor and brought to a peak. Then with a sonic boom, a new sequence began. Satisfied for the time being, I and a few others left the floor for a rest.

The order created by music and improvised social dancing as a vehicle of queer world-making enabled dancers to respond and play with music as an influence and frame. Between different spaces and subjectivities, the lifeworlds produced were different. I experienced these differences through the different musical and movement environments of queer clubs across the city. For instance, the styles of movement and energy were strikingly different between the hard-house soundscape at Twilo and the garage soundscape at the annual celebration of the late Larry Levan at Body & SOUL at Vinyl. At this latter event, many self-proclaimed "old school" (meaning early garage) regulars of Paradise Garage gathered to celebrate the style of music and dance they had enjoyed there and the man who had brought it off. In garage classics, the girl gets to sing her song more often than not, rather than being cut-up and sampled. In contrast to the often restricted, repetitive movement in a hard-house soundscape of beats and samples, exemplified by DJ Danny Tenaglia, for instance, I had the general impression that the movement range was wider, varying from rapid, intricate footwork with the torso tipping and twisting in counterbalance with the feet, to acrobatic leaps, flips, and rippling, full-body contact with the floor; from a voguing style, to African dance-influenced pelvis-torso articulations.

What does the relationship between music and dance produce? Is music the master and we dancers its willing drones? The development of queer-identified dance spaces is synonymous with dance music. In a recent essay on gay men, the music and discourse of disco, and dance clubs, Walter Hughes suggests that:

> Even the subtler critiques of disco implicitly echo homophobic accounts of a simultaneously emerging urban gay male minority: disco is "mindless," "repetitive," "synthetic," "technological" and "commercial," just as the men who dance to it with each other are "unnatural," "trivial," "decadent," "artificial" and "indistinguishable" "clones." (Hughes 1994, 147)

This argument ventriloquized by Hughes catches its tail in the trap of Puritan-capitalism. The dancing body produces nothing; therefore is worth nothing. While this view reveals the prejudices against improvised social dancing and gay men, Hughes understands that the dancing individual cannot resist the empire of the beat which is achieved by its very relentlessness and this, for Hughes, is deeply connected to erotic power:

> The power of the beat to make us dance is commensurate with the power of desire to lead us into sexual acts, even those considered forbidden, unnatural, even unnamable by our culture. Desire, by way of this analogy, is more than either a physical sensation or an internal libidinal force; it becomes a reified external force that can penetrate and establish control over any number of individuals, drawing them into a community of submission to its power. (Hughes 1994, 150)

Hughes internalizes the same oppressive capitalist reading of gay male clubbers that he identifies in reproducing an image of the clubber as surrendering agency to a reified external force. Such readings deny the agency of the dancer, seeing him or her as victim of a (baser) desire located either in or outside the susceptible body and controlling it.

Did club music *make* participants dance, controlling their bodies? In his essay, "Participatory Discrepancies and the Power of Music," musicologist and cultural studies scholar Charles Keil suggests that this power of music lies in the creative tensions and relaxed dynamics that invite the listener/dancer to participate through process (for example, beat, drive, groove) and texture (for example, sound and tone qualities) (Keil 1987, 275). He makes the interesting assertion that the idiosyncratic processual discrepancies within a beat and between any other rhythm sources, including bass, piano, and voice, create "push" or "relaxed dynamism": not only a drive, but a bright, happy sound quality that makes people want to participate. I forced myself to resist and watched individuals at the edge of the dance floor, tracking their increasing involvement with the music and with the group kinesphere from engagement in the beat to dance. There were numerous ways in which this happened. I would like to focus on just two, which I am going to call—following Keil—"processual" and "textual." Neither of these ways of involving bodies with music was mutually exclusive of the other. I observed the first—processual—when the dancer became involved with the drive of the beat. As I watched from the side of the dance floor at Twilo, a dancer started to engage with the beat by shifting his weight from side to side and rocking his pelvis. Gradually, as his whole body became more involved, he isolated his chest from his pelvis, pulling the backbeat through his torso. He clapped his hands softly along with the beat or back beat.[5] In textual involvement, I saw dancers respond to the quality of the track, perhaps joyous or dramatic. A dancer engaged with the music by raising his arms in the air with an upward soaring "whoooa" vocal. Even as I watched, dancers often shifted from one mode of involvement to another, and sometimes operated them simultaneously.

The beat not only penetrated the dancer; dancers penetrated the beat, inserting their kinespheres into it. The progressive drive of the beat contained a dramatic dynamic beyond a flat, regulated measuring of time. If this was less than apparent on listening to a track at home, it was rendered visible and usable when I watched people dance. New dramas emerged from the interaction of dancer and musical text and from between dancers that I was not aware of when I listened to the musical text alone. These dramas resulted from participants' active play with each other and with the musical text. Dancers responded not only to the beat, but also to patterns of tension and release evoked through rhythms and musical chords. They composed new dramas and new possibilities for the music. David Morales' remix of "Goldeneye" by Tina Turner exemplifies the cues DJs served up for dancers. After building up layers of rhythms, which acquainted dancers with the tempo and timbre of the track, and after repetition had made it familiar, the explicit rhythm track was pulled away, leaving the unembellished key signature chords of the harmony chiming out. A key chord sustained itself under the second repeated cycle of these chords to create a dramatic tension of expectation. Dancers acted out this tension, not simply embodying its effects, but producing new and exciting ones through play. They used the power of their own sensual-material moving bodies to act and produce compelling effects of communality, sharing a movement repertoire and a spirit of pleasurable play. Individually and as a mass, dancers created their own dramas within the matrix of the soundscape. Some reveled in their own silence and stillness, but with no less intensity than when they were making large and/or rapid movements. Others took the opportunity to dart around the space in between the temporarily more static dancers. Still others remained on the spot and vibrated in anticipation of what was to come. Within a couple of phrases, the DJ built new, syncopated rhythms on top of the existing phrase, shortening them to a double time to increase the sense of urgency until it broke under the strain and collapsed into a more complex sequence. In a genuinely exciting and moving moment, with the beat as a unifying thread rather than relentless master, the energy of the mass of dancers reached saturation point around me and combined into one great powerful throb, before shattering into hundreds of different points of movement, like a handful of glitter thrown into the air. The effect of these dramas was of a combination of kinespheres that constituted a larger kinesphere of movement to create a community of movement in which the individual's own movement was essential and valued. There was not only "push" inherent in dance music, as Keil identifies, there was also the "pull" of participation, because of both its opposition to alienation from the body, from others, from the environment that is part of the experience of living in a late twentieth-century city, and because of the autonomous pleasure of moving.

The club soundscape's patterns of repetition and variation produced a pleasurable balance between security and novelty. Repetition and variation in movement offered security, novelty, and the opportunity for exchange and empowerment. Because there were no clocks or windows in clubs that measured the passing of time, the effect of drugs, music, and dance made the body the central reference point of another sense of time. This distorted sense of time was affected by the repetition of the beat, phrases, rhythms, breaks, and by the movement. This repetition matrix had four effects. First, the sense of time was measured by music and movement. Second, repetition had a reinforcing effect on movement. Third, repetition had a liberatory effect, as performance theorist Richard Schechner suggests: "It is as if the security of repetition frees the dancer's imagination" (Schechner 1985, 11). Fourth, repetition-accumulation lifted performers: "The spectator's mind tunes to subtle variations that would not be detectable in a structure where attention is directed to narrative or melodic development" (Schechner 1985, 11). Both these contentions are made by Schechner to account for a trance-effect of a collaborative, "collective special theatrical life."

The structure of music and dance across the clubs I visited was characterized by the repetition of motifs with variations and differences combined together in different ways to form a repertoire. By musical motifs, I mean "a short figure of characteristic design that recurs throughout a composition or a section as a unifying element. A motif was distinguished from a theme or subject by being much shorter and generally fragmentary" (Apel 1969, 545), a definition that is applicable to both musical and movement motifs. In movement performance, each repetition of each motif was both first and last time. This was a critical difference in the performance of music and dance. Although repetition of musical motifs contained differences created by the live performance of the DJ, identical repetition was possible and frequent. Only movement performance was never exactly duplicated. This was not only due to the ontology of performance, but also a conscious choice of the dancer as agent. The very nature of social improvised dance and of improvisation per se welcomed, encouraged, and depended upon openness to repetition with differences and to transformation. Dancers engaged in movement motifs, "a short unit that is either dependent on being incorporated into a longer movement sequence (as when a head gesture is used in a complex stepping combination), or it is an independent sequence (such as clapping hands) that is used in conjunction with longer movement sequences" (Friedland 1983, 28). The whole body engaged in social improvised dancing, but not in the same way throughout. At a bare minimum, social improvised dance was based upon at least two movement units: for instance, a rocking pelvis and crossing and uncrossing arms. Difference and repetition were carried both diachronically and synchronically across movement motifs, combinations, and sequences and within the body itself.

Dancers I have observed commonly worked themselves out of one movement motif, often playfully engaging with musical motifs, and, with a new transition, repeated it with a different movement element or quality. At Exhibitchionist, a lesbian party at 2i's on West 14th Street, the border of the West Village and Chelsea, I saw a dancer initiate a repetition of a motif with a small jump. The spring was a new movement element and it affected the quality of her established movement motif. It launched her into a springier variation in which she unraveled a spiral, energetically revolving and twisting to make a Mobius strip out of her movement traces. Next time around, she initiated the motif with a movement triplet on a musical upbeat. The triple bounce imparted a more jittery quality to the same spiral, although the musical motif repeated without variation in structure, content, or quality. In yet other variations, she initiated movement motifs with a jerk of her head or a swing of her arms that set herself off like a spinning top. Each time, the spiral she unraveled with her body was formed by a counterpoint between her torso, arms, and feet. She shifted the weight in her feet in counterpoint to the tilt of her upper body, as she brought one shoulder up, while the other swooped low. She played with the possibilities the repetition of her spiral movement motif offered. They were endless, but her performance wasn't. When she exhausted the possibilities of her kinetic imagination, when she seemed to get bored, or when something new occurred to her, she interjected a new motif, and a new cycle of repetition with variation began again.

As I continued to watch her over fifteen minutes or so, she returned to the original movement motif, using it as a coda. She did so within the same musical track, as if the familiar repetition of musical structure cued repetition of movement structure. Less frequently, she repeated the move, with variations, in a couple of other subsequent musical tracks. Across the changing soundscape, she developed this motif, until it became unrecognizable. Before my eyes, the unraveling spiral transformed. She minimized it, pulling it in closer, reducing the twists, and aligning her upper and lower body. Its direction changed from circular multifocused distributions of energy, to a pumping of energy into and out of the floor. An unraveling spiral transformed in a matter of beats to a fluid rippling up and down her body. Gradually, this changed again. The energy she projected into the floor pushed her feet out until she started to try out steps. A return to her original coda seemed to become a commentary on her development, a base to which she returned to juxtapose how far she had come, and to add even more counterpoint and dynamic to her movement.

As they became more involved with the music, dancers transformed its structural qualities to varying degrees in movement, engaging in compositional practices of increasing levels of intensity that jazz musician Lee Konitz, talking about improvisation in jazz music, distinguishes along a continuum from interpretation to improvisation (Berliner 1994). Konitz's continuum is a useful model because it offers a way to see how dancers worked with the music, and how their increased confidence led to increased involvement and commitment to movement that, in turn, increased individual imaginative possibilities. Success at each level of the continuum provided the basic repertoire, license, and confidence dancers needed to graduate to the next level of involvement, which demanded increased imagination and concentration. As they began to get involved, dancers sometimes restricted themselves to interpretation, entering the musical world along its own path to acquaint themselves with the structural components of its soundscape. They sometimes colored this in various ways by accenting certain beats with a gesture or move, such as clapping or rocking the pelvis. At one moment, I saw a dancer slur and suspend the beat, the next she articulated its every syllable, creating varied textures of lighter and heavier movement accents. Improvised social dancing constantly negotiated individual autonomy within the structures of its environment. However, the cues provided by the environments of music, space, and other bodies and their movement permitted certain freedoms.

Many dancers I observed engaged fragments of a movement repertoire that were sometimes idiosyncratic in relation to the central pulse of the music. These fragments were created, dropped, changed, developed, and/or incorporated into a longer sequence in which the whole body became more and more intensely involved. Many fragments of movement I saw were gestural in response to a quality in the music, including lyrical content. I watched a dancer adopt a mock melodramatic pose by pulling his body to attention, resting the back of his hand on his forehead, and wagging a finger scoldingly on the other hand. As confidence and involvement grew, I sometimes saw some dancers move to the next level of involvement. They started to embellish the musical structure as each one's unique imagination lent distinctive character to their movement. As I watched, I saw a dancer who had become familiar with the track embellish its rhythmic phrasing. He varied this by anticipating or delaying rhythm in one part of the body, while another continued following the beat. I have seen dancers carry the rhythm in their feet, stepping or shifting weight while their torso and arms carried embellished syncopations. Movement intensity increased as dancers started to perform variations, creating individual idiosyncratic movement shapes and patterns whose relationship to the musical shape and pattern remained clearly defined. This seemed to require further concentration. Dancers were intent on both the music and their movement.

Finally, the music and space could become vehicles of autonomous invention. This improvisational mode required a high level of concentration, involvement, and imagination. Often it was not sustained and occurred in short bursts. I saw a dancer become completely immersed in her own artistic creation, transforming the parameters of music and space. She seemed to stay within the environment of music, without ascribing to its dictates of rhythm and pace. She bent down at the waist, until her torso was parallel with her legs. Then she rolled out of her bend by pivoting around her pelvis, and shook herself out with hands on her head. She turned herself over into that bent position again and twisted her arms behind her torso, down her back and legs, pulling and pushing her hands around each other and over and underneath her, and letting that movement carry her down to the floor. She crouched there and repeated her rolling twisting motions with her arms alternately over and underneath her torso and back, until she hugged her knees. Then, with small gestures, she pinched and unpinched her fingers and articulated every joint of her arms as if her hands were butterflies. Her posture and her gestures were original in that they did not ascribe to a typical movement repertoire of axial (vertical spine) movement. Through movement she played with the music; her laid-back attitude and pulse sometimes seemed to counterpoint the insistent and unvarying beat. Yet, within social improvised dancing, I was fast learning that unexpected gestures, attitudes to rhythm, and qualities of movement were part of the form itself.

Her ability to play with music and movement together not only held great aesthetic appeal to both her and to me—her spectator—in its variations, but suggested some shared meaning and value in a queer lifeworld in which play was important. Colin saw play as an important element of his own movement in relation to music:

> I say play or playful because for me I relate to music. I think of it as a dialogue. Sure, certain things are being dictated or suggested by the rhythm but I feel confident enough when I'm dancing to stop all of a sudden, which I think is very cute. That for me is being playful—moving and working with the music rather than just dancing to the music [He strikes a regular beat on every syllable]. Which I think a lot of people do and that's OK but they're just following the music.

The pause or "freeze" he described was an excellent example of movement play. It was, as LeeEllen Friedland so effectively describes in her fieldwork on African-American body-poppers, a "punctuation in active stream of movements and a powerful locus for aesthetic engagement between the performer and nonperformers" (Friedland 1983, 28). As she notes, movement play required skill and earned prestige. But, as I suggest following Attali, composition in such a context as a queer dance club could not be judged on aesthetics but on social integration (Attali 1985). In queer clubs, there was a standard of fierceness. The execution of movements such as the freeze also required and produced confidence. This self-assuredness was a key element of "fierceness." Friedland suggests that the effectiveness of such movements may be that they were unusual and not commonly seen in everyday life. However, I would elucidate this further by suggesting that it was not always incongruous bodily images that produced the effectiveness of this dance. I would suggest that through the observations I have made in queer clubs, effectiveness also related to attitude to movement. It was the confidence or fierceness with which movements were executed, their flowing quality, and their deliberate rupture and restructuring, and the pleasure of execution by the dancer that simultaneously was valued by queer standards of fierceness, and which also empowered the individual within a queer lifeworld. Furthermore, if the currency of fabulousness and of fierceness had its own gold standard to support it, then its effect on the dancer and on his or her witnesses also held power throughout the club and into the everyday world outside.

As mentioned in the previous chapter, through dancing, Stephen empowered himself. Being able to successfully engage in movement play gave him a confidence he used in his everyday life outside of the club. I have watched Stephen and others leave the dance floor and circulate in the club with energy and vigor, engaging friends and the space around them with his fierceness and sheer fabulousness. I have walked through the East Village with him as he proceeded with a sexy bounce, torquing his body when someone called to him, or slyly sidling up to someone on the street, and getting into their stride before cocking his head and greeting them. It was as if the repetition of movement in clubs and the repetition of going to clubs once a week, most weeks, allowed him to commit those sensations of confidence in his body to his body. They became habit, and a valuable resource he drew on in his everyday dealings with others in the club and in his life.[6]

When a dancer worked with the soundscape, he or she worked, not only with the structure, contents, and qualities of the sound itself, but with its history and appropriated meanings. Through music, dancers connected themselves to their own compositional desires and abilities. Their world-making through this connection enabled and articulated ordered relationships with the present and with the past, which embodied agency, creativity, and values to self-fashion through movement. Like the instruments and technologies of music itself, dancing became the tool of performance, rather than its by-product or symptom. But music was not the only structure within which dancers played. The matrices of relationships on the dance floor were not only between dancers and the music, but with each other. Both these relationships shaped ideals of community within lifeworlds in queer clubs.

4

THE ORDER OF PLAY
Choreographing Queer Politics

I know a lot of gay people across communities—clique is a better word. I don't like the term gay community or lesbian community in New York because I don't believe there is just one. That assumes that all gay people share the same values and the same politics and that clearly isn't the case. I really didn't like Crowbar. It attracted a lot of young people I didn't see at the Bar or the Tunnel Bar and that shook me up a little bit. Partly it was competition . . . what are these young guys doing in my neighborhood. In the two years I had been going to these bars I had embraced their history because I had met so many people who would tell me they'd been going to the bar for twenty years. I felt a part of that history through these various cliques. Between these bars there was not a singular community and I was happy I could bridge those communities as a lot of people did. But I knew a lot of people who would say, "I never go to Tunnel Bar, I never go to the Bar." The Crowbar was taking business away from the bars I wanted to support. So I stopped going. (Barrel)

With freedom you can do what you want to do, but maybe do something you don't want to do. In clubs you put on a kind of persona. We want to be different, but then we don't. When you grow up gay, you're an outsider and you want so bad to belong to something. We'll take drugs we wouldn't normally do, we'll have sex we wouldn't do. We'll take more risks, because we want to be part of a scene. (Iain)

≋ OUR LIVES ARE DEFINED by the limits of our imagination. When I reflect upon the stories of informants and their relationships—imagined and realized—with others in the club, a complex, sometimes contradictory texture of desire and reality-making emerges. Some participants wanted to see the club as a space of escape from the outside world; others wanted to see these spaces as prepolitical configurations of community that could blossom into political agency outside. Some saw their activity as an individual self-fashioning; others expressed that their decision to go to a club was born out of desire to be with others like themselves, and still others found any realization of these desires compromised or unfulfilled in clubs. While none of these expressions negated each other, they did present images of the imagined and real club space and of improvised social dancing as complex textures. None of these expressions necessarily had the same resonances for everyone. What were the relationships between individual self-fashioning and notions of community and political agency through the relationships between bodies as they danced? How did meaning in and of a queer lifeworld get constructed not only by the individual dancing, but also by bodies dancing together? I contend that from the physical and verbal articulations of at least some participants, improvised social dancing in queer clubs did not exist outside of everyday life. It drew from it and informed it. What people could imagine kinesthetically and/ or politically, on the dance floor and on the street constructed lifeworlds. I want to explore some of these political aspects by unpacking the view that dance itself is mindless and those who indulge in it are not only guilty of mindlessness, but of a dangerous surrendering of political agency, and how individuals, as active agents of queer world-making, learned how to be with others on the dance floor and in a queer lifeworld through incorporation and realized the shape of both through embodied practices of energy transmittal and movement mimesis.

That complicated term "community" is not one I feel comfortable applying to what I observed and experienced in clubs without giving it a very nuanced definition for two reasons: the limitations of community building as political praxis for gays and lesbians, and the complex configurations of expressed desire, utopian longing, disappointment, and the sheer variety of practices in the club space. In his essay, "Identity and Politics in a 'Postmodern' Gay Culture," Steven Seidman traces the development of queer politics from the gay liberation movement of the early-1970s, and notes the reason for the failure of its dominant agenda of community building based on an ethnic model of identity politics:

> The challenge to the dominance of an ethnic model, with its notion of a unitary gay identity and its emphasis on cultural difference, surfaced from individuals whose lives were not reflected in the dominant representations, social conventions, and political strategies. (Seidman 1993, 117–18)

The margins revolted against the center, only this time the center was not mainstream heterosexual culture, but gay culture, dominated as it was by white, middle-class gay men. Even lesbian politics, orienting away from gay culture toward separatism, was dominated by white, college-educated women who set the agenda. Ever since this failure—and it continues today rather than being set in the amber of 1970s liberation politics—gay politics has grappled with the problem of inclusionary representation, while maintaining the autonomy of individuals' needs and priorities. Through interviews, experiences, and observations, a complex, sometimes contradictory texture emerged in clubs when participants verbally or physically expressed a desire for or experience of community, sometimes through a sense of disappointment or an acknowledgment of dystopia.

I find Richard Dyer's (1992) self-admittedly overschematic categorization of the utopian sensibility and its relation to specific inadequacies in society useful for understanding the utopian promises of dancing in clubs, and how they can fall short of the experience. Dyer neatly identifies social tensions, inadequacies, and absences and what the entertainment economy offers as their utopian solutions. Instead of exhaustion, it promises energy; it replaces dreariness and monotony with an intensity, excitement, and affectivity of living; substitutes the manipulations of advertising, bourgeois democracy, and sex roles with transparency: that is, open, spontaneous, honest communications and relationships; and replaces the experience of fragmentation, which Habermas (1989) identified as one of the causes of the failure of the utopian promise of the public sphere, with the experience of community. Perhaps then this was one of the reasons that many informants evoked a desire for community in its complex expressions. It may be the one promise that informants felt could not be fulfilled in any other space or by other practices involving queers together.

The advantage of this analysis is that it offers some explanation of why entertainment *works*. The weakness of this analysis, according to Dyer, is the absence of class, race, or patriarchy from the left-hand column. But not all informants with whom I spoke emptied all of these needs from their evaluation of social tensions, inadequacies, or absences that a club could or did address. Several informants included one or more of these factors in their evaluation of the utopian promise of queer clubs, recognizing that its failure rested in the failure of the clubs and their patrons to negotiate race, ethnicity, class, and/or patriarchy as an inclusive model of queer world-making. Going to a lesbian club, for instance, did not mean you could get in or, once in, that you would not experience racism or sexism. To the list of factors not always addressed in clubs, I would add heteronormativity, experienced by some informants as a conscious tension within society to their perceived deviance to which queer clubs promised a utopian solution celebrating queerness. However, in relation to queer clubs, homonormativity—that is, the conservative and assimilationist dominant gay culture that seeks to alienate queerness—produced social tensions between itself and queers that were not resolved in some spaces. Disposable income, whiteness, and ideal notions of physical attractiveness produced a sense of belonging and a sense of alienation in different individuals. This gets complicated in queer clubs, many of which have their own normativity: buff Chelsea boys may feel alienated at the East Village queer club Pyramid; white or black men with the "wrong" bodies may feel alienated at Octagon; bears may feel alienated at Twilo, and so on. It is important to note that, perhaps with the exception of community, the ideals of entertainment imply wants that capitalism itself promises to meet. That the utopian solutions of entertainment and of a club may also be the promises of capitalism hints at what may be an unpalatable truth for some. At its core, entertainment, including clubs, may be reactionary and normative unless otherwise consciously kicked against. Informants who critiqued notions of community that were based on economies of capital, including standards of beauty and conspicuous consumption, were also more likely to critique capitalism. In fact, their critiques of certain clubs articulated their critique of capitalism. Informants who enjoyed going to larger, more expensive clubs with their designer bodies and dress, were not apolitical, but seemed to articulate their politics through describing clubs as spaces of self-actualization and realization: be all that you can be, rather than destabilize normativity or make allegiances with other queers, people of color, and women. Yet if the promises of capitalism do not include community, how might a dance club suggest resolutions to this failure?

On top of the complex image presented by the verbal expressions of participants, the movement on the dance floor itself was a constant negotiation of individual creative autonomy and communality. This was due to more than the truism that the literal and metaphorical common ground of these subjectivities was the dance floor, partly because across New York City there was the choice of many dance floors and all informants rejected one or another because a place was "not about them." For instance, Colin was not interested in going to Twilo with its majority white clientele, Tito because the vast majority were a good thirty years younger than he was, Thomas because he felt he could not be open about his HIV status, and Catherine because it was male dominated. When I looked over any dance floor, it initially seemed as if everybody was moving the same way. Yet, as I observed for a time, I began to notice individuals and clusters. I noticed dancers on podiums, go-go dancers, and how those around them oriented themselves in relation to them. My gestalt impression was of a mass of individual movements threaded with contingent interrelations. What made it seem initially as if everybody was doing the same thing was that somehow order was maintained. There were ordered ways of being together that worked on the dance floor to produce individual as well as mass experience. How was this achieved? What rules were in operation and how were they learned, observed, interpreted, and used as the basis for improvisation? By understanding the choreography of the dance floor, can I understand a model for queer community and queer politics?

Choreography is the deliberate patterning of a body or group of bodies using the plastic elements of space, time, and effort. These are traditionally formalized into a score put *onto* the bodies of dancers by a choreographer. Improvisation differs from this model of formal choreography in at least one important respect: while the creative process for a choreographer may take months and precedes its performance, the creative process in improvisation is happening in the very moment of performance. Lynne Anne Blom and L. Tarin Chaplin explain in their work on dance improvisation that "the kinesthetic self is free to partner the imagination impulsively, without preparation or preconception" (Blom and Chaplin, 1988, x). This is broadly true. However, "freedom" does not mean the same thing to all and the execution of this slippery and contingent concept on the dance floor produced different tensions within and between dancing bodies. Blom and Chaplin continue, "Improv implies a lack of constraints, a diversity of possibilities to follow in any direction for as long as the mover pleases" (1988, x). This is the implication, not only of improvisation, but also of freedom. However, on the dance floor, as in any physical arena, there were limitations and constraints on space at least. Participants had to be aware of and observe certain rules; otherwise chaos reigned. Chaos on the dance floor might look something like a brawl between people who have not observed the rules of respecting each others' space or kinesphere. It certainly would not be an attractive space to enter, and quite possibly would be physically dangerous. A bloody nose in a mosh pit may be a badge of accomplishment, but on a dance floor it definitely signals a bad night. Blom and Chaplin round off their initial description of improvisation by stating that:

> It exists outside everyday life, creating its own time-space boundaries, seeking only its own inherent profit and goal. In ordinary life we learn to distinguish the real from the unreal; in play and improv we acknowledge all realities. Make-believe becomes as real as gravity and equally, or more, potent. (xi)

Blom and Chaplin denote this idea from the field of dance they regard as the model for dance improvisation: the work of Steve Paxton, Yvonne Rainer, Trisha Brown, and Anna Halprin in the 1960s.[1] As I am looking at improvised social dancing in queer clubs, I would like to add an important nuance to this. While improvised social dancing had its own profit and goal, it was affected by and affected everyday life. In queer world-making, as in improvisation, make-believe—or what queers can imagine kinesthetically and/or politically, on the dance floor and on the street—could be as real and as potent as gravity.

When I went to a queer dance club, I made a choice to place myself in a particular space and engage myself in particular practices. I chose to shape myself and my relationships through experiencing the movement of my body and the movements of others around me on the dance floor. But am I also choosing to forget and escape? To get into the body is sometimes read as collusive with getting out of the mind. Furthermore, in the case of going to queer dance clubs, a homophobic-inflected capitalist reading asserts that music, drugs, and alcohol are uncritically consumed and an apolitical clone intent on irresponsible hedonism is produced. Alex succinctly describes a certain attitude he experienced, "turn up the music, spoon some more coke up your nose, and take off your condom." What are the cultural prejudices that located improvised social dancing and the pleasure it produced as apolitical and as a surrendering of individual and group agency to the imperative of the party?

Catherine glowed when she told me how excited she was to be going to dance clubs in New York City. Back in Middle America, in the strict religious community in which she was raised, dancing was forbidden. She recalled hiding an outlawed Walkman under her mattress and listening to music after curfew. During these precious stolen times, she coped with the repressions of her home life by imagining herself dancing. She came to New York to find her feet—literally and metaphorically. Her story reminded me that the moral suspicion of dancing is not a historic phenomenon and still exerts a great and pervasive influence over Western thought. The pioneer of kinesics, Ray L. Birdwhistell, suggested that the origins of the mind/body split, which is rooted so firmly in Western society, is a result of a predisposition to diametrically opposed and valued splits (Birdwhistell 1976, 66). Historically, emotion was anatomically located somewhere below the rib cage, opposing rationality, which operated from the head. By association, "bad" became fixed on the body and on the emotions, both being the site of violence, illness, and waste. To be "good" it was necessary to keep any of the evil leaking out of the baser body. The body was monitored for productive, rational output directed by the mind. When the mind lost control of the body, the individual would cease to be productive and controllable, and dangerous chaos would result that threatened to disrupt the social order.

These prejudices are reproduced by a legislative economy that insists with the force of morality that the heteronormative family is the sanctioned economic unit upon which capitalist society is based. The individual animated body is scrutinized by the society that equates its non-task oriented actions with evil excess: the individual who uses their physical capabilities for anything other than production and reproduction is evil. Thus, under the same rubric, a Puritan-capitalist ethic casts both the dancing body and the queer body into the pit of damnation.[2] This imperative has resulted in a deep division between work and leisure. Furthermore, it bifurcates cultural use-value between those practices producing an end, and autotelic practices, whose ends society perceives to be indulgent, hedonistic, and marginal. These "useless," "trivial," or "low" evaluations are then associated with their participants. Therefore, clubbers are stigmatized as "mindless," "primitive," and "immature" because of their pursuit of pleasure dancing in clubs. Clubs themselves are seen as having little cultural or social value. Indeed, the media frequently portrays them as sites of self- and social-destruction.[3]

In the field of lesbian, gay, and queer politics, commentators have expressed alarm that making cultural meaning in a market-mediated environment robs a presumed unitary queer culture of its political power. In short, they surmise that attendance at clubs produces nothing useful politically. Even worse, it is a dangerous distraction by which people immerse themselves in hedonism rather than politics. Recently, gay culture observer Daniel Harris bemoaned the effect of a pervasive late-capitalism ideology of individualism that supersedes social responsibility and opposition to hegemony: "All too often personal empowerment becomes a substitute of social empowerment, self-acceptance for social acceptance, coming out for fighting back" (Harris 1997, 258). Undoubtedly, the ideologies of these times combined with an absence of alternative ideological underpinnings of national political debate and the assimilationist mood of mainstream gay politicking, have rendered queers susceptible to the instantly gratifying self-help rhetoric of commercialism. However, it is precisely because I see struggles for the right to dance in New York City that I sense that an important battle is being waged. The action has moved from the arenas of government to the arenas of popular culture.

Two perspectives reinforce the position that clubbers do not mindlessly engage in trivial, inconsequential activities. First, as queer theorist and political activist Michael Warner notes in a ground-breaking introduction to a collection of essays that identify and coalesce queer theory and politics:

> To a much greater degree than in any comparable movement, the institutions of [queer] culture-building have been market-mediated: bars, discos, special services, newspapers, magazines, phone lines, resorts, urban commercial districts. Nonmarket forms of association that have been central to other movements—churches, kinship, traditional residence—have been less available for queers. (Warner 1993, xvi–xvii)

The third space of recreation has often been the only space in which queers could express themselves in ways often not available in the home or the workplace. Second, I believe that the practice of improvised social dancing offered ways of teaching queers how to be together. It produced paradigms of sociality and kinship in excess of the market and upon which the health of the queer individual and the queer lifeworld depended. It has potential to teach us how to be together at the same time as asserting a creative autonomy—a utopian sensibility that breaks open Dyer's schematic. The impulse to dance revealed a desire to compose a version of the self that moves out of its prescribed column and dances all over the map.

Improvising movement on a dance floor, participants never moved in an empty space. Improvisation developed in complex and beautiful ways from an individual's own body-consciousness, experiences, and memories of moving in everyday life and of moving on other dance floors or on the same floor in times past. It also sprang from those incorporated ways people knew how to be together. This negotiated both the desire of how people wanted to be with another or with a group or mass, and the physical rules they had to observe when they were. Individual movement motifs of fall and recovery, freezes, and the use of two units of movement simultaneously, for instance, gained deeper resonance when considered in this context. Some of these resonances were political. In improvised social dancing, participation broadly produced two kinespheres—of the individual and the group. The negotiation of these kinespheres in relation to music and in relation to others within the group suggested how the choreography of individuals to each other and to the group negotiated the physicality and sociality of queer lifeworlds. Dancers simultaneously worked with their fellow dancers, but could also retreat into a world of their own. Paradoxically, although dancers directed their focus inward, it seemed as if awareness of others in close proximity was maintained or even increased. Thus, the dancer had to measure the space around him or herself, and to be aware of others at the edges of the space they made for themselves on the floor through movement.

Informants often expressed relief when someone got up to dance on a previously empty dance floor, as Dana, an African-American lesbian in her midthirties expressed: "I hate walking into a club and everyone's just sitting around looking at each other and trying to figure out if anyone's looking at them. It's a downer and it's so stupid. What you really need is a few people to get their butts on the floor and get over the fact everyone's gonna look at them for a while. Then more people'll get up and hopefully the party'll get kicking." Dana's words reinforced my impression that most dancers found security and developed energy when on the dance floor with others. So, while not sacrificing individuality, dancers found confidence as part of a group. Space was a physical plastic reality, which dancers shaped. Movement created the space of the dancer—their kinesphere—in the soundscape and on the dance floor. Too much space, in the case of an empty dance floor, and people seemed timid of breaking the emptiness. That is, unless they could dance with a group of friends who offered some security dancing together. I observed that people played with movement if they had the space to do so—both on the floor and in the music. On a tightly packed dance floor, less play was obvious.

The variations in levels of involvement and the movement styles and the intensity a group of people produced on any dance floor I observed contributed to the gestalt effect of a mass of individualized movement. As a function of queer world-making, levels of involvement from interpretation of the beat to embellishment through to improvisation were ways in which dancers could build their confidence, evoking a sense of both security and creativity in and between individuals. As an articulation of queer world-making, the improvisational movement of individuals was integral to the mass: it constituted it. For instance, a woman I observed one night at 2i's danced near a participant who was improvising freely with the music and the space around her. She gave her space and preserved her own. She moved more closely on the beat, bringing her feet together on the first beat of the rhythmic phrase, and pushing each arm across her torso, while twisting her shoulders to counterpoint her pelvis. She seemed less confident of experimenting with movement in comparison with the other dancer. She started moving self-consciously and remained axial, but, gradually, her confidence seemed to grow, and she invested her movements with more energy and intensity. She seemed to work more with the music, rather than hiding behind it. Although the difference in moves, style, and intensity of these women's movements produced them as individuals to my eye, their spatial awareness of each other made it seem to me as if they were not isolated from each other and indirectly worked together. Occasionally, the more reserved dancer glanced over at the more experimental one. Although neither made eye contact with the other, they gave each other enough space and appeared to appreciate each other's presence on the almost empty dance floor.

In their work on dance improvisation, Blom and Chaplin suggest that the combined elements of kinesthetic awareness, phrasing, forming, and relating contribute to the experiential body of knowledge that I have defined as twofold drawing from the experience of the everyday body and from previous improvised social dancing experience. Our experience of moving in the world is a vital mode in which we learn about ourselves and about our world. This knowledge is both incorporated and embodied: it is brought into our experience through the body and is expressed through it. Such physical agency is not mindless as the body itself has its own intelligence and memory: when we lift a new object, we draw on muscle memories of lifting to anticipate our necessary physical performance. The body provides constant feedback to the brain to judge spatial parameters, distance, and size. It perceives the position of body parts, and processes and stores information about laterality, gravity, verticality, balance, tensions, and dynamics, as well as integrating and coordinating rhythm, tempo, and sequences of movements. All these activities of perceiving the self and others are integral to everyday life, but on the dance floor, dancers were more aware of using their kinesthetic awareness, not only to prevent themselves from falling or hitting someone else, but also to create movement.

Occasionally, dancers unintentionally lost their balance, or accidentally made contact with others around them. From observation and experience, there were different responses to this from other dancers. Often when I saw or experienced accidental contact, the person contacted offered reassurance that they were not irritated by smiling and it seemed that people tolerated and even expected some infringement of intimate space. However, I also observed that there was a limit to the amount of times contact was accepted. If a person was unable to follow rules of dance floor etiquette—often through being involved in their own movement to the point of ignoring others, perhaps affected by drugs and alcohol—then people around expressed irritation, moved away, or in a couple of instances I witnessed, their irritation was such that their own play state was broken and they left the dance floor altogether.

Dancers also worked from their own body knowledge of movement linkage, transitions, and organization, using this knowledge to create forms that responded to the music, to the impetus of movement itself, and to others close by. Dancers were influenced by all these parameters and this was one of the reasons for the impression of order that pervaded my observation of the dance floor as a whole. However, the relationship of the dancer to all these three influences of music, their movement, and the movement of others close by did not result in uniformity of movement style. I want to focus particular attention on the effects of the last of these parameters I have mentioned—the influence of others around the individual dancer—in order to investigate how dancers choreographed themselves in relation to each other.

Dancers participated in each others' movements, even when, on a dance floor, there was only limited formal partnering. Dancers picked up on each others' rhythms and seemed to follow, lead, complement, and/or counterpoint them. Blom and Chaplin suggest that this results from "kinesthetic empathy": that when dancers see each other moving, they know "on a deep level about the delight, calm, or frustration they are experiencing [. . .] It allows us to [. . .] identify with him in the shared experience of movement" (Blom and Chaplin 1988, 23). This experience seemed to be indicated in both participants' retold experiences and in my own. Tito Mesa recalled a particular dancer who would impart a certain feeling to those watching him:

> Oh, Michael Beck. That's a name to remember, Michael Beck. That was the first dancer—fan dancer—in New York City. Nobody fucking danced like Michael Beck. He was my inspiration. You saw this man and you have

to stop and salute. Besides that, he was beautiful. He could go all night all over his body, dressing his body with his fans. He was so gentle, no attitude or whatever. Watching him, I felt such joy, such peace.

However, I contend that such kinesthetic empathy was not only based on identification as Blom and Chaplin suggest. Dancers may not always have known what another was experiencing when they watched each other dance. They interpreted others' movement through knowledge of their own movement experience. Some dancers felt alienated from others if they seemed to be experiencing what they did not.

Dancers received and achieved a level of energy from each other, but they also incorporated others' moves into their own repertoire through mimesis and adaptation. These techniques produced and articulated knowledge of the shared rules of sociality. I engaged in mimesis in my ethnographic research. I would try to copy styles of movement I found intriguing or compelling when I was dancing at clubs, as I noted in my fieldnotes:

> Often when I see a movement, I try to duplicate it, try it in my own body. This can be very helpful, but it also presents problems, which can also be productive. I watched these muscle guys and one was doing some really interesting movement. I tried to copy it, but felt weak, like I was a bad photocopy of a bad photocopy. Gender and muscularity have a lot to do with it. His dancing body is visibly and experientially so different from mine. I became very aware of how weak my left side has become especially (Fieldnote: Sound Factory Bar, 11/29/96).

The rule of this ethnography, at least, is first you do it, then you understand it; not only because you can reproduce another's movements, but because you can't ever exactly. In sensing through my body's auto-feedback that I couldn't reproduce someone else's movement, I learned that my gender and muscularity not only precipitated my failure, but also produced my difference. I produced a different movement effect in my body even if I duplicated the moves themselves.

As drama was produced between dancers and the musical text, so it was also produced between bodies. I want to demonstrate examples of how participants picked up on each others' movements, adapted them into their own movement style and/or complemented them. I saw a dancer move low next to someone whose movements were high and in the air. Another dancer moved on the beat, while another emphasized the back beat. Occasionally, an informal contest or challenge began between dancers. One performed a phrase of movements, and the next picked up their dominant or last moves, or complemented it, and developed it through their own phrase. Each playfully seemed to try to outdo the other. I saw this more formally in the challenge circles that formed at certain clubs, for instance at Café Con Leche—a mixed midtown club populated predominantly by Latinos. In these circumstances, an order was maintained. Each dancer signaled that he or she was ready to go into the circle for a virtuoso turn by pacing around inside its inner ring of participant-observers. The dancer's entrance sometimes overlapped with the previous dancer's presence in the space. In these circumstances, he or she danced with them or next to them until the other dropped out, not unlike the mixing of tracks over each other until one emerged dominant. But other less formalized partnering or interrelations occurred between dancers. People danced together apart, picking up on each other's energy and moves and using them as resources for their own movement and energy.

At clubs such as Escuelita and Krash on Astoria Boulevard in Queens, I noticed different attitudes to dance compared to the relationship of the individual to the mass in clubs such as Twilo and Arena. There was more partnering, for instance. The participants I saw made more contact with each other, both eye contact and physical touching. On the floor at other spaces, I saw a mass of individuals of small clusters; at Escuelita and Krash I more often saw a mass of partners. This was not at all times, but when a salsa or merengue track started, dancers rearranged themselves on the floor through subtle and not so subtle shifts of their bodies, their attitudes, and their focuses onto each other. Dancers touched each other more, not only through physical contact, as they grabbed hold of each other's hands, shoulders, or hips, but through orienting themselves closely around another, working in and out of their kinesphere, around them and up and down them. The participants I saw did not represent sexual acts through a recognized lexicon, but produced the effect of creative sexiness through contact, playfully catching each others' eyes and/or holding an intense gaze, and moving close to each other. The rhythmic phrasing of Latin music and the style of its dance evoked stepping footwork: often participants tilted their hips at counterpoint with their torsos, initiated movement in the pelvis, and crossed their feet over each other in small flowing steps.

One time at Escuelita, my friend Juan pulled me into a merengue with him. I didn't know how to dance the merengue as a formal step, but went with the rhythm, picked up on what other couples were doing, incorporated it, and followed his physical cues relayed through his hands as they gently pushed mine to nudge me into a turn. I was used to dancing in a club for a while without getting tired, but after just a minute or so, the fronts of my thighs were screaming for mercy. Executing tight, intense steps rapidly, I really felt how this dance differed from the freer, individualistic improvised dance I was more used to doing. I held my center of gravity higher in my body, rather than dropped low into an open pelvis and fairly static feet. (Usually I kept my feet static or close to the floor so I could feel across my personal floor space without stamping on or kicking another dancer.) Just holding the posture of arms up and holding anothers' hands, head high, spine erect yet flexible, hips angled backward, really put strain on my body. But it was also fun; I certainly laughed a lot. While there was something secure about playing with my own body as I concentrated on my own movement, there were also new adventures and possibilities to be had in dancing with another. This may be part of the attraction of Escuelita and Krash and Latin dance styles in general when I have seen them appropriated at other non-Latino clubs. Even at different spaces, I have seen and experienced a certain joy shared between two people when they danced in relation to each other.

This incorporation of moves was both functional and expressive. It was a way participants learned how to be with others and it was simultaneously expressive of the pleasure of being with others. I asked many participants to recall how they felt on entering a queer club for the first time. To a person they all responded that they were anxious. Iain's response was typical:

> I wasn't completely out. I remember going to my first gay club in about 1982 and being scared to death. It was fear that I would actually have to connect with another gay man, 'cos I really hadn't in that setting before. 'Cos everyone seemed to be in control there, whereas outside they weren't. 'Cos all the gay men were there as a group. I remember sitting on steps and thinking, "Please nobody talk to me." I didn't know what to do, what rules to follow, how you were supposed to go about meeting people.

For Iain, having knowledge of the rules was vital to operate in the space and to have control over the possibilities he encountered for interrelationships. How could he be powerful as an individual gay man if he didn't know the rules that produced the order of gay sociality? The specialized rules of sociality in a gay club were a school in which he learned the rules of the wider gay lifeworld. In other words, these rules were not so particular to the club at all; in fact, they informed his behavior outside the club. I want to demonstrate five instances of how participants shared knowledge of movement partly so you can see the diversity of experience, relationship, and movement this exchange created. First, one individual was taught how to play with movement by others. Second, a crowd transmitted shared knowledge through their responses to music. Third, participants used body knowledge to orient themselves in relation to the crowd. Fourth, participants used the knowledge of the rules of personal space within the crowd, before showing some of the ways being together on a dance floor produced social interaction. Fifth, I suggest how a queer space projected rules of sociality, which resulted in the rejection of outsiders who did not value an exchange of physical closeness. All of these used incorporation through mimesis and transmittal in different ways.

Before participants could experiment with order, they learned it by copying. Mimesis was explicit as in consciously showing another how to dance and thus how to use their own bodies to project desire, for instance, at the same time as making oneself the object of desire. Barrel recalled dancing at a club and being instructed on how to modify his movement. His friends choreographed him: "Don't dance like this," he demonstrated with a flailing gesture jumping up and down like an excited child. "Dance like this," and he showed a more contained groove. He ground his pelvis slow and low, looking around him as if scanning others on the dance floor and making eye contact with absent others when he rocked over to the far edge of his kinesphere. Then he playfully pulled his eyes away as his gyration took him in the other direction, back into the center of his kinesphere, and out again to the other side. There he demonstrated making eye contact with others, before returning to his other side. I asked him why he thought his friends showed him to dance this way:

> BARREL: Because before I looked like a kid at a high school dance. Now I looked tougher, and they showed me how to cruise and dance at the same time.
> FB: Who were they? Other gay men?
> B: [laughs] No, my butch lesbian friends!
> FB: So, butch lesbians taught you how to be a gay man?
> B: I don't know about that. I had a pretty good idea. But they certainly showed me how to be queer.

FB: What does that mean?

B: How to fit in with other queers. But also how to be special. How to get people to look at me—the people I wanted to desire me. I learned how to be tough and playful, sometimes guys can't do both. And figuring out how to dance like that, I figured out how to be like that when I wasn't dancing. It's all in the body once you've got it.

Participants on the dance floor used dance to socialize themselves to an environment made up of other queers through the transmittal of shared knowledge of these texts. The collective anticipation and responses of dancers to musical features and effects affected the transmittal of the rules of a queer lifeworld. It was through experience of their own bodies and others' that dancers learned how to respond to the two primary texts of the club—the space and the music, and to insert themselves into them. When Alex first went onto the dance floor of Paradise Garage, he felt the full force of the presence of bodies, their shared knowledge of the musical text, and their expectations and responses:

> It was the first time I'd been on the floor dancing. And the floor would dance as a whole, as a group. Everybody knew the parts of the song and a part of the song would come up, or there'd be a break in the music and "hey" and everybody's arms would go up, "hey!" There would be hundreds of people, all at the same time and the lights would flash and confetti would blow out. And everybody knew it—that this was going to happen at this time in this song and they were waiting. So it was this kind of energy in the room. People would anticipate parts of records; it would be this big explosion.

The dance floor was a space and improvised social dancing an act in which people organized themselves in their own way as a collective in which the individual members became an inseparable part of the human mass, through an increased awareness of their "sensual-material bodily unity" (Connerton 1989, 50). Alex incorporated not only individual movement motifs and styles, but through raising his hands in the air at a certain point, for instance, he folded himself into this experience of collectivity.

As he told me his story, Alex was surprised to make the connection that this was the first time he had danced at a club. No longer was he running from floor to floor catching different scenes, as he had done at Danceteria, his regular haunt. For the first time he felt part of a larger movement through dancing together with people. Dancing with others offered him a new invigorating experience of his own body. He was able to create his own kinesphere at the same time as feeling part of a larger mass. When he relived this experience, he became more animated. He flexed his torso, waved his arms, and shifted his weight in his chair, as if becoming aware of his own weight again. His face lit up. His energy palpably changed as he radiated the feeling through his memory of it. I picked it up in my own body and became infused with the energy of his body memory. Not only was he performing the past in his theater of memory, but he also was interpreting it in the moment of performance. By performing the memory, he made a connection. He paused and reflected silently on this for a moment, a smile hovering on his lips. "Wow, all those years going to clubs, and I'd never danced." He carried the memory of that experience with him in his everyday life. It offered him a new model, not only of his own body, but of being with others, which he compared to other experiences of being in his body and with others.

Participants used body knowledge in another way to orient themselves to the crowd. Bodies sensed and understood—read—energy, a reading we used to orient ourselves in a dark club, an environment of disorientation. We used this sense to choose where we wanted to be. At Tunnel, I moved through the club, sensing the energy of the crowd to locate the true center of the space, which was not determined by architectural design. I sensed the saturation of energy near the center of the dance floor. Colin also used his body-sense to orient himself. He preferred not to be at ground zero. He had changed over the years and so had his desires. He wanted something different from going to dance. Where he once sought out the experience of being in the densely packed center of the dance floor, more recently he desired space. He desired to be with others, but not hemmed in by them. Therefore he sought out less densely populated spaces on the dance floor:

> In Octagon, spatial dynamics are different than in other spaces, I've noticed. There's more interior, you know, guys bopping. Just standing to the side and moving to the music and dancing but not really investing, not really going out into the floor. There's the inner group or core that can get into it and make the most investment with their bodies. Then there's another ring watching those in the middle, and there's another ring of us at the side watching both groups. Ten years ago I was right in the middle and now I'm at the side. Out of the hot spot. I don't like to be cramped.

He found greater personal freedom to extend his kinesphere and his energy at the margins. But others sought out the center. Yet others moved from center to periphery and back again. A dancer chose what relationship he or she wanted to have with other bodies—whether to be closely packed in a tight kinesphere, which was almost inseparable from the group movement, or to have more individualized space.

In the dancing I observed, there were cultural rules and preferences for creating a personal kinesphere and articulating it. Fluency of kinespheric awareness—being able to create and enjoy one's own space at the same time as moving with other people—was a powerful cultural pattern that shaped movement. From outside and inside the crowd at S.O.S., a women's dance party at Silverados, a straight strip club on West 20th Street and Fifth Avenue, I found it impossible to focus on individual dancers, as we were all dancing so close, but it was possible to pick up on the qualities within the mass of movements around me. It throbbed and pulsed to the rhythm, holding together tightly within the space. Within the mass, participants incorporated the energy of movement, rather than the individual moves of those around them. Emphasis tended to be on continuity of energy flow and on rhythmic impulses, rather than on the specific positioning of body parts. No one individual claimed more territory than was offered. Because of the restrictive space, floor patterns were tightly controlled: the floor space covered by an individual never extended beyond a step forward, backward, or to either side of a central position. Participants executed backward steps only to regain ground lost by stepping forward. In this way, the dancers held a tightly defined territory, with no unexpected blind lunges backward that would have resulted in the social and physical awkwardness of blocking or encroaching on another's territory—unless someone intended to get into someone's space, of course. How much space each person was allowed depended on whether they were alone: two friends dancing together got to control their spaces plus the space between them, while individuals had very little space. There was some heavy cruising and sex-play going on. I saw couples differentiate themselves from the mass of individuals as they focused on each other by moving into each other's intimate space. They generally remained face on, but some couples pressed butt into abdomen or nudged and rolled shoulders into a partner's chest. Thus, within the tightly defined public space of the dance floor, space was again subdivided into private spaces, formed partly out of necessity, partly out of social dancing etiquette or order, and partly out of a desire to get closer to someone.

Lisa, an Asian-American lesbian in her late twenties, expressed how the common ground of dancing together could overcome some of the inhibitions people may have had about approaching each other off the dance floor:

> I think it's really hard to meet people at clubs. I did meet someone who is a good friend of mine now. We just started talking because we were the only two people on the dance floor and we realized we had stuff in common. But generally I think that it's hard for women to meet each other. There's a lot of reasons. I think women tend to be more protective, more inhibited, I don't know if women want to put themselves out there. It takes a lot of energy to put yourself out there and meet someone unless they have some background information, unless they get the dish on this person from someone, but you can't if you just see someone who's attractive in a club.

Improvised social dancing offered a realm of security by providing other ways of projecting self than through the gaze. Dancing offered more numerous, different, playful, and creative ways to make contact with another, enabling participants to overcome reservations they had, giving common ground.

For economic and aesthetic reasons, queer spaces such as Crowbar and Velvet were smaller than gay clubs like Twilo and Arena. This feature not only held together a critical mass of queerness rather than diffusing it, but it demanded physical closeness, which was valued by participants, like Stephen:

> They'd come rolling in to Crowbar complaining, "Twilo was this, and Twilo was that," but they wanted to get out of that big space, truly anonymous—anonymous in the worst sense, and truly—I can't think of the word—umm, there was no touch. There was no . . . It was too big, you know?

Participants had to work together. They had to dance together. They had to touch:

> Bars are really just too talkative, and queerness is about the physical. We're talking about the physicality of the space, that's what the language is. And in other big spaces, it's not just the dancing, you have to use other senses: the ocular, how one's dressed. When you walk in these [queer] spaces, who you walk in and kiss, that establishes who you are. You walk in and say hello

to the bartender, and if he says hello back and gives you a hug or a kiss even, or if he maybe starts making you a drink, people see that. And something is established there, who you are in that space. Then you walk in and kiss the most fabulous dancers or even, they come to you when they see you're at the door. No conversation is had. It changes how spaces are used.

In a larger space, participants could become lost and anonymous. For some this was the attraction. But in smaller queer spaces, participants valued feeling an integral part of the energy of the event through physical closeness. Not only did this physical intimacy affect participants' sense of their own bodies, but also of their relationships to others around them. The sense of being together in queer spaces was more than the coincidence of being in the same space at the same time.

But this too is complicated when gay or queer spaces were also used for straight parties. One comparison is particularly interesting in terms of the use of space and physical closeness. Susan Tompkin, who was Bruce Mailman's assistant when he ran the Saint, noticed a phenomenon on the dance floor: "It could hold a lot more gay men than straight people. Gay men don't mind being so close together." (In Dunlap 1995.) Stephen noted that the particular cultural patterns of queer sociality in Crowbar manifested themselves as physical intimacy:

Gay people are more touchy than most people. Not touchy, feely, but in such a very sexualized space, people felt the need to touch in a way that was sexual, in a way that was power. I'm thinking about the way I've been with perfect strangers and touch and it's to greet, "How are you doing," and they'd touch you back in a way that was cool. You're allowed to go past personal boundaries and that was OK. And sometimes they'd start dancing with you and you'd start dancing with them.

In some spaces, for informants such as Stephen, gayness was based on an understanding about physicality. But not all, as Stephen indicated that there are some places in which the attitude he encountered was more expressive of "OK, you touched me once, don't do it again," a feature also noted by Tito:

We called these people the Paco Rabanne people, people who never sweat. The beauties of New York, and they have the face and the body, "Look at me, but don't touch me and don't talk to me." Those people did not belong in these clubs because we were the people who love to dance. If we

bumped them, they'd say "Ugh, how disgusting, you're all sweaty." We
hated them. "We're here to get sweaty, bitch. If you can't handle it, get
out."

People who carried such attitudes into what Stephen defined as more
queer spaces, were regarded as outsiders by regulars who did not appreciate their need to distance themselves from other people. They were
outside a desired-for or experienced community of dance. Participants
articulated the rules of sociality in physical terms, in opening up, or protecting one's own kinesphere. The kinesphere, and the individual's
awareness and attitude to it, were the agents of embodiment and transmittal. Stephen desired this kinesthetic, playful model of queer interrelations. Through these patterns of physicality, he felt empowered. To
him, this physicality was the embodied performance of the kind of gayness he valued and a way of being and knowing himself as queer.

Exchange was the motor that drove social organization. In many instances in clubs, such as the experience narrated by Stephen, value
seemed to be determined by the exchange itself, rather than by the in-
trinsic value of what was exchanged. The nature of the transactions described by Alex, Stephen, and myself were social. More than this, they exhibited the value of exchanges of particular embodied forms of sociality,
which, while not particular to queer social practices and spaces, were im-
bued with a particular force for people who felt alienated from heteronormative and capitalistic exchange economies. Stephen emphasized
that Crowbar—the club in which he had these positive experiences—attracted a great many working class participants who felt marginalized by
the increasing gentrification of its East Village location. The values of
these exchanges were not the same and their meanings did not have the
same resonances for everyone, but the need to find ways of being together was a need for queer kinship that may not have been available in
other arenas of biological family, workplace, or public places. What was
valued was not a product but an experience of knowing spatial and musical texts and how to respond to them, of creating a kinesphere, of composition, of being in various levels of proximity to others and physically
interacting with them. The processes of incorporation and embodiment, transmittal and mimesis valorized particular forms of being with
each other. What was being vigorously transmitted was not simply the desire to be part of a great mass of collective energy, but the value of individual creative difference.

All informants expressed the desire and effect of being with other queers: "I guess what I want is to be with others like me" (Alex); "There's something really powerful about being in a room full of other women" (Lisa). These expressions can be understood as prefigurative articulations of the meaning and value of community. Informants articulated community through numbers—a group or mass of people, and similarity—"others like me." Informants articulated expressions of community in terms of what they wanted from a club. Several also articulated the experience of being with a mass of people on a dance floor through numbers and similarity, but articulated numbers using terms such as "whole" and "everybody," rather than "others," and in terms of the energy a mass of people produced. They experienced similarity, not only in terms of gender, sexuality, ethnicity, or race, but in terms of shared knowledge expressed through movement. To decide to go to a club was more than a way to get physically close to others, more than the function of the desire to be with others. The movement relationship between people on the dance floor was expressive of being with other queers.

Dancing together to music, some participants expressed a sense of connectedness with others and of pride in that achievement. Stephen wasn't the only one who got his sense of empowerment and gayness from dancing in a club. Tito also talked about this:

> The Saint people were the people who loved to dance. They communicated through the spirit of dancing. Through music I'm connected to the whole world. I embrace my gayness, I embrace my happiness, I know who I am. I open a path. The Saint opened my eyes. We don't have to go in the dark anymore and masturbate and suck each others' dicks and hide. Finally we can say, come over to my party, enjoy this life. The doors are open. You already had it, but you didn't notice it before—that you had this in you, that this was always in you. But the Saint made you aware, my God, I'm very proud of what I am, and not because I've become a member of a social club, I was already a member before I was born, but now I realize I have the right to be gay and celebrate through music; an ocean of human beings all together as one. It's the most beautiful communion that I ever experienced in my life. We were all one soul, that's the feeling that you felt when you walked through those doors and into that ocean.

At the same time as they developed movement in relation to music, participants developed a relationship with their own bodies, with the space around them, and with other dancers. This development performed not only an experiential body of knowledge of queerness in the single body unit, but it performed an experiential body of knowledge that dancers shared.

These third spaces of recreation offered a potentially more supportive environment than the domestic or the work space, but this could not be so without the practices within them. The physicality of these spaces embodied and transmitted values of alternative kinship, Alex remembered:

> Your identity comes from the family, I was on the outside of my family. I needed to go and find kids who liked what I listened to. My mom hated what I listened to. She'd come in and rip the posters off my wall. I needed to go and find family to get something that I wasn't getting at home and I found it in New York nightlife with other young kids who were searching, with the same need to be loved. That's why they were there and that's where we found it. We found each other. Families did get created and especially working at the Boy Bar—that was my family. The MC was kinda like dad. And it was like, "How do I be gay? How do I exist in this world? How do I battle between, I wanna be who I am and be a freak and dress this way, but how do I find boys who like me. How do I exist?" And here is a place where I do, and I can ask these questions and I exist.

While politicians and moral majoritarians adhere to a Puritan-capitalist ethos of family values of patriarchy, hierarchy, and homogeneity, queer kinship in clubs was based on particular forms of physicality—intimacy, togetherness, a critical mass of energy, participation, and sexiness. In offering support too often lacking in the American family, these club spaces became home and peers became family. The third space of recreation thus was part of a physical and social network, which participants understood as home. These clubs were also spaces in which work was done. Thus, the spaces of home and work were incorporated into the third space, challenging the assumptions of boundaries between the three, and exposing their separation within a Puritan-capitalist ethos that aimed to control and prescribe productive activities of the body and their relative values. Queer clubs queered these assumptions.

Modern intellectual and practical gay history is perhaps primarily marked by a struggle to develop an inclusive, yet profligate operation of "identity" and "community." Informants of color objected to the assumption that individuals who shared a same-sex object desire in a homophobic society shared a common experience, outlook, and set of values and interests. Rather than sharing a core gay identity around which race or class added nuance, an individual could be simultaneously gay, female, Latina, a mother, and working class, for example, each identification being shaped by and shaping the others. Attention on race, class, and gender does not imply alliance or intersection, but rather "a fantasized space where all embodied identities could be visibly represented as parallel forms of identity" (Warner 1993, xix). While aspiring to a "representational politics of inclusion and a drama of authentic embodiment" this pluralism reified identity and spoke of inclusion as though it were synonymous with equality and freedom, "reducing power to a formalism of membership" (Warner 1993, xix). Politically and intellectually, "queerness" proposes a radical generalization that rejects interest-politics in favor of a more thorough resistance to regimes of the normal. Appealing to one's sexual, gender, or ethnic identity as the ground of community is rejected because of its inherent instabilities and exclusions. However, when informants used the terms "identity" and "community" in interviews, they used them in two ways, one with a sense of a historical truth (as opposed to fact), the other utopic. In other words, they expressed identity and community as experience and as need. Some participants I interviewed regarded these as both self-limiting and enabling. The limits and power of identity and community were reflected in the spaces and practices described. Lisa, using both the experiential and utopic mode, described community in these spaces:

> Ideally, it would be more word of mouth, networks of friends. I don't know what that community would look like. It might not necessarily be queer. It would be an interesting mix of people. Nightclub community tends to feel forced. It's not really community 'cos it's advertised through newspapers, and so you might have different groups and cliques but do those communities really start to open up their borders and find community in a club? Downstairs at the Clit Club they used to have a pool table and all these women used to congregate around there. It felt weird because it felt like I couldn't go in there. I could have, but I just didn't feel comfortable. But I also felt bad because I felt that maybe they felt they couldn't come upstairs.

Her engagement with the concept of community expressed her awareness of its limitations and of false consciousness. Yet, when she was on the dance floor with others, she sensed a togetherness and a common ground. By paying attention to spaces and cultural practices within them, people were working with and against, above and beyond what political agendas have mapped out on a battlefield of identity politics.

To conclude, queer theorists Lauren Berlant and Michael Warner recently asserted that the radical aspirations of a queer world-making project are to build "not just a safe zone for queer sex but the changed possibilities of identity, intelligibility, publics, culture, and sex that appear when the heterosexual couple is no longer the referent or the privileged example of sexual culture" (Berlant and Warner 1998, 548). The heterosexual couple remains a privatized unit, while in a queer lifeworld, participants felt joy and shared in the expression of a public knowledge. It was this experience that was valued. The choreography of participants in a queer dance club produced the effect of a mixed texture between individual and group kinespheres and desires and realities that was not homogenous or uncomplicated, not even open for experimentation all the time. They produced different kinds of pleasures as well as frustrations and disappointments. In choosing to go to a certain club and choosing to involve themselves to a lesser or greater degree with others there, dancers were incorporating and embodying an ethics of the self and ethics of sociality simultaneously.[4] Politics attends to the making of the social world. Choreographing interrelations between the self and the other and the individual and the mass in the club devised a queer lifeworld, which informed its imagination and realization outside of the club. Both spaces were political in this sense at least. What participants could dance had the real power of gravity wherever their feet carried them.

⦊⦊ 5

ONLY WHEN I LOSE MYSELF IN SOMEONE ELSE
Desire, Mimesis, and Transcendence

[At Limelight] there were all these pictures on the wall of guys and their erections. And everyone would be drinking looking at the erections. And upstairs they had the sex room. So I went up there and everybody was crammed into this little room and you couldn't see anybody's faces and there was all this moaning and groaning and heavy breathing. And I thought, "This is so strange. There are all these people downstairs trying to meet people and there are all these people upstairs doing this most intimate act but they can't see each other." So I thought, I'll do a little experiment. Let me see if I can go downstairs and meet somebody. So I went downstairs and ordered myself a drink and I just sat on the sofa, very much by myself, trying desperately to make eye contact. For an hour I couldn't make eye contact with anybody. Everyone at the bar was looking at the dance floor or the go-go boys or the erections on the wall. So nobody was even looking at each other. When I was younger there was con-stant looking—a constant flow of cruising going on with your eyes. And I thought, what happened?

(Iain)

The other night I was at the door and one of the bartenders whose girlfriend had just broken up with her was hanging out with this gay friend of hers and they were getting really shit-faced drunk. Next thing I know this bartender gets up on the bar and starts taking her clothes off and dancing. Next thing I know she pulls this gay friend of hers up on the bar and his shirt goes off, her shirt's off, her pants are off, she takes his pants off, and all I saw were his pants off and him completely naked on the bar, and the girls just freaking out and getting really pissed off. I understand why they are upset as there are very few spaces that are safe and they can say "This is my space and I don't have to see that." A couple of girls left and one of them was in tears and wanted her money back. But after that happened, the atmosphere in the bar changed one hundred per cent. It went from everyone just standing around like a high-school dance to everybody just going wild. Because I guess they figured that they couldn't do anything more embarrassing than what they had just seen on that bar.

(Edie)

≋ ONE OF THE MOST famous descriptions of dancing suggests that it is a vertical expression of a horizontal desire. I want to explore more particularly how individuals learned how to be with others on the dance floor and in a queer lifeworld through practices of energy transmittal and movement mimesis by looking at some examples of how this was executed in relationships between bodies negotiating desire. There are a number of reasons I want to look at this field. First, in looking at desire I hope to avoid reifying the queer imagination—kinesthetic and/or political—as an object, reemphasizing queer world-making as process. Second, I want to explore the ambivalent feelings some informants expressed about sex performances in clubs. Third, the sexual politics of representation are contested in clubs themselves. Finally, these performances act as both environmental and choreographic features. They were often the most consciously choreographed movements. On the dance floor, participants choreographed themselves as objects and subjects of desire. Desire informed relations between bodies on the dance floor to produce a choreographed effect. Desire impelled a body to emerge through movement and establish a rhetoric of being through self-fashioning. I look at some examples of how this was executed in relationships between bodies negotiating desire. I look at the use and limitations of lexicons of sexual moves and erotic movement styles in strippers, go-go dancers, and participants on the dance floor and the relationships between them, as well as considering the political resonances of expressing queer sexuality publicly. Finally, I consider how transcendence of the self-conscious body and its limitations at the same time as working within the physical realities of flesh, space, and time might offer an elusive but powerful political vision.

Representations of sex in movement were common in clubs as part of the movement repertoire of go-go dancers and participants on the dance floor. The purposes of having go-go dancers or strippers in a dance club were motivational, erotic, aesthetic, economic, and political. They marked the environment as pro-sex. This had a special weight in some lesbian spaces, which attempted to promote autonomous female-to-female desire at the same time as negotiating both the model of desire as the masculine objectification of women's bodies and the feminist agenda that identified it. Women have few public arenas of female-to-female desire. Several female informants expressed the need for assurances that if they do look, that their object wants to be looked at and desired by other women. Lisa was an Asian-American lesbian in her late twenties who critiqued the strip performances she witnessed at Angels, a women-only strip club in Tribeca, which was closed down by the city under the zoning legislations enforced in 1998:

> At Angels, this is not always strippers who want to work there. It's Harmony [a straight strip club with the same owner] strippers and they have to work there. It's powered with stripping because it is so coded with the heterosexual gaze. I don't want to reduce anything to stereotypes but maybe it might be more interesting if you have lesbian strippers. I don't know if you could make an announcement to say these are actual lesbians. If they looked like lesbians too.

Some participants read performances of sexuality, looking for "realness" rather than the reproduction of overdetermined cultural codes of sex that also hold heteronormative currency. The erotic power of dance was also created by the spectator as much as by the dancer herself and thus was dependent, not only on the movement of a dancer, but upon interrelationships between the dancer on the podium and the dancer/observer on the dance floor.

D.A Miller writes that "perhaps the most salient index to male homosexuality, socially speaking, consists precisely in how a man looks at other men" (Miller 1991, 131). Some women, according to informants, have difficulty looking at other women. The gaze has been so overdetermined as male by feminist theoreticians that some women going to lesbian clubs seemed to equate a look of female-to-female desire with a masculine objectification of women. Politics affected the relationship of bodies to one another, between the podium and the dance floor, as Edie observed:

> What really affects the community and the bar scene and the pick-up scene is the feminist movement. It was always saying that the bar scene was bad and it was patriarchal and objectified women. These one-night stands were degrading to women and if you pick someone up in a bar you're not picking them up according to who they are, but on aesthetic and drunken principles. I find a lot of women find go-go dancers and cruising very offensive.

In looking at other women dancing, participants could construct objects of desire that they might not be able to do on the street. However, some informants critiqued other performances within clubs that were difficult to accept because they presented a mass-mediated erotic ideal object of the body and movement. Paradoxically, these performances seemed less able to negotiate the flow and sociality of desire between people because of their very self-conscious attitude to movement and use of a codified lexicon: representation of what you were supposed to desire seemed sometimes to limit that flow of desire. Representation of sexual movement had the power to alienate some people at some times as well as to "pull" them into participation. Some spectators used the performances of strippers and go-go dancers to release themselves from inhibitions and some were reminded of them.

Ella and Edie contrasted the effect go-go dancers had on their observers in Meow Mix, a downtown lesbian bar populated mainly by young white feminists and Her/she Bar, a lesbian club dominated by women of color, both African-American and Latina. Both informants felt that feminist politics were configured differently in each of these clubs, which resulted in more enjoyment and play with representations of sex in dancing in Her/she Bar than in Meow Mix. They interpreted this as having something to do with the politics of Meow Mix being more informed by a feminist critique of the male gaze and the objectification of women's bodies. Ella, a bisexual clubgoer in her twenties, also compared the style of erotic performance dancing at Angels to Her/she Bar:

> I don't know if you've ever been to Angels—that's supposed to be about live sexuality and it so isn't. It's about artifice. When I first went to Her/she Bar it blew me away. This go-go dancer was so beautiful I couldn't believe she existed in my reality. She was doing this crazy solo dance, with the splits and cartwheels, who knows what the hell she was doing out there. And women were so invested in the gaze. Desire was the connective tissue in a way I've never seen it in Angels where it's so mechanical. I don't know if this woman was a lesbian, but I've never before seen a strip show where the exchange was equal, the agency was working in a really cool way. It was about desire, not commodity, and not about desire as commodity. It seemed "real" real sexuality.

Responses to these performances and to dancing among participants on the dance floor that incorporated the lexicon of sexual movement were informed by wider sexual politics. But such performances might also affect politics, as Catherine suggested. She changed her views after witnessing pro-sex performances of both go-go dancers and other participants in lesbian clubs: "Here are these women, and they are sexy and working it, and this is an option for me too. I can dress sexy and dance like that and flirt and play and enjoy my body and others' like that and not have to feel bad about not being a 'real' lesbian or a 'real' feminist or whatever that's supposed to mean in some circles." Maybe through experiencing different ways of being together, some like Catherine could use movement to empower themselves to make changes in their political beliefs and values.

As well as choreographing the gaze, performances of overtly sexual dancing also choreographed the audience. Most queer clubs I visited in New York City from 1995 to 1998, whether for men or women, had some type of go-go dancing, whether explicitly sexual, as in the case of strippers, or less so, as in the case of a dancer on a podium. The presence of these dancers marked the politics of the space as pro-sex rather than shackling desire to exploitation, and imparted an increased sexual charge to the environment. However, this charge was sometimes configured differently: one within an exchange economy based on commodification and payment, and the other within an exchange economy based on less commodified pleasures. In the following examples from my observations and experiences, I investigate how these differences manifest themselves in the relationships between exotic dancers in clubs and other participants. How did one relationship produce an individual, private customer and the other a crowd of dancers?

Up on the podium at S.O.S., the go-go dancer's eyes were open, but she was not looking at any of us in the audience. Her engagement with the beat of the music was different from the mass of dancers on the main floor. She moved around in a small arc and drew attention to herself by exaggerating her walk, her pace measured on a half-beat. This beat was accentuated when measured against the faster bobbing and bouncing rhythm of the crowd below. Gazing at the floor or upwards toward the ceiling, a long vertical metal pole oriented and steadied her. She wrapped her arms and one leg around this pole. With feet static, her wrists led the flow of her relaxed hands. First, her hands glided up and down the pole, followed by a similar hand motion up and down her own torso. The similarity of movement between the pole and herself described and objectified her own body as phallus (power). She drew her audience into her diagetic space with the directness of her gaze. She manipulated our gaze over her body with her own hands. She was director and actor of our gaze over her body, but the script was prewritten. As her hands cupped her breasts, she flexed and pushed her shoulders forward and back, projecting and withdrawing the always forbidden, but exaggeratedly marked possibility of touch. When she stopped, it was less a break than a dropping away: she stepped down from the podium as the rhythm ground and shimmied on without her. She abandoned the beat and disappeared from view.

Architecturally, the scopophilic focus of Silverados—the strip club where S.O.S. was a once a week party for women—was the dance floor. From a raised bar women surveyed its occupants. The music stopped and a disembodied female voice called for the dance floor to be cleared for the show, with lap-dances to follow. Several impassive-looking women stepped up onto the floor, appropriating it from a space of public dance to a space of public gaze and private desire. They each claimed a spot on the floor and stood inactive until the first slow, lyrical bars of the music, which contrasted with the faster, bouncier house music participants had been dancing to just a few minutes before. On cue they performed their acts. A few women leaned against poles, their feet static, and pressed their buttocks outward, and, as the only part of their anatomy moving, they were the intended center of focus. Apart from walking from one spot to another to display themselves to another section of the audience, the dancers' feet rarely moved and when they walked, their walk was casual and unstylized. Another couple held themselves up against each other and one of them rubbed her face across the others' breasts, but with no weight or effort in her movement. The quality of contact—be it with the floor, themselves, or with each other—remained uncommitted, neither deliberately light or strong, never thrown, never supported by another, and never risked. The only engagement was spatially directed toward the customers. From their play with their cash, their customers' pleasure came from being able to buy and show they could possess a private sex performance in public. For example, one held a five-dollar bill out for a performer on all fours to lick. Another performer stood with her back to a group of spectators, her legs apart, and slowly bent over to reach out for the security of the floor below with her hands, reaching out for the approval of the audience with her butt. The targeted audience member demonstrated her approval in the expected way, responding to the cue by folding dollar bills over lacy elastic like washing on a line. These seemed less to be sexual movements than financial transactions: like an ATM in reverse. There was no redundancy in these movements, which raised them above a professionally executed functional level to one full of "the richness of the communicative process" (Bird-whistell 1970, 86). They were strictly choreographed using formal lexicons of moves and gestures on cue. The relationship between audience and dancers was strictly choreographed on a call and response pattern. In the performances, a cue was given and a response was immediate: the performer bent over and the cash was paid.

There was little variation from the lexicon, which some informants, like Lisa, found clichéd and limited to performing stereotypical ideals of female sexuality:

> I think it could be just as interesting if they didn't have professional strippers doing the typical moves like Demi Moore does [in the movie *Striptease*]. It might be interesting if they asked women at the club to strip or have contests. It's a performance of one kind of female sexuality. The way I have seen women dance, it's supposed to be a performance of a feminine sexuality because it's supposed to be about being looked at. The movements are coded as feminine.

Some of the performances were mimesis of sexual acts, for instance, cunnilingus. However, their visual composition, orchestration, and movement quality suggested a soft-core live mimesis of a soft-core film mimesis, rather than a public presentation of a private act. For instance, three women positioned themselves so that one lay face up with her legs held upward in midair while another woman crawled toward her crotch and lapped at it from five inches away like a cat with myopia. Meanwhile, the third woman straddled the second with her back to the site of always deferred contact between mouth and crotch, and, by her open-thigh position and direct sweeping downward arm movements, she simultaneously accentuated her crotch and the second woman's buttocks as a site of our focus and desire. Their representation of sex turned their moves into commodities to be exchanged. Gesture and posture were exchanged and valued as commodity, rather than as autotelic experience of desire.

The role of go-go dancers was not only to produce an audience of spectators, but also to encourage people to dance. Typically, these dancers were positioned on a small stage as at the Clit Club, or a podium to the side of the dance floor, as at Escuelita, or sometimes on a podium or stage in the center of the dance floor, as at Limelight and Twilo. Typically, go-go dancers performed at least two sets of about twenty minutes to an hour. Sometimes, I noticed they did their first or all sets before the dance floor had reached its zenith of energy. Their performances seemed to be strategically timed to encourage people into the dance floor space, whether to observe them or to dance. Once the dance floor was in full flow these dancers did less performance. One go-go dancer stated that he finished no later than three A.M. as he did not want to work all night at a party that went on until the morning, such as Arena or Limelight, where he worked. But I also noticed that when the party was in full flow, dancers took over the podiums themselves, losing their inhibitions and becoming "stars." In addition, when dancers were in full flow, they were more focused on themselves and less inclined to focus on go-go dancers.

Up on podiums, go-go dancers sometimes seemed removed and distant from the crowd, their bound energy in contrast to club patrons who seemed more integrated with the crowd and moving with a freer flowing energy when they danced on podiums. Go-go dancers exhibited more professionalism, and perhaps a sense of censorship, dictated at least in part by the city's restrictions on sex performances, for which a club could be rezoned as a sex establishment and closed. At Tunnel, a male go-go dancer was twice removed from the social dancers in the club for their view: he was raised on a platform and he was naked apart from boots, a bandanna, and a small white towel which he held around his waist. He untucked it, held the ends out to one side of his hips, and rocked his weight rhythmically from one leg to another. He retained tight control over his own movement, with no looseness. His flow movement was bound: his energy extended little beyond his own pumped and taut skin. It couldn't. He had to keep hold of the towel to cover his genitals. While he hid it from the prying eyes of Mayor Rudy Guiliani's sex-establishment zoning ordinances, [1] he also concealed those parts the Nautilus machine could not reach. His body was hard, but his dick was not. He attempted to shelter the evidence of the rupture of fantasy. He might not have been turned on, despite his movement lexicon. His movement was the representation of arousal, not the arousal itself or its expression.

As an ex-go-go dancer, Colin identified his function and his pleasure as motivating others to dance. He mobilized his knowledge of a stylized sex lexicon, at the same time as self-censoring his movement and relationships with others to protect himself from unwanted attention:

> COLIN: I figured out what I would and wouldn't allow to happen. What kind of a go-go dancer I would be. Not just a dancer, but a go-go dancer. And the way that I danced is different from now. In most clubs now, it's not

even about the body, but more specifically about dicks. It's part of the change and it's a shame in the way it's about someone staring at some guy, rather than motivating the dance. And that for me is the best club, that has dancers not there to be obsessed over, but there to make you dance. You used to get tips and that was great, but now you have guys with dollar bills hanging out of their jockstraps and that's different, right? They are part of the club environment, its energy. They weren't just there for you to look at.

FB: When you were on the podium would you dance differently than if you were on the dance floor?

C: Yes. You realize that you're part of the entertainment, so you're more outwardly focused. There was a subconscious attempt to be sexy, sensual, whatever, whereas when I'm dancing out there on my own the motive for being there is not necessarily to be that. I'd adopt a few characteristic gestures or moves, things that you think may be appealing to the crowd. For me a lot of it had to do with the gaze. I would actually look at people, make eye contact. And I'd be dancing with you across the room. Make contact, connections visually. Body isolations in general I think in my mind can be very sensual. Playing as well, with the tempo, fast, slow, that's sexy too. Which I may do on my own, dancing on the floor like everyone else, but I wouldn't be so conscious and so aware of an audience, trying to figure out what would make them move.

Not all go-go dancers I observed affected a distanced or indifferent stance to dancers on the dance floor. As I watched a go-go dancer work the room at Crowbar, I noticed that participants picked up on his energy level and sometimes playfully adapted his moves and danced them back at him, or at others, or for his own pleasure. Go-go dancers often emphasized and accentuated movements already happening on the floor, heightening them. Colin suggested that he deliberately used his gaze to connect with people when he was on a podium, more so than when he was dancing on the dance floor, out of go-go boy performance consciousness. Lisa also compared go-go dancers who demanded the ocular attention of participants with other ways of making contact on the dance floor:

> It's like someone is on a pedestal when they're on stage, rather than someone on the floor. They're distant, apart, and doing something else from the rest of us. It's good when we just work together. I think women don't make eye contact with each other, so I think a lot of flirting might happen by emulating each other's movements in a playful way, getting closer to someone.

More overtly on the dance floor, movement can be used to signal and demonstrate sexual desire, as Edie noticed:

FB: What are people performing when they dance?
EDIE: Half the time they're performing sex. Half the time they are performing how good they are in bed. I think it's very conscious. Especially when you get the butcher dykes—you can see that strut. You can see the way they'll walk up to their woman and they try and dance. I took my ex-girlfriend and I kept watching the way people would interact with her and a lot of women would walk up and they'd pretty much show her what they'd do to her if they got her in bed. They'd come up from behind, put their hands on the woman's hips and start grinding into her. The more flexible women will manage to find a way to let her know that they would go down on her. They'll get really low and get their faces right by their crotch. Or they'll run their hands near the body.

To the spectator, a person's lexicon of sex moves could attract or paradoxically distance them. But how a person moved was highly attractive to many informants: "I'll look and if I see something I'll copy it. Maybe because I like that person. Or maybe 'cos I'm attracted to that person, I'll pay special attention to how they move. I guess it's a bit of both. But how they move is real important—that's why they're attractive" (Dana). On the dance floor, representation of desire was not just manifested by certain moves, but by a certain consciousness of moving, as Stephen articulated: "The one who knows he can dance. He knows he's fierce, he knows he can work his way, and the boys just love him, and that's how you know there's something up with this shit. They all want this boy. I've seen that." The theatricality of presence and the agency it implied colluded to affect both presentation and representation: presentation of self and representation of sexual potency: "If someone dances well, I kinda think that they're going to be hot in bed, just because they show they have a real sense of their body. It's not just that they're flexible or whatever, it's ... it's that they know how to have pleasure" (Mark). In such instances, it was not the codified representations of sex that entered into the circulation of desire and from which the bodies of spectator and performer emerged.

Dance scholar Cynthia Novack identifies the improvised social dance movement qualities, style and structure of internal focus, ongoing energy flow, and extemporariness with the values and qualities of self-expression, freedom, egalitarianism, and spontaneity (Novack 1988). As attitudes to sex and sexuality change across time and different cultural positions, this relationship can be traced comparatively on the dance floor from formalized partnering to the individualized movement of today's dance clubs. The formal gender roles of structured social dances such as the tango or merengue with their strict regulation of intimacy compare with the emphasis of release in improvised social dance, which reflects the sexual ethics of expressive and personal freedom. At Krash, a mainly Latino club for gay men and lesbians in Queens, the flow of house music was broken up with more formal merengue sections in which dancers danced more formalized steps in more formal gender roles: one was the woman and one was the man, regardless of biological sex. A performance on stage sanctioned the playing out of these sex roles. An MC called up a couple, and announced that the butch had a question for her femme. "Will you marry me?" The femme glowed and the crowd applauded enthusiastically. This scene seemed to equate gay liberation with heteronormative sanctioned couplings reflected in formalized gender-role courtship rituals in dance.

This scene of formal dance partnering contrasted with an observation I made at S.O.S. of a couple dancing together. For the first few minutes after the stripping ended, the dance floor remained empty. Then a couple took to the floor, moving more freely around each other rather than centered on a pole or on a part of their own or the other's anatomy. They gently stamped out the beat, which they bounced through their whole bodies from head to feet before being earthed in the dance floor. As one raised her arms up and isolated her torso and hips in a gyrating motion, her partner directed her arms toward her without touching her and at the same time bounced deeper into the other's lower kinesphere. They created a complementary movement variation that united them as a couple, without one leading and another following in a more formalized gendered relationship. Their focus was on each other, and when they made eye contact, they held it for a moment while the hint of a smile passed across their lips.

So far, I have focused on how participants negotiated the club texts of music, the crowd, body knowledge, shared knowledge, lexicons of movement, and dance floor relations to choreograph and thereby produce and articulate different notions of interrelationality. Movement embodied an intent to be involved with others. As queer world-making, the agency of the individual was not sacrificed to the mass. Individuals found their own space within the group, and the shape and energy of the group itself reflected the variety and diversity of bodies and experiences within it. Body politics affected the club and the practices of improvised social dance, and also had potential to affect politics. But the promise of improvised social dancing was not just to realize a material body, but to transcend the body and its politics as obstacles, producing notions and practices of political agency, community, and utopian imagination. Dancers worked with music, space, individual and shared knowledge, and with each other to transcend the limitations of the physical body, judged by society and by peers according to measures of normativity, beauty, and productivity—sexual or otherwise. Participants could overcome their self-consciousness and work, not only with the sonic and physical realities around them, but with a personal and political vision of what they wanted to achieve.

While manipulating the physical realities of space, time, one's own body, and the bodies of others, some participants spoke of a desire or an experience of transcending the self-conscious body and its limitations. Did this offer a political vision? Did the dissolution of the self in the pleasure of the flow of movement offer possibilities for the emergence of new consciousnesses? Judith Butler writes:

> Desire is the site in which demand and need are never reconciled, and this makes of desire a permanently vexed affair. Further, desire is never fulfilled, for its fulfillment would entail a full return to that primary pleasure, and that return would dissolve the very subject which is the condition of desire itself. (Butler 1995, 381)

What if, rather than making of desire a "permanently vexed affair," the very impossibility of reconciliation, of closing the circuit of desire, allowed a space of constantly refiguring possibilities to remain open? What if this is one of the attractions of social improvised dance as queer world-making?

The dissolution of the subject was an expressed goal of improvised social dancing for some participants. As I watched dancers, they did not seem to represent acts on stage, they presented themselves. The source of these effects was not located in the illusions of representation achieved through the performing body, but rather in the play of the performing body itself. This was never so apparent as at the moments when the performance took off. These were the moments at which self-consciousness dissolved (Csikszentmihalyi 1990). As such, these performances were never reproductive, but genuinely productive. The goal of some of the dancers with whom I spoke was to achieve that state of being in the ever unfolding present, free from external or internalized judgment. This sensation of self-realization, of reaching something inside and being able to bring it out creatively through the sensation of moving your body, produced self-knowledge. Through self-knowledge the participant connected with others and made meaning on the dance floor. This sense of empowerment was not exterior or discursive. If the dancer was able to meet the challenge of creating with his or her own body a feeling of un-self-conscious pleasure, the sensation of moving produced knowledge and empowerment. The repetition of the pulse of music and movement, the opportunities for variations, interpretation, embellishment, and development within social improvised dance created a framework in which possibilities could be realized. The social character of this improvisation opened a space for intersubjectivities to be developed and practiced.

Paradoxically, the sensation of dissolution made the person experiencing it less conscious of their surroundings, while an observer may have become more aware of that dancer in a group of more self-conscious movers. Ariel observes:

> I made a connection with someone at Axis. They had this drag show. I got there fairly early I think, and it was just dancing. At one o'clock the show started, and that was the only point at which the music stopped. Everyone's crowding around and watching the stage. It was at that point that I started hooking up with someone. But afterwards we were talking and he said, "You now, you just seemed so unapproachable on the dance floor. People were staring at you and you know you're one of those people that people just watch." It's so weird, 'cos I don't think about that often, it's like I'm not performing for others. It's not like I'm performing for you, I'm thinking about me. I'm in my own world when I dance. And then as soon as the music stopped it became an entirely different space. All of a sudden, it wasn't a dance club for me, it was a social environment. All of a sudden then, I'm a person again. And then all of a sudden there are other people—one of whom I hooked up with.

The dancer/storyteller, Ariel, was less concerned with representation achieved through the performing body than with the play of the performing body itself. Ariel's goals had changed; he didn't go to clubs anymore to make an outward connection, in the sense of seeking sex; now his desires were to achieve a different sort of goal—a connection with himself beyond the physical:

When I say it's exercise, it's a spiritual exercise too. I used to be active in the church, believe it or not. It's spiritual because . . . it's hard to explain . . . but when you're going into yourself in your dancing body, your moving body, you're trying to touch something that's inside of you, right? And so my spirituality was always for me very strong, but not because I related directly to the Catholic church or to the ceremonies or rituals that were going on, but I always had an intense relationship to a God-like figure, and that's never left me and that's an interior thing that wasn't so much involved in the exterior. It's not like I'm dancing to God, mind you. But I feel that type of interiority going through me. There's a moment when I can see myself, and my flesh and my muscles and my bones, and reflect . . . you know, I'm moving [looks at arms] and I'm living. This is the blood that's going through me. For some reason, there's a connection there that I feel.

Dance could produce a high in which the self-consciousness of body-as-obstacle dissolved and a new body emerged with a new empowering consciousness of the body as self. Ariel had an idea of what he wanted to achieve through dance, which was less aesthetic, less judged on exterior models, and more on internal ones:

FB: Do you have an image of yourself in your mind as you're moving?
ARIEL: Yeah, yeah, I would say so. It's a memorable image, it's in your body. It's almost as if there's a template there of how you should be dancing. And you want to achieve that at that night, that evening, that moment, you want to get into that. I remember this point in an evening where I'm just tired or worn out and I'm wondering, OK, is it time to go, have I done my deed basically? And then I'm no, no, no, and I keep going because I haven't reached that high. And I think a lot of my drug use was about that: I was trying to reach some state. It wasn't necessarily psychological, or emotional, or some of those reasons people do drugs for—I was still trying to reach some weird template is how I describe it—some vision, some image of an existence, of where I want to reach that night, whether it was the drugs or the dance. And so the drug thing has passed by, but that's still what I'm trying to reach. I don't want to go home that evening without really trying my damnedest to get to that point and it just brings me further into myself, but again, that's what I love about dancing—trying to reach that point. And I love it when you reach that moment when you can't even imagine stopping.

Through dance, Ariel wanted to achieve a state in which the obstacle of physical or even emotional fatigue was no longer an issue. He wanted to achieve a transcendence of himself as an oppressed object of power and self-oppressing subject through dance. To him, the process of transcendence was just as important as the product. The whole point was that here on the dance floor and in his body was an open space, full of potential. But the transcendence of the body was not a transcendence of order; it implied a different order that liberated the individual from the work and the home body through play. The order of this play, where the body was in tune with its own rhythm and the consciousness was freed from day-to-day worries produced—if you like—a more perfect state of being. Improvised social dancing could make one body into another. The body was obstacle, instrument, and goal. It was through the pleasure of dance that some participants sought the opportunity to shake off the body of the home and work, and started to realize the self-fashioned third body of self-achieved power. In *Homo Ludens: A Study of the Play Element in Culture,* his influential contribution to the theory of human creativity, Johan Huizinga (1950, 9) corroborates these features of the nature of play by stating that

> as a regularly recurring relaxation, it becomes the accompaniment, the complement, in fact an integral part of life in general. It adorns life, amplifies it, and is to that extent a necessity both for the individual—as a life function—and for society by reason of the meaning it contains, its significance, its expressive value, its spiritual and social associations, in short, as a culture function. The expression of it satisfies all kinds of communal ideals.

This expression of communal ideals is also part of the promise of improvised social dancing. It's another "template" or ideal way of being together that dancers attempted to achieve.

> We are all condemned to silence—unless we create our own relation with the world and try to tie other people into the meaning we thus create. This is what composing is. Doing solely for the sake of doing, without trying artificially to recreate the old codes in order to reinsert communication into them. Inventing new codes, inventing the message at the same time as the language. Playing for one's own pleasure, which alone can create the conditions for new communication. [. . .] it relates to the emergence of the free act, self-transcendence, pleasure in being instead of having. (Attali 1985, 134)

Attali's comments get at the perceived underlying utopian promise of improvised social dancing in queer clubs. It also expresses the promise and power of queer lifeworlds. For improvised social dancing in queer clubs as queer world-making promised a form of social exchange based on improvised composition, rather than the reproduction of a commodity: self-invention, "inventing new codes, inventing the message at the same time as the language. Playing for one's own pleasure, which alone can create the conditions for new communication . . . ," this is the praxis on the dance floor of Teresa de Lauretis' (1991, iv) theoretical promise of queerness, "to recast or reinvent the terms of our sexualities, to construct another discursive horizon, another way of thinking the sexual." The very ephemerality of social improvised dancing composed in the moment of performance held this promise.

Dancing in a queer club was both a suspension and escape from the normativity of everyday life and yet brought movement from it to construct or rehearse the possibilities for everyday life. These practices constructed lifeworlds as a production in the moment of a space of possibilities, which remained fluid and moving by means of the dancing body, as it improvised from moment to moment. The suspension of everyday life did not trivialize the practices; rather, as Richard Schechner (1985, 6) writes,

> [performance consciousness] activates alternatives: "this" and "that" are both operative simultaneously. In ordinary life people live out destinies. [. . .] But performance consciousness is subjunctive, full of alternatives and potentiality. During rehearsals especially, alternatives are kept alive, the work is intentionally unsettled. The celebration of contingency—a true, if temporary, triumph over death and destiny—describes even ritual performances.

This was an opportunity, never a certainty. But improvised social dancing in a queer club offered this opportunity in the face of its seeming impossibility in other spaces. If the opportunity was realized, or at least the desire for realization experienced, this rehearsed a political imagination by providing a template for knowledge of the self and community with others. Why might this have particular urgency for queers? Stephen Mullaney has historically identified the term "rehearsal" as being almost synonymous with "performance" except in one particular instance: when performing in front of the embodied representatives of the law for the purposes of censorship (Mullaney 1988). Queers knowingly perform in this larger theater of power, but rather than being its objects, they make themselves the subjects of this power. These club spaces and practices were of performance, of theater, precisely because they fulfilled the meaning of these terms in Schechner's sense of being "laboratories" in which "what if" was the defining principle. Small wonder then, that participants described their club experience in utopic terms. While challenging the idea that dancing in a queer club was simply for its own sake, the utopian vision of the ideal relationship with your own body and with others around you and its potential for affecting everyday life was not always fulfilled. The order or relationship may be dystopic. The relationship or order of the body and community may also be of alienation or of the commodity to its consumer. But whether with another person or with one's multiple subjectivities and bodies, whether a social or personal ideal was achieved, desire was articulated by all informants. These were visions of what could be. Social improvised dancing in a queer club did not only mobilize the past, it expressed the future.

⫷⫷ 6

CLOSER
Crackdown, Community, and the Physicality of Queerness

Tonight on TV, I saw a late night advertisement opposing Ruth Messenger's mayoral campaign paid for by the friends of the incumbent, Rudy Guiliani. It had quotes pasted up over grainy (visual media shorthand for sleazy) images of XXX establishments. The quotes from Messenger read something like, "Sex shops add to the character of neighborhoods." Then women on the street — not of the street — say how these stores demean and degrade women. They finish with their horror at Messenger's quote: "She said that?"

So I had to get out.

The bar of Velvet — Foxy's home — was dark and narrow. In the back performance room a topless skinny tattooed boy was dancing listlessly with a hula-hoop. A wholesome-looking girl wearing blue jeans and a purse slung across her shoulders got up on the podium and started to perform an awesome cheerleader routine with the hula, transforming it into some swirling vortex of energy with her in its middle. She expertly threw it up and caught it, spun it over from one arm to the other, then round her neck, her waist, and her thighs. "Beautiful People" by Marilyn Manson clattered and howled over her performance. She was no pro, but her show was so spirited that the queer crowd among whom she was incongruous cheered her and did not seem to mind when she dropped the hoop. That was, until a man in a red T-shirt with a pager told her to stop. She got down, but later danced with the go-go boy up on the podium. Again the man rushed in and told her to stop. After he returned to the front, I asked her what he said to her. She told me she was told she had to stop dancing because the bar had no cabaret license. "It's like Footloose and it's bullshit. I'm from fucking Montana and I can't believe this. This is New York City for Christ's sake, and I'm not allowed to dance." Master of Ceremonies Justin Bond sauntered up with a microphone and she repeated her tirade. An activist had been distributing leaflets about a rally outside Guiliani's office on Fiftieth Street and Lexington Avenue that Wednesday to protest the clampdown on night life. He spoke into the microphone to ask people to come. "As if we ever go to Fiftieth Street," retorted Justin. (Fieldnote: 9/27/97)

≋ A DANCE SPACE always exists on license. Nightlife is a third space where participants come together, sometimes in the hope of building lifeworlds. Was this the reason why, despite the great financial and cultural capital clubs brought to New York City, they were being cracked down on in the 1990s by the local authorities? How did they fit into the "quality of life" agenda pushed by the mayor's office as it attempted to re-draw cognitive maps of New York City by criminalizing some activities and groups? Small doubt that the renewed vigor invested in queer spaces as spaces of resistance and rehearsal for new possibilities was a response to this as well as a very conscious connection to the queer history of gay and lesbian spaces in New York City: to the memory of the "Golden Age" of New York City nightlife of the 1970s and 1980s, when self-fashioned downtown superstars danced together with media celebrities. The new queer clubs also kicked against dominant gay spaces and their worship of idealized maleness and whiteness. But why was there a need for them at this moment? What drove them and what pleasures were on the menu?

From an economic perspective, any crackdown on clubs would seem to be akin to neutering the goose that laid the golden egg. Clubs offered very real economic benefits to New York City. In 1996, an estimated 24.3 million people patronized almost three hundred New York clubs, exceeding the combined attendance of Broadway theater, city sports teams, the Metropolitan Museum of Art, and the Empire State Building. The total estimated benefit for the city was more than one billion dollars.[1] This estimated income did not include the trickle-down effect of music and clothes sales. New York City's clubs solidified its reputation as the night life city of the world, shining like a beacon for party-seeking tourists, who also spent their cash on accommodation, food, and transport. New York's cultural capital was further augmented as its clubs were playgrounds of culture, as the ground from which celebrities such as Madonna, Bette Midler, RuPaul, Lou Reed, John Zorn, Talking Heads, Keith Haring, Kenny Scharf, Jean-Michael Basquiat, and Fab 5 Freddy emerged. Underground dance clubs incubated musical and dance movements that swept the globe—from bebop to the Twist through hip-hop, punk, and garage, as well as gestating many fashion trends. But in clubs all over the city that never sleeps, people were not talking about the latest white hot scene, but what had been raided, fined, or shut down. Community opposition, a poor public image, and a city administration that came down hard on clubs as part of its quality of life campaign disproportionately affected queer clubs for two reasons. First, because on the list of establishments harassed or closed down, queer spaces were overrepresented. Second, for queers, especially queers of color and women, denied representational power in other spheres, the stakes of closing down spaces they gather in were high.

Andrew Rasiej, co-founder of the New York Nightlife Association, and owner of Irving Plaza, a live music and nightclub venue, remarked in a 1997 article in the *Village Voice* that the crackdown was a direct result of the real estate boom in Manhattan, and the gentrification of previously commercial and low income, often ethnic neighborhoods.[2] The pressure exerted on clubs came from three sources: from the mayor, from enforcement agencies such as the police, the fire department, and the Board of Health inspectors, and from organized local community groups. As part of New York City Mayor Rudolph Guiliani's high-profile "Strategy '97" push to fight crime and insure his reelection, the mayor targeted dance clubs identified by the police as "a magnet for drug sales, underage drinking, loud music, and other conditions, which create an atmosphere conducive to crime."[3] What were the reasons for this increased attention? Why were archaic licensing laws being enforced with new urgency and with what results?

To contextualize this strategy within queer world-making, in 1994 the Republican administration of New York City under Guiliani proposed zoning regulations for "adult establishments" that threatened to radically affect queer lifeworlds.[4] Activist groups such as Sex Panic! feared that gay neighborhoods and blocks such as Christopher Street and the West Village and Chelsea would be dissolved. Gay spaces such as bars, bookstores, and clubs defined as "adult establishments" according to the definitions of the City of New York City Planning Council would be forced to relocate to areas less accessible for potential customers. In order to remain open in their current locations, such establishments would have to purge themselves of material and performances defined as "adult" (see Appendix D), the presence of which would subject them to the zoning laws. In this context, the Strategy '97 quality of life agenda could be seen as an example of the politics of space being actively used to curtail the existence and articulation of queer lifeworlds. This was no idle preelection posturing. As well as enforcing the zoning laws and "Disneyfying" districts such as Times Square, another, older weapon was mobilized that used the politics of movement to control, not just the spaces, but the bodies of the people who went to them. Contemporaneous with the imposition of zoning laws, the local political authorities and enforcement agencies instigated a noticeable crackdown on bars and dance clubs, including those catering to a queer clientele under licensing laws restricting public dancing. While on the books for a number of years, these laws were now subject to unprecedented enforcement. They stated that go-go dancers (pretty much defined in practice as anyone on a podium) could not perform at an establishment without a cabaret license. If this was not enough, three or more customers "moving rhythmically" in an establishment unlicensed for dancing also constituted a violation. As the opening anecdote illustrates, this made security personnel very nervous indeed. More than once over this period, I and other friends were urged to cease and desist "moving rhythmically" in bars—even those with DJs who entrapped us by playing Stevie Wonder! Several times challenges by security lead to bizarre arguments about how much of a sway, or a swing of the arms, or twist of the pelvis constituted a violation. Queer public sex was not the only body practice outlawed in attempts to control and erase the construction and articulation of queer lifeworlds. The mayor's office itself was actively using the politics of space and movement to engage in world-making. But the world envisioned was one in which the family was the sanctioned unit and Disney was the seller of stories.

The New York Department for Consumer Affairs issued cabaret licenses only after dozens of other permits, certificates, and licenses had been acquired and inspections passed (these are overseen by the Department of Buildings, the municipal electrical department, the Fire Department, and Department of Health). The various agencies that regulated the club and bar business—the State Liquor Authority (SLA), the Department of Health, the Department of Buildings, and the Police and Fire Departments—entered a new and very public phase of activity. After the Happyland fire of 1990 in which eighty-seven people died in a Bronx club, the Fire Department set up a Social Club Task Force to make sure establishments complied with city safety guidelines. However, it was only from 1996 that citations for "disorderly premises" by the police increased as a result of a ramping up of political pressure from both the mayor's office as a result of the quality of life campaign and local communities as a response to the real estate boom. Locally, members of community boards worried about the effect that clubs and their patrons had on property prices, while the mayor's office focused its efforts on attracting big business to the newly scrubbed Big Apple.

As rents achieved astronomical levels, propelled upward by the real estate boom, the frustration of community groups increased. Many felt businesses benefiting local communities were being forced out and replaced by bars and clubs that served "outsiders." Members of these groups, as active voters, turned their concerns into effective action. Their powers of opposition were increased in 1993 when Queens state senator Frank Padavan helped pass a bill giving community boards a greater say in the SLA's awarding of liquor licenses. Known as the "five hundred-foot rule," the law aimed to prevent the saturation of neighborhoods with bars and clubs. An establishment had to hold a license for on-premises liquor sales. To obtain one, the owner had to get approval from the community board, which considered the nature of the establishment, the owner's reputation, the legal record of any related liquor-serving establishments, and whether the new business was opening within five hundred feet or less of three or more establishments. Community Boards' recommendations factored in SLA decisions, as well as in decisions to award cabaret licenses in their neighborhood.[5]

Neighborhood groups, such as the Save Avenue A Society in the East Village (their members sit on Community Board Three) used their new powers to stop the opening of new bars and to obstruct the renewal of existing liquor and cabaret licenses, making it harder than ever to open a new club or renew the license of an existing one. One 1997 estimate put the cost of opening up a new bar as $100,000 extra in legal fees alone.[6] New York was a city where only entrepreneurs with deep pockets could afford to open a club. In addition, community groups' numerous and various complaints to the police about noise, drug use, parking problems, and cruising had drastic results. For example, neighborhood opposition to Edelweiss, a renowned transvestite club in the Hell's Kitchen district of Manhattan west of Times Square, helped to get the place padlocked in March 1997, on the grounds that it attracted prostitution.

There was no doubt that crime levels decreased in the new, improved New York City. Whoever seized the credit for this mined political gold. The police contended that this lower crime rate was the result of their aggressive pursuit of petty public offenses. The "broken window" theory behind this strategy, first adopted by Police Commissioner William Bratton, held that suppressing the symptoms of public disorder discouraged major crime. However, commentators voiced uneasiness about the implications of this policy:

> If you fix a broken window, the theory goes, vandals won't be tempted to break every window in sight. That sounds right until you substitute people for panes of glass. What happens when the symptom of disorder is a group

that doesn't fit into the neighborhood? Or when their behavior is bad for business? (Goldstein 1997, 38–39)

As a result of this strategy the number of arrests for misdemeanors such as pot smoking, graffiti writing, and playing a boombox in a public space soared and, according to officers at Legal Aid, the great majority involved poor people and people of color, provoking the question, who diagnoses the symptoms of public disorder? Whose quality of life was being protected?

When police cracked down on prostitution in Chelsea in 1996–97, gay men cruising around the waterfront bars were next. The Anti-Violence Project of New York City reported a huge increase in arrests for public lewdness in the same period.[7] In many cases, according to Christine Quinn, executive director of AVP, police were targeting men they saw necking, or merely cruising, on certain streets. When it comes to quality of life offenses, queers and people of color can seem suspicious, not just to the police, but to communities and to the city. However, this begs the question, what do we mean when we talk of "community" and "citizenship" in New York City in the 1990s? The rights of property owners and business proprietors were asserted over other groups who may use urban space and who were less politically organized.

All of the above had rights to use public space. However, fear of the very differences that define New York City has been a machine too easily used in the service of homogenizing the population. Elected officials mobilized fears of "antisocial," "antifamily," and "immoral" practices as well as local community, business, and corporate fears of falling property values. In this climate, clubgoers felt under constant surveillance. The police raided establishments and sometimes indiscriminately issued summons. The press reported a club's citations, no matter how minor. Security personnel were under increasing pressure to conduct prolonged and extensive searches for illegal substances and weapons. Club closures created good press for the Guiliani administration. The perceived and real edgy aesthetic of dance clubs did not hold much appeal to the family-friendly New York the mayor tried to convince voters and corporate interests such as Disney he had single-handedly delivered.[8] Sensational moralistic exposés in the media—such as Jack Newfield's series of columns in the *New York Post*—used raids, citations, and sensational coverage of club-owner Peter Gatien's drug-conspiracy indictment and club promoter Michael Alig's indictment in a grisly murder case involving another clubgoer[9] to portray clubland as a seething hotbed of violence, noise, and drugs, thus feeding the concerns of "good citizens."[10]

The closure of clubs—with the attendant loss of jobs—did not generate political heat. Club owners and industry stars such as DJ Junior Vasquez had no political base; they delivered no votes. The multimillion dollar nightlife industry did not have a lobbyist, made few political contributions, and its members were often openly suspicious of each other. Clubs that drove revitalization in formerly derelict districts were now more likely to be regarded as spawners of criminality than antidotes to it. Club life was often transient, as many clubs were not supposed to be permanent, so clubbers were used to being uprooted and moving on. The bartenders, busboys, bouncers, dancers, and partygoers were not your typical Guiliani voters, if they voted at all. Many were not New Yorkers, some too young to vote. In comparison, local community groups were well organized, vocal, and stocked with voters.

One of the consequences of this "quality of life" campaign was the politically expedient criminalization of certain groups and practices. Although not every affected establishment catered to a queer clientele, several such bars and clubs ran afoul of these new regulations and newly enforced laws, producing a widespread feeling among many clubbers that a homophobic and racist bias was at least partly responsible for this crackdown. News of raids and closures spread through the bars, clubs, coffee shops, and meeting places of queer lifeworlds. The image of the safe space within New York City and of the security that sometimes capitalism appeared to promise was left standing in its shabby attire in the harsh strip light of reality. The safe space that attracted queers and people of color revealed itself as an illusion when authority figures such as the police and fire officers raided a club, started counting heads, and asked for identification from each patron. In addition, many queer establishments were borderline profitable and numerous fines for violations resulted in closure. Stephen recalled exactly how his favorite dance space, Crowbar, eventually closed, as a typical endgame of the harassment of queer spaces:[11]

It was the death of a thousand cuts. It was like AIDS. AIDS isn't a disease, AIDS is a number of cumulative diseases. And that's what's happened to a lot of gay public spaces that they cracked down on. It wasn't just a cabaret license. It's "that'll be fifteen hundred dollars." And then there was the fire department, which was another arm of the city. They would raid a place saying there were too many people in the space, and then they'd be busted for loudness, and then other places would be busted for the backroom. There were a thousand different things that all came together—it was harassment at a very high and a very stressful level for the owners and folks there. I mean, it is a gay bar and a queer space, but also the people in it are working class, who have a tenuous relationship to authority, as it is—white or black. There were all these grungy people, artists, dancers, who already had a tenuous relationship to authority. All you have to do is on a Friday, Saturday night when it's bumping and grinding, have five fully decked out fire department folks come in. You know, it's a damper. No more dancing, and everybody's like, "I'm outta here."

Closures of queer spaces on the grounds of infringement of licensing regulations were seen by queers as a direct attack. The thousand cuts effect caused the closure of Cake (a small gay bar/dance venue on Avenue B between Sixth and Seventh Streets) that closed on April 19th, 1997, under the weight of fines for offenses such as overcrowding and obstruction of view (establishments with windows are required to maintain a clear line of sight from the outside, a vexed question in relation to queer bars that want to offer a safe space where queer patrons do not have to look out onto the straight world, or to be exposed to a potentially hostile gaze from outside). In response, Jackie 60, the long-running club famous for its eclectic crowd and inventive weekly themes, presented a two-act play drawing parallels between the "Taking of Cake" and the Stonewall riots, which sparked up in response to a police raid on a queer bar. Mistress Formika, one of the club's hosts, fumed in an article in *Time Out,* a magazine that lists New York events, "They're looking for any excuse to close these bars down" (Goldstone 1997, 12), a sentiment shared by many queer clubgoers who link the crackdown to control and the cultural cleansing of New York. The space reopened as a straight bar, as did the space formerly known as Crowbar.

People felt racial tension was also reflected in the harassment of clubs. One promoter told *Time Out* magazine that the police asked him not to have hip-hop nights at his club. When the Tunnel relaunched its Sunday night as a hip-hop party in 1996, the police set up a roadblock across Eleventh Avenue at 27th Street and searched the cars of anybody who looked like they were going to the party, looking for drugs, guns, and stolen cellular phones—not a uniform strategy employed for all clubs in New York City. Patrons of clubs such as the predominantly Latino Escuelita read police presence as homophobic and racist oppression. As I stood in line outside this club on a Thursday night, patrons could not help but notice a police van parked directly outside the door. Police officers stood watching as door people checked patrons for identification. "I bet they aren't standing outside some swanky white, straight bar in Soho," a clubgoer said, voicing the opinions of others who concurred. "Haven't you got anything better to do? Where are you when we're being attacked in the streets?" one person grumbled. Police often responded to the concerns of local residents and business owners. In at least one building in affluent Tribeca, across the street from Vinyl, a group of concerned residents put up posters asking residents to register objections to the club. One of the concerns listed along with noise, parking, and drug use, was that the club's hip-hop event attracted undesirables to the neighborhood who might affect property values and quality of life.

The New York City crackdown occurred at the same time that locally and nationally gay neoconservatives focused their attacks on the gay club scene. Since the early 1980s, neoconservatives claimed that the social movements of the 1960s were to blame for the ills of contemporary life, and tried to roll back the gains of civil rights, feminism, and gay liberation. During the same period of liberalization, popular social dance forms had shifted from formalized dances that strictly regulated intimacy and gender roles to looser, improvised forms that expressed greater personal freedom and autonomy—the Twist being the most famous example. These forms caused moral panic in mainstream culture because they were linked to libidinous sexuality and through that to thinly veiled fears of blackness, miscegenation, and the need to protect young people and women in particular from their baser—darker— selves. During the 1970s, large dance parties and clubs located in urban centers such as San Francisco and New York were engines and symptoms of gay pride. These events and their projection of a certain gay lifestyle provoked the disapproval of some gay critics who felt liberation was wasted in "frivolous" activity.[12] But in the 1980s and 1990s gay neoconservatives had a new stick with which to beat club life, as they claimed that these events and their attendant practices of promiscuous sex and drug-taking resulted in AIDS.

In 1997's *Sexual Ecology: AIDS and the Destiny of Gay Men,* Gabriel Rotello argued that gay male anonymous sex offended nature, ecology, and the social order, and that monogamy was the natural, ecological, socially responsible cure for gay men's ills and a protection against AIDS. In national forums such as *The New Republic, The Atlantic Monthly, The New York Times Magazine, The Weekly Standard, The Nation, Newsweek,* National Public Radio, and the *Charlie Rose* show, Rotello, along with Andrew Sullivan,

Larry Kramer, Michelangelo Signorile, and Bruce Bawer threw scorn on queer bars and clubs and harangued queers for their "excesses": excesses they claimed were both self-destructive and threatened to destroy the chance of acceptance of homosexuality by mainstream society. These writers typified clubs as products of low self-esteem and tied them to promiscuity and drug abuse, setting up models of the good gay and the bad queer in opposition to each other.[13] The good gay settles into a respectable career and a monogamous relationship. (Sullivan [1995] argues gay politics should be reduced to two issues: military service and marriage.) The bad queer works to get high and fucks in backrooms and bathhouses. As far as lesbian sexuality is concerned, these male writers cleaned it up and silenced it. If they mentioned it at all, they spoke for it, but in order to use a selective model of lesbian monogamy as a sexless wedge against queer culture. This assimilationist force in gay politics partly resulted from increasing dependence on fundraising and media jockeying. One symptom in the nineties was the gay press's negative portrayal of how one gay fundraising party form—the circuit party—transmogrified into an albatross around the neck of sections of gays and lesbians seeking acceptance from mainstream heterosexual society.

The gay party circuit was an international calendar of gay parties, which included the Winter Party in Miami and the Black Party in New York in March; the Palm Springs (CA) White Party and Cherry Jubilee in Washington, D.C., in April; Hotlanta in Atlanta and the Morning Party in Fire Island, New York, in August; the Black and Blue Party in Montreal and the San Francisco Hell Ball in October; and the White Party in Miami in November. Typically, these parties were held in large venues or outdoors and charged hefty entry prices from $60 upward. As reported in *Out,* a national gay magazine, the circuit scene was undergoing a change in the mid to late 1990s that raised troubling questions and blasted long-simmering controversies about drug use and unsafe sex into the open. After almost a decade of parties geared almost entirely toward fund-raising for AIDS charities, circuit parties received negative press for their domination by a new breed of for-profit entrepreneurs. In 1997, American Airlines quietly announced it was ending its sponsorship of four circuit parties, including the blossom season Cherry Jubilee in Washington, D.C., and the Easter-time Palm Springs White Party. B. J. Stiles, president of the National AIDS Fund, which distributed philanthropic monies for corporations like tobacco giant Philip Morris, remarked in an interview with *Out* that "what we're hearing from corporations is that they're becoming skeptical and anxious about these parties.

They want to know if they are legitimate, or if they're something they want to avoid with a ten-foot pole" (McKinley 1998, 92). The fear that some promoters were profiting from AIDS philanthropy by advertising that "a portion of the profits benefit AIDS groups," while being unspecific about what portion and which groups, had a chilling effect on public image-conscious corporate sponsorship for AIDS groups, at a time when even the gay press was creating an impression of hedonism with sensationalized reports of drug overdoses. AIDS groups that relied on these parties for a large slice of their income knew that raising money for AIDS was difficult under the best of circumstances, and these were not the best of circumstances. Drug induced medical emergencies and arrests at circuit parties were a public-relations nightmare for sponsors, including Gay Men's Health Crisis, which had to do damage control after a young man was evacuated from its 1996 Morning Party in the Pines on Fire Island after falling into a GHB-induced coma.[14] After the 1997 Fire Island Morning Party, the gay press reported the drug-related collapse of several men, with the customary responses from organizers that, at a party of that size, four incidents—none serious—was an excellent record. These media responses and counterresponses became part of a regular public relations dance performed for high stakes in front of sponsors and sections of the gay media who felt that images of partying—read drug-using and anonymous sex-seeking men—damaged efforts for cultural and political acceptance of homosexuality. Subsequent to these incidents, GMHC canceled the Morning Party altogether, despite the funds it raised.

If circuit parties and the men who loved them were scorned by more assimilationist gays in the United States, then the latter had unlikely allies in radical queers and those who shared a fond nostalgia for other spaces and times, but who avoided circuit parties for different reasons, many having to do with an inherent distaste of their elitism, as Iain describes:

> I had a friend who got into all the circuit parties 'cos that was an elitist thing and he wanted to be part of an elitist gay culture. It's not a class thing but a ratings thing. It's class but not in money, but in beauty and being seen at the right clubs, with the right people in the right clothes.

With their high ticket prices, luxurious surroundings, celebrity population, the best DJs with the best sound systems, the latest remixes, and, of course, the most Adonis-like idealized men, circuit parties were associated with elitism by several informants. And it was an accusation, not a recommendation. A large part of their objections involved not just the lack of access to those who couldn't afford the entry, but a certain body elitism that marginalized other bodies.

Gays obviously exist in every income bracket and come in all shapes and sizes, but some informants felt marginalized by pervasive images of buffness, whiteness, and wealth in the gay media and advertising. Barrel talked about how, as a dominant image, the young buff body marginalized other gay bodies, making them less desirable and less desired:

> That look has become so defining of what gays look like. It has defined your sexuality. Everybody wants to look the same because they want to be desired. That's the image that these [circuit and other large clubs such as Twilo] parties are putting out, you need to look like this to be part of our group, and to have sex at all. At Squeezebox [a queer club] it's interesting to be skinny. I'll never have a big buff body and I don't want someone telling me I don't belong because I don't have a big buff body.

Alex tracked a change in desirable gay bodies over time through pornography:

> If you look at porno in the late '70s and up to the '80s and look at how the body changed. The boys' bodies in porn changed from the '70s thin but wiry into the '80s hairdo, more buff, and bigger and more American looking. Straight boys were working out and doing that look before the gay boys were.

He identified this body image with a desire to evacuate the cultural stereotype of the swishy, limp-wristed queen, suggesting that its effect on a certain gay population might be tied to a desire to look straight, that is, not to conform to a stereotype of gayness. The preeminence of representations of the buff gay body seemed to amount to compelling evidence of the assertion of certain types of hegemonic gay masculinity, which measured what not to be (i.e., effeminate) as well as projecting an ideal. This body was fashioned at the gym and displayed on the dance floor of many gay clubs in New York City. Tanning, waxing, shaving, and oiling the body were other cosmetic aids to visibility. Abs, preferably waxed, were the essential accessories at circuit parties and at large parties such as Juniorverse at Twilo and Arena at the Palladium. Sitting in the chill-out area of Arena, my two gamine companions, Jay and Richard, squeezed each other tight. "Oh, I'm so glad you don't look like those boys," murmured one to another, surveying the homogeneous mass of muscled frames before us. "I'd get scared that you'd walk into that crowd and I'd never find you again." We laughed, but our laughter commented upon the astonishing similarity of bodies in the club. Almost all had bodies toned like classical Greek statues, stripped to the waist with short-cropped hair, and little or no facial hair. Most were white. Mimesis seemed to be the name of this bodybuilding game. To occupy the position of desire represented by bodies in advertising, the media, and in the club, gay men constructed themselves into the object of their own desire.

Iain associated the gay male ideal body image and the pressure it exerted on young men, with the pressure women have felt being subjected to images of the ideal female body in the media:

> I look at HX [*Homo Extra*] and *Next* and think if I were a young kid, that would just depress me to hell to go out. As a man and as a gay man, one of the problems I had was self-esteem and I think, my God, if I was younger and had to put up with the expectations I felt I had to meet. It's like women today, if you don't have this perfect body and these perfect tits, then you're not attractive in our society.

In connecting gay men and women together under the burden of low self-esteem, he identified one of the polymorphous mechanisms of power through which cultural prejudices against these members of the population operate: the pressure to physically conform to an ideal in order to be accepted. Difference was avoided. In this representational economy, the body became another product that marked itself as gay—desired by other gay men and thus marked as desiring them. This body reproduced and consumed itself in its own image, as Alex pointed out:

> And that's not fair of a community that's supposed to embrace diversity. It does not. It's just like the rest of American culture. It wants to mainstream. It want to merge with the rest of America. It wants it so bad. A lot of what gay culture is about is money. Buy an outfit. My friend had to have leather pants for the Black Party that cost him four hundred dollars. That's what they want. You're not going thrift shop buying for something for twenty bucks, you're going to the gay shop. You buy the gay outfit like the gay Ken doll in the window. It's hilarious and it makes me really sad.

However, there were those who could not acquire that body and those other markings of a certain commodified gayness. Others, like Ariel, were turned off by the homogenizing effects of commodification. Under this rubric, gay identifications in New York City could be seen as a series of product choices—including what clubs you choose to go to:

> I feel for the first time in my life I really have to pick and stick to it. When I go to most clubs, it's very gay and I feel like I'm fitting this piece in this puzzle. In Seattle, the places I'd be hanging out where there'd be so much play going on weren't defined as gay or straight, they were defined as Goth. It was very reassuring because I never felt I had to choose or be seen a certain way. Part of that is just having the mystery of it. People not knowing, questioning—that's the exciting part of it for me.

Alex remarked tellingly that "Going to a club is like shopping." The historian John D'Emilio (1993) tracked how capitalism created the material conditions for homosexual desire to express itself by freeing individuals to make a living through wage labor, instead of within an interdependent family unit. Patterns of living evolved that allowed individuals to survive beyond the confines of the family.[15] In addition to wage labor, the rise of consumerism and the ability to create and re-create oneself has also played a significant role in the development of gay communities within the urban landscape.

According to Iain, approaching age forty at the time of our discussion, other modes of the physical play of desire from which other bodies might have emerged had been lost. He reflected nostalgically:

> When I first went out we weren't in the buff era yet. People didn't walk around with their shirts off. It was about who you eyed and a little cruising scene going on. Back then it was more the face . . . so it was still physical . . . but I don't remember feeling so self-conscious. Now I feel like I really don't belong.

Several informants noted that a body of physical play that emerged through how people moved or looked at each other was succeeded by a body that did not move, play, or operate physically in the same way. In the clubs, some informants, like Stephen, felt that the purpose of coming to dance had been forgotten:

> People are more aware of their bodies now, but it's too uptight. Now people are more concerned about how they look, rather than, boy, I'm enjoying this music. We'd get messy dancing and we didn't care.

This tension was expressed through style. In an urban gay culture, style was particularly substantive. In his 1987 essay, "The Gay Decades," Frank Rich discussed the phenomenon of the distinctive cultural energy of gay male culture (until recently, lesbian culture has not had as much visibility or impact on the mainstream) breaking from the margins to the center. He identified what he saw as an increasing infiltration of gay lifestyle and sensibility into hetero-America, from social life (clubs such as Studio 54) to pop culture (Bette Midler and Dynasty) to fashion (buff Calvin Klein underwear models). Rich concluded that all of this pointed to "the most dramatic cultural assimilation of our time": the homosexualization of straight culture.[16] In his eyes, through this process urban gay culture lost the very edge that defined it. Advertisers scouted out the possibilities for appealing to the attractive PINK market: Professional Income, No Kids. Therefore, the representation the gay community received of itself and what it should desire was predominantly white, apparently healthy—read HIV-negative, young men (no queens, tranvestites, or transgendereds, please, and not too butch—bears need not apply), of a certain physique (no skinny fags or chubby queens), and enjoying the privileges of their whiteness, youth, beauty, health, and disposable income—a cruise holiday perhaps or an intimate dinner for two at a Chelsea restaurant. As Daniel Mendelsohn bemoaned in *New York* magazine in 1996, "Gay culture has gone from *épater*-ing *les bourgeois* to aping them." He suggested that, in the intervening decade since Rich's essay, the phenomenon he described has been inverted: the most dramatic cultural assimilation of our time has been the heterosexualization of gay culture. "As homosexuality has moved, however slowly, toward the mainstream, there's been less and less for gay culture to do what it's best at, which is to stand on the margins and throw shade." Whether it was the theatrical activism of ACT UP, or the over-the-top glamour of drag, or a way of walking down the street or calling out to other gay friends, gay style was all about performance, sometimes for an appreciative audience and sometimes not. Gay style was critique, and in defining itself through whiteness, buffness, and a model of gay masculinity, in coming to clubs not to dance but to be admired, that defining edge was lost. Some informants felt the loss of certain types of pleasure and recovered them by re-eroticizing them in queer spaces.

Alex and his friends had enjoyed the scene-setting glamour of clubs such as Danceteria and Area in the 1980s, with their incorporation of different types of music, art, and the expression of individual style he called "pulling a look." They opened the queer club Squeezebox in 1994 partly in response to a homogenization of gay style, which Alex saw as without style in the queer sense of style celebrating difference. In typical New York fashion, he associated this with a neighborhood. Thus, "Eighth Avenue" stood for "Chelsea"—a downtown neighborhood with many businesses catering toward a gay male constituency:

> You'd go [to a queer club] and because it wasn't so commodified, there were these really outrageous people pulling these looks and it wouldn't be this half-assed thing. It would be cartoonish and over the top. It wouldn't be like this Eighth Avenue idea of how it should be. They'd make their own celebrities and you'd be this kid and you'd be a downtown celebrity.

Whereas approval was granted in dominant gay spaces to those similar to a certain constituency, queer spaces valued and celebrated difference or freakiness. Squeezebox was intended to be a place where freaks could fit in, Alex described:

> I can come wearing make-up, I can come with my hair dyed red, nobody cared, everyone was, "wow, you look great, love it! I want more, give me more! More lipstick—here's some lipstick. More eyeshadow? Here, I want more, more of it. Your lapel on your jacket is that wide, well, make it bigger. If you can be that much of a freak, be more of a freak. Let it out." Here are people who not just wanted, but needed to be this way. They needed to perform and here was a way for them to do it. Here was a place these kids could do it outside of Hollywood and they could be stars. The energy was amazing because of all these different people who came and got involved.

In Squeezebox and other places such as Foxy and Studio Filthy Whore, rock chicks mingled with retro drag whores, queer-core punks, and goths. Alex worked the door in these spaces and his policy was based on an inclusive ideology. He saw the fact that he let John Kennedy Junior in as proof of this. Furthermore, John-John couldn't sip Jaegermeister in a VIP area separated from the queer throng. In a smaller space like Squeezebox, Alex pointed out, the critical mass of bodies was maintained, compared with larger clubs where people could get lost and hide if they wanted to:

> In Squeezebox, there is this core group of people who come and, especially in the beginning, it was a really sexy crowd, people in tight clothes,

boys in make up, everybody being androgynous, sexy, showing skin, showing their body, and then you have people on the outside of that who came
to look. When there's a big club, the core group gets lost. The lookers are
looking at the lookers not looking at the freaks in the middle that make
the scene what it is. And that's why there's a VIP area, and Squeezebox has
no VIP area—it's too small, so everybody's forced into working together.

The culture of these spaces was a process of tension between
"freakiness" and "normality." Participants defined queerness by what
they were not—normalized, homogenized, and mass-reproduced.
Thus, they also defined themselves against capitalism. But it would be
reductionist to claim that these practices resulted from oppression
alone. For any queer world-making was part oppositional, part pleasure, and—of course—part the pleasure of opposition. Patrons found
pleasure from fitting into a queer space, not just rejecting a non-queer
space.

Many of these queer spaces had drag shows or some patrons came in
drag. Drag is the epitome of queer style-as-critique. Alex describes how
the tension between mainstream gay culture and queer culture produced different kinds of drag with different referents:

> The drag at the time [1980s] was Upper East Side socialites. And at Boy
> Bar, people started doing southern white trash—the women they grew up
> on trailer parks with. And people came in with ratty hair with hayseed in
> their mouths. Boy Bar and Pyramid started playing with different ideas.
> Like drag doesn't have to be beautiful, it can be about ugly and it can be
> about white trash and all these other things.

In these spaces, drag was performed as a transgression of what drag was
supposed to be. Structurally, a show could be recognizably a drag show
cabaret, but performers subverted its content. In doing this, Alex said,
performers subverted not just "Upper East Side" drag, but ideal notions
of beauty and femininity:

> Sometimes these shows would be about seedier things . . . Fellini, John
> Waters-esque, about white trash. Sometimes about abuse. About unwanted
> pregnancies. These themes are not normal. It's not about getting up and
> doing a Judy Garland tune. It's saying I'm not going to accept what this is
> supposed to be and I'm going to fuck with it. I'm going to take the struc-
> ture of a drag show and I'm gonna present something that's not usually

presented, and that's what made it exciting. It becomes a very DIY queer sort of thing because it's not toeing the line.

Queer drag often incorporated topical political commentary and presented a space of transgression for the audience members. As participants in the performance, they felt its liberatory force to subvert mainstream gay and straight notions of gender and beauty. Did queer drag of this type subvert mainstream gay notions of style? Could it subvert concepts of gay and straight sexuality?

At the Clit Club the music stopped and a performance began. From dancing together, we focused our attention on the small stage. Mo B. Dick—a well-known drag king on the scene—he of the familiar pompadour quiff, gold tooth, and pencil(ed) moustache, leered at the ladies, but below the neck, she was clothed in femme drag: a pink slip and high heeled pumps. His butch partner wore leather and jeans and a chest wig. To the rock 'n' roll strains of "Are You a Boy or a Girl?" they performed a gender-fuck relationship, culminating in Mo B. adjusting her underwear to allow a dildo to hang between her thighs. At the climax of the performance, she simulated fucking her partner. Such a performance subverted not only notions of sex, gender, and female and lesbian sexuality, but also the audience's preconceptions about drag kings—that they are just about butch, straight masculinity. For instance, when Lisa performed her lounge-singer drag persona, she made him gay. There was more than one type of chick with a dick.

> I really like drag kings. There are a lot of possibilities for that. It's not so much gender-subversion as the idea that you could have a women's space that's totally about dicks. As opposed to saying that a women's space is all about the female body, which is reduced to female genitalia and female sexuality, which is supposed to work a certain way.

Drag kings freed sexuality from biological sex or gender roles. The roles of penetrator and penetrated were revealed as performances rather than predetermined by chromosomes.

Queer drag permitted transgressive play, not only with what gender signified, but also with what lesbian and gay sexuality was supposed to mean. When Alex and his friends got together to discuss what kind of place they wanted Squeezebox to be, they all desired a fun, queer, playful, "anything goes" place. Alex enjoyed the playful flirtatiousness he remembered in Danceteria and Area: he could flirt with a guy without knowing—or maybe caring—if he was gay or straight. He could be kissing a girl in the bar, and then a boy in the backroom, and move from place to place. He could engage with people in ways he felt he couldn't in dominant gay or straight spaces. Stephen remembered that at Crowbar, notions of what "gay" and "straight" sexuality meant in dominant spaces were also played with: "Some straight bands would come, well, straight, but queer, you know, some of them had stories with some of the boys. And I saw—once or twice—some of the [gay] boys with girls. So it was truly queer in terms of sexuality."

When participants played genderfuck, gayfuck, and lesbianfuck, they eroticized what was taboo in other spaces, putting it back on the menu. This play embodied a strategy of eroticizing signs of heteronormative and homonormative oppression. For example, the unglamorous neighborhoods in which leather bars were located, once symbolizing the insignificant social status of their patrons, came to symbolize their daring and adventurousness. In another powerful example of the strategy of eroticization, queer spaces celebrated and reeroticized "immoral" behavior and put sleaze back on the agenda, making it desirable again. The return of sleaze enacted a powerful response to the political climate of New York City at that time, in which the mayor, city agencies, local interest groups, legislators, the media, and corporations were trying to culturally cleanse the city of sleaze.

In 1994–1995 there was a second wave of closings of sex clubs after the AIDS panic of the 1980s. He's Gotta Have It, Zone DK, and other gay sex clubs were padlocked, due to media outcry and a mayor determined to recreate a family-oriented city that would attract corporate investment and tourism. Within mainstream gay culture, the attempts of neoconservative gay writers to exorcise sleaze, and by some tenuous association, AIDS from gay public life, lead to a demand for a cleansing of gay culture. But what was taboo was ripe for eroticization. Chi Chi Valenti, promoter of the long-running Jackie 60, affirmed the vital presence of sleaze in queer clubs: "I certainly think of sleaze as a major element. It was missing from clubs in the '80s. It brings back a gay sensibility, formerly exhausted by AIDS, in a time of safer forms of sex, but it's still nasty" (Goldstone 1997, 11). How did sleaze manifest itself in queer clubs?

In small spaces in locations in the East Village and the Meat Packing District (the industrial zone along the West Side waterfront around Eleventh to Sixteenth Streets), away from the Eighth Avenue strip, club nights with names like Studio Filthy Whore (a smart parody of Studio

54), Skin, Social Toilet, Twisted!, Foxy, Trannie Chasers, and Cocksuckers & Buttfuckers, proliferated in the mid-1990s. Typically, DJs played rock and roll favorites rather than the latest house remix and a bevy of unusual go-go dancers and other performers entertained the crowd, from queercore punk bands to seventy-year-old strippers. Many clubs had theme nights to keep the party fresh and exciting and encouraged partygoers to participate by "pulling a look." So Jackie 60, for instance, had homages to Fellini, cybersex, and a parody of Michael Alig as Bugsy Segal where participants were encouraged to dress up in accordance with the theme. At Cake, one night of the week was called Cream and had performances in sleazy contests. Hustler on Thursday nights would encourage participants to pick each other up and go down to the basement. Foxy ran a queer take on "Search for a Star." For a five dollar entrance fee, partygoers would receive five hundred "Foxy dollars." MC Justin Bond would announce that a contestant had offered to perform a naked protest song perhaps, or some bizarre demonstration of scrotum stretching—and audience members offered the asking price in Foxy dollars and even upped the ante. At the end of the night, the contestant with the most Foxy dollars won a cash prize.

The aesthetic and ideology of sleaze cultivated by these clubs attracted people who saw trips to these spaces as slumming. Lisa observed how this revealed a subtle tension between the middle-class glitz of larger clubs and a working class drive pushing queer spaces:

> I don't see money getting in the way as much as class. Working class women will save the money if they want to go. I know a lot of working class women who go to clubs tend to be a little older—in their twenties up. The people who seem the most tight with money going out seem to be the young girls from NYU at Meow Mix, even though their parents are sending them to an expensive place. But I think that that's white middle-class kids taking on the attitude of being poor. It's the attraction of the whole punk DIY thing. They have the luxury of being poor. I think a lot of working-class women and women of color will save the money. That'll be their thing for the month.

The class experience of these spaces manifested itself in several ways. Promoters did not work for profit and had limited resources, hence the DIY culture of queer; partygoers paid five to ten dollars to go to a queer club, but not the twenty-five dollars and upward to go to Twilo—sixty dollars and upward for circuit parties. They also felt more comfortable wearing a jumble of clothing, rather than the latest expensive label, and they usually could not afford such items. Stephen balked at calling Crowbar "slummy," but acknowledged that some bourgeois boys from salon-type events such as held at Flamingo East on Wednesday nights would come to this space for other reasons:

> Crowbar wasn't slummy, but—I can't put my finger on it—the subtle nuances, 'cos it wasn't slumming, but a lot of boys from the West, Chelsea boys would come, and maybe they followed their racialized, sexualized interest. Flamingo East was more bourgeois. People would smell of cologne and look nice and stand around with cocktails talking. Crowbar, honey, you came to dance, and you were gonna sweat your ass off. You were not wearing your shit like that.

This working class ethic also meant that clubs functioned as third spaces:

> You know, not everyone has the luxury of going back to their own apartment. A lot of people live with their family, or in the streets. That's why the backroom is so important. You can explore your sexuality and get off and hang out, but in a safe space.

Barrel describes how, as clubs became homes in the absence of other resources, fellow clubgoers were family in the absence or withdrawal of other social ties.

> By maintaining my center in the East Village rather than Chelsea or these other gay neighborhoods, I always thought of myself as being queer as something that was subversive and transgressive from being gay. It was a more working class value. My parents are middle class but my grandparents aren't. I never really identified with my middle class family. I always felt that being queer was being different. I always wanted to be erased from my family. I had dreams that if they didn't love me I would be free and could escape.

As long as economic privilege is linked to race, gay men and lesbians of color will face difficulties in severing their ties to heterosexual families and defining their own neighborhoods. But despite these difficulties, queers of color have defined their own club spaces, away from fanfare or mainstream vehicles of publicity. News of these spaces spread by word of mouth; therefore, these spaces had underground cachet. This epithet held value in being outside of mainstream vehicles of publicity and the types of club populated by tourists to the city.

Gay culture's emphasis on sexuality both reflected and reinforced racial, as well as class, hierarchies. Jermaine remembered the popularity with African-Americans and Latinos of clubs he used to frequent in the borough of Queens, such as Freda's Hideaway and Billy the Kid, and he suggested one reason why gay men of color rarely ventured to gay clubs such as the Saint:

> You must remember that the Saint was for rich, middle-class white men. No tacky drag queens. It's like they were Harvard and wanted their own club. Membership promised exclusivity. It was supposed to keep certain people out. It was expensive to be a member, and then the tickets were really pricey. And honey, we couldn't afford that. That decided who was desirable in that space.

Colin felt that economics was not the only reason why some black informants did not find white-dominated gay clubs attractive.

> I went to Splash [a gay bar in Chelsea] and it was not about me. And I didn't want to be a part of it. I don't do the Chelsea thing anymore and part of it is finding out what's going on other than that. Suspect [a dance club for gay men of color] I discovered through word of mouth. Now it's starting to appear in a few magazines but there's no big publicity, which is interesting in the gay community. It's more underground, more secretive, hence the name. The black male body is always suspicious and also the black male body that looks straight, but it's not.

This knowledge of the underground scene gave Colin a choice and it gave him pleasure. Clubgoers became more selective given choices. Colin had a list of places he didn't go. The places he frequented were black and Latino, such as the Warehouse in the Bronx; Krash in Queens; Octagon, Escuelita, and Suspect in Manhattan. He enjoyed going to places that were about him, about his body, his blackness, and about the hip-hop music he enjoyed. All of these clubs and events were located in marginal spaces in the city. Two were in the boroughs, and the three in Manhattan were outside of the hotspots of mainstream nightlife, such as Greenwich Village, Chelsea, the West Village, and the East Village. (Octagon was located at 33rd Street and Eleventh Avenue; Escuelita at 39th Street and Eighth Avenue; and only Suspect, held in Nowbar at Seventh

Avenue South and Leroy Street, was at the southwest edge of the gay West Village. The latter of these took place on Sunday night, not on a mainstream party night such as Thursday, Friday, or Saturday.)

The presence of Latino clubs such as Escuelita and Krash on Colin's list is worth a closer look. Colin identified himself as "different" from whiteness and heterosexuality, as well as African-American. He felt comfortable in clubs whose patrons were a mix of African-American, black Latino, and Hispanic Latino. These clubs manifested the opportunity for dynamic and playful modes of self-consciousness. In *Culture and Truth,* ethnographer Renato Rosaldo (1989) uses the powerful metaphor of "border crossings" to envision the formation of ethnicity as a process of "intercultural borrowing and lending." In Escuelita and Krash, pleasure was created through border crossings, in the intersection of music and dance through the remixing of traditional music—salsa and merengue—with house beats and breaks, and in their juxtaposition with contemporary hip-hop and house music. These had implications for the emergence of new forms of cultural and political identity in which common bonds formed between gay Latinos of different experiences and gay African-Americans. These were also resistances to the "reductive multicultural pluralism" that José Esteban Muñoz (1998, 196) suggests is deployed against people of color in the United States as well as a response to whiteness.

I visited lesbian spaces such as the predominantly white Meow Mix and events such as Her/she Bar, which had a more mixed clientele of Latinas, blacks, Asians, and whites, and Flava at Club Farenheit, an event advertised for black "sistas." Edie suggested that the comparatively fewer lesbian clubs in New York City had the effect of segregating the community racially and on class lines. Black, white, and Asian women highlighted three differences they noticed between predominantly white lesbian spaces such as Meow Mix and spaces dominated by Latina or black bodies and music.

For one, Ella observed that dress codes were different:

> If I had to generalize, I'd say that clubs that don't have women of color going to them tend to have more of a range of dress and a range of masculine/feminine dress. The type of femininity is more varied and reminds me more of how straight women of color will dress in that feminine way, with those type of clothes. Whereas in Meow Mix it's more this grunge thing. And you walk through the East Village [where Meow Mix is located] and a lot of the times you can't even tell who's straight or gay 'cos everyone's dressed in this asexual grunge thing.

Second, Edie and Ella both noticed a freer, more playful expression of sexuality:

> At Meow Mix, it's more of a young feminist crowd and it's very cliquey, 'cos there are so many regulars. So it's like if you're not in their group you can't approach them. Whereas at Crazy Nanny's and Clit Club, it's a free for all. It's dancing and people can do that more. Like Her/she bar, the women are a lot more open sexually. I remember one night and one of them got right off the stage and started making out with a woman in the audience, you wouldn't see that at Meow Mix. At Crazy Nanny's you could see that it was the women of color who would watch [go-go dancers] and the white women would just glance by (Edie).

> At Her/she bar, everyone was really into the go-go dancers. They weren't scared to be caught looking, like I've seen more middle-class white girls do. And everyone was dancing together, really hot. Someone asked me to dance. That's never happened in a white space (Ella).

Third, according to Lisa, in spaces such as Flava at Club Farenheit and Her/she Bar, DJs played more rap, rhythm and blues, and hip-hop:

> There is a lot of music different from what's played in white lesbian clubs. There is a lot of rap music and it seems like it is what the DJ wants, and not censored because someone might think the lyrics are mysogynistic. There is a different kind of relationship than there might be in a mainstream lesbian club, there would be some sexual lyrics sung by men about fucking women, that would maybe objectify a woman's body.

The implication of this last statement seems to be that in a space less influenced by white lesbian-feminist politics, participants were more willing to playfully appropriate the meanings of lyrics and genres of music. Participants suggested that these differences existed because lesbians of color found little cultural support or solidarity with the white middle-class lesbians who dominated the political ground and representations, as expressed by Dana, an African-American lesbian: "While they were having meetings and reading books, we were dancing." These differences reflected how lesbians of color crucially drew on black and Latina cultural forms and practices perhaps more in these spaces than dominant lesbian forms, which might include, for instance, a rejection of signs of femininity, as well as music and movement associated with a male-centered objectification of women.

In clubs for gay men of color, such as Octagon, Suspect, and Escuelita, dance had a particular value in an economy that Stephen suggested might not even be about gayness:

> I have a lot of currency in a dance space. I'm a good dancer. I like dancing, I'm very comfortable with my body. And I know that I have a great deal of currency and power in those spaces. Sometimes there's too much for folks, and that's where you see the integrity of boundaries, that you know there's the solid boundary, and then there's the blur. Meaning that the black folks understood each other and wanted that. You're looking at black culture, not just black gay culture. Those things shift and change within the blink of an eye but sometimes you are looking at black culture and not just black gay culture, and that's about enjoyment of the body and incredible love of excess in the body and they would go off on itself. The need to have these duels that were playful, that was completely beyond dancing forms for the white folks. They just didn't get it. It was completely beyond them and the currency would change. It would be . . . bafflement. Complete bafflement.

Stephen linked being able to dance with cultural capital:

> The one who knows he can dance. He knows he's fierce, he knows he can work his way, and the white boys just love him, and that's how you know there's something up with this shit. They all want this boy. I've seen that. He loves to show that off, sometimes for the black boys, sometimes for the white boys, and it's a racial thing for him, even though his primary desire might be for black or Latino boys.

Stuart Hall writes that, denied access to other forms of cultural capital or the means to produce it, black people have used their bodies as the only asset they have had (in Wallace 1992, 29). Colin articulated that the expectation for a black body to be able to dance well, also happened at the expense of other possible expectations. "Oh yes, well, in Milwaukee growing up in high school, there was this thing that we black folk knew how to dance. We couldn't be a Rhodes scholar, but we knew how to dance." Stephen knew he traded powerful currency on the dance floor as a good dancer, which had little value in other spaces where dance was not so compelling a source of power, for instance, in a more talk-oriented bar, in the workplace, or in the street. He saw the dance floor as one of the few spaces in which a black participant could be read as powerful.

Colin noted that in some clubs for gay men of color like Suspect or upstairs in the hip-hop room at Octagon, dance style reflected values of an imperative black masculinity:

> In certain spaces there is a double marking of the black body, which is always already in motion. It's interesting—those folks who won't move too much. 'Cos in certain black clubs you don't move to excess. You move in moderation and those who are excessive are just feminine, bottom. Like upstairs at Octogon or Suspect . . . Do you know that song "They Won't Dance No More" by Goodie Mob. It goes "They don't dance no more/ they don't dance no more/all they do is this/all they do is this." Which is about how folks aren't dancing anymore. The types of dances popular in black culture are very contained. They're not expansive.

In "Black Macho Revisited: Reflections of a SNAP! Queen," Marlon Riggs (1991, 254) laid the blame for black America's pervasive cultural homophobia on a desperate need for a convenient Other "*within* the community, yet not truly *of* the community":

> An Other to which blame for the chronic identity crises affecting the black psyche can be readily displaced, an indispensable Other which functions as the lowest common denominator of the abject, the base line of transgression beyond which a Black Man is no longer a man, no longer black, an essential Other against which black men and boys maturing, struggling with self-doubt, anxiety, feelings of political, economic, social, and sexual inadequacy—even impotence—can always measure themselves and by comparison seem strong, adept, empowered, superior.

The anxieties Riggs named may be even more urgent among black gay men. Riggs' description of black macho is extraordinary adept at describing the attitudes of the weight and shape of dancers I observed in the spaces mentioned as he uses physical and spatial movement metaphors:

> By the tenets of black macho, true masculinity admits *little or no space* for self-interrogation or multiple subjectivities around race. Black macho prescribes an *inflexible* ideal: Strong black men—"Afrocentric" black men— *don't flinch,* don't weaken, don't take blame or shit, take charge, *step-to* when challenged, and defend themselves without pause for self-doubt. Black macho *counterpoises* this warrior model of masculinity with the emasculated Other: the Other as punk, sissy, Negro faggot, a status with which

any man, not just those who are in fact gay, can be, and are, branded should one deviate from rigidly prescribed codes of hypermasculine conduct [my italics] (Riggs 1991, 257).

This type of movement in spaces for black gay men spoke, "We may be gay, but at least we're not queer": embodying the emasculated Other of black macho. The term "gay" was often stigmatized in the argot of clubs such as Suspect. Men spoke of their "SSL" or "Same Sex Lover," but were less easy using the term "gay."

Clubs ethnically mixed between black and white remained elusive. Even in spaces such as Clit Club and Her/she Bar, participants tended to keep to their own spaces within the club. They tended to respond differently to different cues. At Clit Club, the floor filled up with black women when a hip-hop track was played and the racial mix changed yet again with another music style. Many of the participants with whom I spoke desired greater racial mixing in gay and queer clubs, and expressed pleasure in seeing different bodies and attitudes to dancing and in hearing different music. Beyond this, there was also a desire for alliance building, as Lisa said:

> I would like there to be more women of color in clubs, not just one racially specific. That would be interesting because I think a lot of times people get so racially segregated. There is this fiction that people of color have no possible ways of working together or have no history together except being black together through colonization in imperialist countries and being thrown together. So I think that could be really transformative.

Sharing a history together in gay or queer dance spaces, sharing practices of opposition and pleasure, could transform the segregated, institutionalized packets of gay culture into a powerful alliance, Lisa continued:

> For me part of being in a utopic space is about being in a space in which racial inflected culture can be expressed. Rather than bourgeois culture. Whether it's queer or not. Actually the term queer is very much contradictory to bourgeois culture. That's nice to see, it's important to see a variety. It's nice because you see hip-hop hour on television, and this is supposed to be African-American culture. It's nice to see other forms of African-American culture or Asian American culture, and that there's some variety. That it's not all institutions, which a lot of hip hop culture is. It's totally canned, false, like "alternative," or "punk."

Bourgeois culture, by this reasoning, appropriates, sanitizes, and homogenizes the signs of marginality, making them institutions of consumerism, and thus politically nonthreatening. Part of the energy of queer, black, and Latino culture derives from maintaining difference from dominant culture, and maybe, utopically, rather than realistically, from maintaining difference within gay culture. In New York City, as in any location, class and sometimes ethnicity was often related to the neighborhood in which you lived. Stephen used his connection to the locations he lived and played in to make connections to class and to queerness:

> STEPHEN: I've always liked the East Village. I've always found sublets or something here, so that made my connection to queerness, not just gay, but queerness in New York City to the East Village.
> FB: What is it about the East Village that made it particularly queer in contrast to other spaces?
> S: Well, the class thing, people . . . a mix of races, a mix of class and race. A mix of different colors, being African-American, being black. I was comfortable. There were mixing African-American and Latino communities relating together and that was an experience that didn't exist in the Midwest or the West Coast, where I was as much. In bars in New York—that's where I really realized the connections between African-Americans and Latinos. At college, there was a strong connection, a very needed connection for survival against white folks. So that was a connection for me. That was at the racial level. At the sexual level, queer Latinos and African-Americans were overlapping just as strongly . . . but I found there was a connection there historically in New York and that allowed a lot of folks to come here and gather together.

Stephen's model of queerness was based on the space of the East Village, most particularly in his favorite club, Crowbar, in which a mix of sexual subjectivities, genders, colors, and class, and the bodies bearing and resisting these inscriptions would gather to dance. He recognized queerness as predicated on difference and accommodation rather than homogeneity and assimilation. For him, the East Village historically offered such a space.

The utopian mix of queer clubs included heterosexuals as well as gays. According to Lisa, "Walking around the East Village, you can't even tell who's straight and who's gay." The inscriptions on the bodies occupying these spaces were blurred, often deliberately in acts of play in both dress and behavior. These cognitive maps represented difference and blurring. Mark noted that the unconformity of queer spaces attracted many heterosexuals:

> The Pyramid was about being there and creating a scene and being a freak. It was also a haven for straight people who knew they wanted something else and could handle it. Some can't: "We can't come in here because there are gay people in this space." And some straight people are drawn to it because it's a free space and they can do whatever they want without being questioned. I just hope gay space continues to be like that, that they become queer spaces where all freaks find a home.

In these spaces, "straight" was not used only to refer to heterosexuals. Therefore, a "freak" could be heterosexual, but welcome. In *Disidentifications: Queers of Color and the Performance of Politics,* José Esteban Muñoz reads "pasty normals" (after performance artist Jack Smith's memorable identification) as not just straights, but "the dark side of homosexuality": that "normalcy is not strictly endemic to heterosexuality" (1999, xii). To extend this reading, I would add that just as not all homosexuals are exotic or freaky, not all self-identified heterosexuals are "normal." Queer spaces such as Squeezebox were genuinely queer in that the space was a critical crossing for straights and gays who did not subscribe to "normalcy." Heterosexuals also felt the pressure to conform to notions of appropriate sexual behavior and also rebelled against it. However, queer sexualities also entered into a consumerist economy—they could not exist outside of these fields of power, and queerness and the bodies of queers could become a commodity that could be bought. For instance, when lesbian sexuality has been imagined and appropriated by straight male fantasy, a lesbian club as a safe space is threatened, as Edie, a door person, ruefully acknowledged:

> We can't tell men they can't come in, or else we get sued, which means as soon as you get five or six men in there, women stop touching each other because they don't feel safe. I've seen men walk up and stare at women making out. One man literally went up and kissed a woman and said, "Come home with me and my wife." And I had to throw him out. *Chasing Amy* [an independent film in which a man falls in love with and gets a lesbian] is a major thorn in our side. We'll have twenty-three year old guys who'll come and say, "Hey, I drove all the way from Ohio to go to this bar." And you know they're serious. They're so excited and you say, "I'm sorry you wasted a trip, 'cos I'm not letting you in." They saw the movie where an

average guy managed to seduce some really hot lesbian, and that was the bar they did it in.

The representations of lesbians in popular culture, whether in straight male porn or in fashion spreads or music, were exchanged for the real bodies of women. Edie continued:

> Not just men, but straight women tend to see a lesbian community as something they can commodify. They claim ownership over lesbians. They come in and say, "I don't mind lesbians, I think they're really hot actually." I'm going to say, "You know what, that's not your decision to make." My favorite is when a group of guys try to get in to meet lesbian prostitutes, 'cos they think they can buy them. And if we're having a slow night and a straight couple comes in and it's obvious they're coming in looking for a threesome, I'll charge them twenty bucks each to come in. And then tell them if I catch them looking at anyone, I'll throw them out. And then I'll make them tip extra, the bartenders will charge more. And I'll do that because they're willing to spend the money to "buy" the lesbian experience.

Straight-gay mixing in queer spaces was predicated on queer rules, in contrast to the reversal of this power dynamic outside of the club.

Informants used memories, experiences, and utopic imaginations to offer resistance to current "quality of life" and homonormative agendas, and to rediscover and reinvent pleasures that heteronormativity and homonormativity attempted to disrupt and erase. This knowledge of crisis and of resistance to it was often expressed through nostalgia and in self-proclaimed queer spaces. The strategies of resistance didn't just include reeroticization, but forms already in use in clubs, such as style, mixing, and proximity. However, informants recognized all of these as conscious strategies, and all had a sense of the politics of memory, style, and space. Sex and pleasure became markers of identity and community. This had two implications. First, some informants knew how crucial gender, race, ethnicity, and class were to the formation of queer identity. Second, bearing this in mind, as hegemonic forces sought to curtail sex and pleasure, the moves to close down clubs where these markers of identity and community were valued and permitted were felt most acutely by those most vulnerable and most sensitive to closures: those with fewer collective capital resources. Identity and community thus were expressed in terms of citizenship-rights and in terms of the integrity and necessity of New York's nightlife, rather than narrowly confined to already unsatisfactory lesbian and gay identity politics. The concept of lifeworld was apt to understand these queer dance clubs and how vital embodiment was to queerness. These spaces were sites for the production and circulation of discursive and embodied discourses that were critical of and yet that reinforced normative distinctions between blackness and whiteness, and among gayness, "normalcy," and queerness, for instance. Informants expressed the notion of a plurality of lifeworlds, which in practice opened the possibility, but not always the realization, of individuals and groups producing sites of interaction and intersection among race, ethnicity, class, and gender.

These queer spaces also reflected the model of lifeworld suggested by queer theorists Lauren Berlant and Michael Warner (1998, 558) who assert that a lifeworld differs from community and group because it "necessarily includes more people than can be identified, more spaces than can be mapped beyond a few reference points, modes of feeling that can be learned rather than experienced as a birthright." As Bruce Robbins (1993, xvii) contends, this notion of lifeworld invokes "identity," but does so with "more emphasis on actions and their consequences than on the nature or characteristics of the actors." Therefore, identity was not fixed, but tied to movement and its contexts. Dancers made interventions in their self-fashioning through movement, sometimes kicking against normativity, sometimes not, and sometimes writing new rules.

⫷ 7

MR. MESA'S TICKET
Memory and Dance at the Body Positive T-Dance

My mother—who has a son who will die before her—will say, "Well, son, you could go across the street and a bus will hit you, or a brick will come down from the roof and will kill you." And I say, "Mother, I wish that happened to me. They sell us a ticket and I have the ticket, you don't have it." To me, I see AIDS as a jail and as a death row. Everyday, when I have a cough or a fever, they call and say, "Mr. Mesa, we will execute you tonight." And when I have a fever, they sit me in the chair with all the cables. Then the executioner says, "Sorry Mr. Mesa, it's not working today. You have to go back to your room." That's the difference. It's like, you know . . . I wish it was tonight, but then tonight doesn't happen. It's a ticket, and that ticket is not returnable. I cannot say to you, [gestures with outstretched hand], "Can you have this ticket back please and give me my money?" That's what I try to make my mother understand.   (Tito)

It's funny; this story comes to my mind. It's about three years ago—the T-Dance was at Sound Factory Bar. This man who was watching me from the times of the Saint—probably my age—I don't remember his name, but I'll never forget his face. I was on the stage dancing, and finally he approached me, and said, "Do you know I've been watching you for years, and every time I come here—I come just to watch you dance—and I go home so happy that one of us is still here." And I thought, "Thank you." I never realized . . . I dance for myself, I dance for the universe, for all of us in the world with AIDS. But he was so . . . he looked so sick, like he was having chemotherapy or something, and I said, "Wait a minute,"—I was exhausted, "If you wait one minute while I pick up the next . . . you know, with the music . . . the next dance will be just for you." I danced. I think I was floating on air. And then I came back. We gave this hug to each other. It was so amazing . . . And I was realizing then the effect on the people of

the dancing and the presence of a dancer. It's funny because when Body
Positive moved to Webster Hall, this beautiful man came to me with a
young man. And he said "Hi Tito," and I said, "My God! I can't believe it's
you!" He said, "I'm taking the new medicine and it's working for me." I
mean, this is a new human being, and "Tito, I have a boyfriend now." We
get so wrapped up in the dance that we forget that people are watching,
and they're really watching. To me, I don't know why, but I have that story
in my brains for the longest time. I don't remember his name—with all
these pills, my brain is like Swiss cheese.

TITO MESA HAS been living with HIV and AIDS since 1985. On one
of the last warm October evenings of 1997, we sat together in his East
Village studio apartment, and drank tea surrounded by the accumulated
artifacts of his fifty years. They included a photograph of his drag alter-
ego, Monique; his collection of home-made fans for dancing; and a
Tibetan monk's skull, inlaid with silver eyes, ears, and nose. When he
gently prized open the flip-top skull, small bits of colored paper spilt
onto the floor. Each one had a name inscribed upon it. "Ahh," he said,
picking one up, "Harry! How wonderful for you to pop out today." He
kept the names of all his friends who had passed away in this skull. "That
way," he explained with a chuckle, "they're always in my head." I first saw
Tito on the dance floor of Roxy at the Body Positive T-Dance, a once-
monthly event for HIV-positive gay men and their friends, and, like the
man in the story, was shy of approaching him: he seemed so glorious and
so involved in his movement as he danced with his golden winglike fans.

This space and the practices within that served to create it celebrated
survival, and memorialized those who had passed on. I have come to
read *memorial* as a complicated term, in which not only the past, but also
the present moment, and the future possibilities of a life with HIV and
AIDS were articulated through the performance of the dancer. In the
theater of memory performed through improvised social dance, people
like Tito recalled memories of times past and people passed on. How
might the past be kept and performed in the body and how did these
theaters of memory envision the future? The term *memorial* also has powerful implications for the practice of ethnography itself. As the Body Positive T-Dance no longer existed at the time of writing, to what extent is
this chapter a memorial to it? To what extent is this work a "salvage ethnography" with a disappearing object (the T-dance and its patrons) saved
in the text? (Clifford and Marcus 1986, 112). What is the relationship

between salvage ethnography and the eagerness of participants to have these stories and experiences recorded for the future, with the resonance that certain relationships to death imply?

Body Positive was a New York City-based nonprofit organization with offices in most major cities in the United States. The organization offered a number of services to HIV-infected and HIV-affected people. It published a monthly free paper, the *Body Positive,* in which articles covered new medical developments, government and private funding issues, book and film reviews, poetry, letters, editorials, "kvetches," classifieds, advertisements for drugs and services, and information about events of interest to people with HIV. These events included peer workshops and the Body Positive T-Dance for HIV-positive gay men and their friends, which the organization ran with the help of volunteers. Body Positive's mission was to offer support to people who had a positive serostatus in common, including their HIV negative partners, families, and friends. AIDS resources could not only be counted in the money that went toward research, or Medicaid provisions, or legal assistance. Some people infected and affected by HIV/AIDS expressed a need to form communities to help and support each other.

In 1993, a couple of young HIV-positive gay men decided to set up a tea-dance (called in this instance a "T-Dance") for themselves and for their peers. A tea-dance is an early Sunday evening dance party form established within the gay male community in New York City. The abbreviation of "tea" to "T" recalled those precious infection-fighting T-cells the retrovirus destroys. To the extent that the template for this event was taken from an entertainment form already established and recognized among some but not all groups of urban gay men, compounded by the dance's location in three downtown venues over time, any claims that the participants of this event were representative of a wider "HIV community" are problematic. How can there be any claim for the existence of such a citywide community, when the needs of those sexual, gendered, age, racial, and ethnic populations living with HIV could be so distinct from each other?

Occasionally as he danced Tito looked at me and smiled. Maybe he wondered what I was doing here, on this dance floor full of men, mostly older than I was, almost all HIV-positive. I first went to the Body Positive T-Dance in 1995 with a couple of friends who were regulars. I was an observer as well as partygoer and friend to some of the participants. Female and HIV-negative. Insider and outsider. My presence in this space already problematized the notion of an HIV community. So my use of the term "HIV community" is somewhat complicated and needs to be explained. Although this research was based in downtown Manhattan, many of the participants came to the event from other areas within New York City and from outside it. There was an *awareness* of sharing a way of life among the participants in that community and a desire to identify oneself with other people with HIV. Having HIV did not mean an individual automatically chose to identify themselves with other people with HIV, or even that he or she regarded serostatus as a mark of identity.

Thomas Weise, one of the organizers of the event, was concerned with getting more women and people of color to attend the T-Dance (he estimated about twenty African-American men were in a group of one thousand he claimed were on the mailing list). Within the gay activist movement, white men have historically foregrounded their concerns and enacted a color-blindness that makes many gay men of color feel that differences in experience affected by their ethnicity and race have not been addressed. This led to the creation of spaces by gay men of color in which these specific concerns were foregrounded.[1] The practice of going to a club and a T-Dance event itself might not be an inviting or familiar practice for many of those Thomas wished to reach. Downtown Manhattan, with its cultural heritage and image as a center for the arts (specifically the avant-garde) and entertainment (of a trendy, young nature), was neither a familiar nor a comfortable location for many who lived elsewhere. Accessibility to such events and services was dictated not only by location, but also by class, race, sexuality, and gender issues, as well as the habits of everyday life. For instance, going to a dance club of a Sunday evening was not feasible or attractive for many. Living with HIV/AIDS, individuals felt economic, cultural, and personal pressures preventing them from attending or desiring to attend this event. The conditions and experiences of a life for gay men with HIV do share several commonalities: discrimination and fear from both straight and sometimes gay society; the common assault of opportunistic infections such as Karposi's Sarcoma, cryptosporidium, and pneumonia, and the medication required to control and treat them, and its side effects; and the difficulties of negotiating an active sex life. An emphasis on the commonalities of experience of life with HIV/AIDS should not erase the very real differences of those experiences of women, African-Americans, Hispanics, and/or children from the predominantly white gay and bisexual men who attend the dance. The awareness of commonalities relied upon systems of communication between individuals, as well as accessibility to wider media. The desire to identify with a peer community was not universal. To add nuance to this, the forms of community-building the dance enacted built upon gay activism since the late 1960s with practice of coming out to one's peers. The value participants placed on egalitarian interaction informs my use of the term "community," more than the commonalities of location, time, and serostatus.

As historians such as George Chauncey and John D'Emilio have plotted, New York has a long and diverse gay history (Chauncey 1994; John D'Emilio 1983). Gay men from all over the United States and the world came to the city to share in that legacy and to establish connections with other gays. All of the informants for this chapter came to New York from elsewhere. One informant, Will Wright, came to New York from Wisconsin in 1979. His description of the gay party scene at that time suggested a pre-AIDS innocence that found expression in the club scene:

> Real high energy parties, lots of drugs, sex [. . .] We knew there was something, but we didn't know what it was. It was an article in *The New York Times* in 1979 about Karposi's Sarcoma, and it said about this rare sort of skin disease that young gay men were getting. I tried to find out about it and my friend said it's rare and not to worry about it now. "If it's anything we'll find out later." And we certainly did.

The gay club scene changed in response to HIV/AIDS. Will suggested that in the 1970s, gay clubs and parties were a form of initiation into a gay life and that older gay mentors showed younger gay men not only how to own their sexualities, but also how to party: to be "glamorous" and "expressive." There were now fewer gay mentors, and he regretted the passing of that time of mentorship to one of what he saw as peer conformity. He concluded that this passing has resulted in "gym-bunny cloning": the uniformity of pumped body-types, clothing, and restricted, unexpressive, and "unimaginative" dance styles in evidence at many gay clubs in New York City. AIDS removed almost an entire generation of gay men from a gay social lifeworld. To Tito, the effect of meeting an old face in a place like the Body Positive T-Dance was moving and meaningful: "Incredible . . . someone from my age saying, 'You are one of the only witnesses from my time.'" The men who attended the Body Positive parties I went to tended to be an older set than those who packed out gay clubs such as Roxy, Arena, or Twilo on a Saturday night. Informants identified themselves as the survivors of a ravaged population.

Since the beginning of the crisis, gay men with HIV or AIDS came to New York City to benefit from the medical, legal, and social support offered by organizations such as Gay Men's Health Crisis, the medical expertise in hospitals such as St. Vincent's, and the support of other people with HIV/ AIDS. Organizations such as Stand Up and Body Positive held numerous workshops where people with HIV could meet. Although many of those with whom I spoke testified to the importance of these events for support, information, and counseling, Tito remarked that sometimes he needed to take a vacation from these aspects of a life with AIDS:

> In the beginning, when I got this disease, I used to attend every single meeting, and I'm not saying it's wrong or it's right, but AIDS becomes such an issue. Today I'm bitching about my liver, and tomorrow someone is bitching about something else. I said, "No way!" I love this virus. I made a deal with the virus and I said, "You're going to live with me. There's room for the two of us in here. I'm going to take a vacation and I'm not going to go to meetings anymore. I'm not going to go to talks anymore, and I'm not going to go to research anymore, talking about what are these pills and what are these effects. I'm going to take a vacation. I want to keep living a full life. And that's what I do. I keep dancing.

But where to dance? In many gay bars and clubs in New York City, a body marked with AIDS or the visible effects of its medication was sometimes shunned due to certain ideals of beauty, and out of fear and denial: "They don't want us to spoil their good time by reminding them [that] there are real problems here [. . .] That [AIDS] could be a result of their party" (Thomas). In a 1991 article in the now defunct local gay magazine *NYQ*, Charles Barber asked readers to consider that those people with HIV and PWAs (People with AIDS) who once thrived in the bar and the club now socialized in churches, hospitals, and conference rooms. He traced what he termed "AIDS Apartheid": that the circulations of resistance and pleasure in gay clubs, always operating as elitist, exclusionary, and savagely hierarchized economies, had changed again in response to AIDS: "Walls have gone up, and lines have been drawn: some of us are in, and some of us are out."

At most gay dance clubs, you knew whether you were "in" or "out" when you arrived at the velvet rope, but the economy of desirability also circulated through the exchange of other capital. Many of the larger gay dance clubs charged entrance fees of twenty dollars and upward, a prohibitively expensive amount, particularly to those surviving on government disability allowances granted to PWAs. At the Body Positive T-Dance, there was no body-beautiful door policy and entrance was based on a five-dollar suggested donation per person, with the money raised going toward the organization. This donation system assured participants who already felt exploited by pharmaceutical companies, insurance firms, and many other sectors of the so-called AIDS industry that any profit was used for people with HIV and AIDS. Mark Cicero, the DJ at this party, worked for the cost of expenses. His usual fee was over one hundred dollars an hour. All the hosts were volunteers, giving of their own time to make this event special. They expressed the sense that they were giving something back to an HIV community through their participation and receiving something in return. As Thomas said, "Helping others . . . gives me a reason to live."

How was going to the Body Positive T-Dance different than going to other gay clubs in the city? Both spaces and activities could be described as alternatives to a dominant culture. In both spaces, dance was a fabulous and fun method to explode out of the normative disciplining of compulsory heterosexuality. Both could be said to build and articulate community, but, as Will explained, going to the T-Dance performed repetitions with critical differences:

> It kind of raises your consciousness to a common level. And that's immediately, before you walk through the door. Comparison: when you walk into Twilo, you're trying to fit in. You're looking for that common ground, you're looking for your friends, or the people who are doing the same drugs as you, or whatever. You're looking for that common consciousness. So you start there with the Body Positive dance, with this general pervasive consciousness, and you go to another level with it. [. . .] You slip through all the mundane that you would go through if you were going to a regular club [. . .] Like when I was clubbing, before I went out, I would usually gather at somebody's house [. . .] we'd put our make-up on [chuckles and gestures sniffing drugs], and dress ourselves, and shoot the shit, and call whoever else, and sort of got that going before we went to the club. And then when we got to the club, we'd try to get that together again. But with the Body Positive dance it's, "Oh, I'll meet you at the dance."

Tito suggested that the main differences between going to a club for HIV-positive gay men, and going to others, reflected his changes of attitude about himself after his diagnosis: "I don't have to pretend anymore.

I don't have to wear the right clothes. I don't have to impress you any-more. I have to be me and take care of myself."

Care of the self also required care of the body and, for some of those with whom I spoke, like Will, it also required cessation of drug use:

> We with HIV can't really do drugs. Well, we do drugs. We do lots and lots of drugs! [He laughs] But not the same kind of drugs we did when we were going to clubs. It's a whole other social perspective. The social thing is not to get messed up and this is all where we've been before, you know, which, for some of us, is why we got to where we are today.

Will said he stopped going to clubs when he developed full-blown AIDS, partly because he blamed his clubbing lifestyle for his infection with HIV, if only indirectly. He blamed his gay club lifestyle for distracting him from taking care of himself physically and spiritually, as he attempted to lose himself in heights of social euphoria available in clubs through dancing with a mass of people to trancelike rhythms, taking drugs, and having numerous anonymous sexual encounters. He felt that at the Body Positive T-Dance, his interactions with other individuals were more "heart-to-heart" than anonymously euphoric. Once again, Will ex-plained this through his activities on the dance floor:

> The interaction of other people on the dance floor is very important to me. And how they're dancing. A lot of times, I'll go to the Body Positive T-Dance, and I'll watch people dancing first, 'cos I have to get inspired. And I'll find somebody there where I'll find an appealing motion, and I watch them, and sort of get into a mode or a rhythm, and then try to connect that also to the DJ. More than I would at Twilo. At Twilo, I get into what-ever the head of the DJ is, or try to. Sometimes you just can't. But more at Twilo you're dancing your own thing, not so much with other people around you. At Body Positive T-Dance, I feel more of a connection with the people around me and with their dancing. There's more space, so I guess there's a lot more room for expression.

Freedom to move was enabled by more than a spatial reality. Informants such as Will suggested that support from peers, rather than from the ef-fects of drugs, freed a pathway for personal expression.

The spatial metaphor of "coming out" was initially a debutante ball term. The debutante taking her first steps onto the dance floor was not coming out *of* something (a closet perhaps), but coming out *into* society.

Someone's first steps into a gay club performed a coming out into gay society. Some informants expressed the belief that walking into the Body Positive T-Dance enacted a coming out as HIV-positive to a peer group. Will admitted that at first he didn't want to go because he was in denial of his serostatus and of the ways he had to change his life if he was going to survive. He did not want to self-identify as HIV-positive and foster community with other gay men with HIV: "I thought guys with AIDS were sick and gaunt and didn't want to see them, because I'd be like them one day." For Will, deciding to attend the Body Positive T-Dance was one of the ways he claimed this identification.

Until 1997, when the T-Dance was held at the Sound Factory Bar, patrons made their entrance to the bar/dance floor area through a heavy, lush red velvet curtain that had to be pulled aside with some force, making entrances dynamic and eye-catching. More recently, with the move of the T-Dance to Webster Hall (due to the Sound Factory Bar's refurbishment as a trendy bar), patrons walked into an open hallway where they were greeted by at least one of the hosts. At some point in the evening, most of the patrons I observed stopped at the table in the hall to sign onto a mailing list, pick up information on Body Positive, and/or to pick up safer sex materials such as leaflets and condoms before going into the dance floor area. These activities indexed the functions of the event for information gathering, communicating with peers, and socializing, with the possibility of finding a sexual partner. The dance was a special event, occurring once a month. For some of the men with whom I spoke, it was the only dance or HIV-focused event to which they came, at which they received information about services available, and knowingly interacted with other gay men with HIV or AIDS. This was the only event of its kind in the area and, in keeping with New York's history, brought gay men into the city even for a few hours, seeking what they could not find elsewhere. The mailing list served an important function and included locations as far away as upstate New York, New Jersey, and Pennsylvania. Although the Body Positive T-Dance was advertised in local papers such as the *Village Voice,* and in gay entertainment magazines like *Homo Xtra* and *Next,* it was a special event, and therefore easy to miss as it was not held every night or on the same night every week. From 1994–96, the T-Dance was held weekly, but organizers felt it was too difficult to make special. They felt patrons were bored and were not bothering to come, as they knew it would be on again the following week. However, one of the reasons people were falling away from the party may have been the effects of the new treatment regimes based on protease inhibitors. HIV was starting to be looked upon more as a manageable disease. Furthermore, the ravaged AIDS body, so visible in New York City through the 1980s, became less so. Less visibly marked by AIDS, people might have wanted to loosen their identification as HIV-positive to themselves and to others.

After the Sound Factory Bar closed in January 1997, the event moved to Webster Hall, not a landmark on the gay club map. There were soon problems. Patrons felt exploited by the high drink prices and the initial lack of bottled water, essential for anyone with a compromised immune system as tap water in New York City carries potentially dangerous parasites and bacteria. Some informants even avoided ice cubes for this reason. From September 1997 to January 1998, the T-Dance was held in the Roxy, the venue of large scale gay dance parties. The club was located on the west side of Chelsea, in a strip of blocks hugging the Hudson River, full of industrial units, garages, and car shops. But within this area's dark folds nestled several gay bars such as the Spike, the Eagle, and the Lure, patronized by leathermen and their admirers, a not-exclusively older set than those patrons of the bars in the more central area of Chelsea between Fifth and Eighth Avenues. The piers—an active cruising area for decades—were close by. It was a particularly marked location on the gay male map of New York City, which, although marginal on the cognitive map of many New Yorkers, occupied a central position for and exercised a strong pull on some sections of the gay male population, locally, regionally, and nationally.

The cab turfed me out at an ominously empty doorway. The neighborhood seemed deserted. Did I have the right address and what was I supposed to do if I didn't, I wondered as the cab turned a corner and disappeared from sight. In the stillness of Sunday evening I strained to hear the telltale thump-thump-thump of the bass that might offer at least some sense of security that somewhere behind these infuriatingly nondescript industrial walls a party was in full swing. I chose the only open doorway and found myself on in a long, wide passageway, which gently sloped upward. I could tell it was the right place as I walked past the discarded carcasses of metal detectors and redundant velvet ropes. Yet they remained unactivated and curiously abstract without the human crush that gave them their function, like artifacts on those television shows in which panelists try to guess the long-forgotten function of an object. I felt no small relief when Thomas Weise, one of the organizers of the party, greeted me at the top of the passage. Finally I began to detect music and the old anxieties of seeking and belonging began to fade. The set-up was similar to other Body Positive T-Dances held previously at Sound Factory Bar and Webster Hall. The area before reaching the bar and the dance floor was set up as a meeting place with sofas around tables carrying HIV and AIDS information, the *Body Positive* newspaper, condoms, and the mailing list. But inside the club was a different matter. Whereas in Sound Factory Bar and Webster Hall the organizers had been able to use a smaller, more intimate space, it was a bad night at the Roxy if less than a few thousand found their way through the entrance. The dance floor was of a size that could make a 767 look lonely. The T-Dance regularly brought in about two to three hundred participants. The organizers solved this by pulling some heavy drapes around the portion of the dance floor nearest the bar, partitioning a more intimate space.

Pulling people into a tighter space can be essential to the success of a party. After all, partying is about mixing and mingling. Its initial nervous energy is partly a symptom of the anxieties this produces: Do I look OK? Who's that? Is he "with" that guy, or just with him? When do I tell him I'm HIV positive? At the T-Dance at least, this latter anxiety was alleviated as well as the effects of rejection based on serostatus, as Will observed:

> Since I was feeling a little better, I wanted to engage in the possibility of having sexual activity and I didn't want to deal with the positive issue. I had lesions on my body, and if someone got naked with me, baby, they knew. "Oh, what's that?" "Oh, well . . . I'm positive, I have lesions," and in the negative society, the reaction is usually, umm . . . swift. You see the look on the face of the person go blank [mimes] and it's coming face-to-face with your own denial that you experience, and all the horrors of that denial come back to you. You feel like a turtle that's been shocked and you go into your shell.

The HIV-positive man, vilified in the media as victim of his own pleasure, either is a threat to the dominant negative society if he does have sex, or he is deposited somewhere outside of the possibility of sex. But the atmosphere of the Body Positive party was sex positive. The go-go boys shook up a storm on their podiums, and the sensual dancing of the crowd and the cruising that I saw suggested this. Even the music, sweeter and less full-force hard-house than at other gay clubs, constructed an environment that invited interaction. Not everyone only came to dance.

Tito Mesa arrived at six o'clock sharp with his collection of fans. He was joined by his fellow fan dancers throughout the early part of the evening. Some stayed for the full event and others only for an hour. They claimed the space as they warmed up, smudging the air with soft whirling fans, as if cleansing it of traces of previous events. Through their movement, they performed the shifting of a space of a dominant gay culture to an alternative space focused around a seropositive status. Within dominant gay culture parties, Mark says, "AIDS is behind an iron curtain, it's there somewhere about the dance floor, but nobody talks about it, and nobody would dare to mention it." In front of the velvet curtain at Roxy, the fan dancers prepared the space for themselves and their fellow dancers. They swept into the space with their fluid energy, throwing it before them, pulling it from behind them. They built up energy between them, twirling and spiraling around each other.

The origins of fan dancing were vague. The stories dancers told about them were personally and spiritually evocative. Tito explained that he saw his first fan dancer in the Trocadero, a gay club in San Francisco: "I was impressed with how you can express the feelings of the body and the music, but extended, expanded like the winds and the soul." Each dancer built his own fans out of sticks and fabric, constructing them to suit his body height, shape, weight, and ability. Many built more than one set of fans and brought several to each event. Tito remembered a time when he and his then-lover tried to figure out how to make them after seeing them in San Francisco in the 1980s. They went into their closets and cut up coat hangers and old worn sheets. Then they laid them on the floor and started to glue. The learning process of fan dancing, Tito said, was the most painful experience he said he had ever been through. For the first year, the pain in his wrists was excruciating. There were other reasons for his agony: he was unable to feel the pain building due to the numbing effects of cocaine: "This was in the early eighties; you dance and people are watching you, and they come with coke, and say 'Have!' And you just sniff, and someone says, 'Lick here!' You lick there."

Lying on the floor, the fans looked like prosaic, homemade contraptions. But in the hands of a dancer, they transformed themselves and the dancer into poetry of energy, light, and motion. There were ways of holding the fans to perform different motions. By holding the fans toward the node where all the spokes met, Tito manipulated them into a dazzling presentational display. When he held the fans by their outer edges, he could roll them over his own body, moving them behind, over and along it with an action like the articulation of wings. He brought his hands together and worked the fans, as if holding some fantastic bird.

Each fan dancer had his own technique. Simon, with his long limbs and ballet training, dropped his head and spine into the diving arcs he carved through his kinesphere with his fans. Tito, small, muscular, and pugnacious, ripped his fans through the space around him. Ivan, with his softer chiffon scarves weighted at one end (known as flags), exploded into breathtaking spins, twirling his flags in beautiful furls at ninety degree angles down the length of his body. In a slow transition between musical tracks, Chris, tall and long-limbed, dropped down to his knees, letting his huge golden fan fall and caress his body.

The first fans I held were constructed with wooden sticks, which were quite rigid and allowed movement in planes over the top of, parallel, and adjacent to my body. The second pair were made of wire coathangers and were less stable, more articulated. They seemed to weigh my arms down at the same time as being more flexible. I gripped the first spoke of the fan. The edge of the flap of fabric between the first and second spoke was reinforced with cord or glue to prevent tearing. The friction between the skin of the fingers and this part of the fan caused the terrible blisters all dancers suffer when they first started working with the fans. (Tito taped his fingers and thumbs, as well as wearing cycling gloves, which, with his cycle shorts and hat, were his sartorial trademark since his days in the Saint in the 1980s.) Tito showed me how to hold the fans with my index finger straight along the spoke at the edge and my other three fingers curled around it. By pushing down and away with my index finger and then pulling back with my other fingers, I began slowly and haltingly to work one fan at a time in a figure eight. If the movement was voice, I would be stuttering. I felt as if the motion was an isolated twisting at the end of my arms, originating in my shoulders and elbows, whereas Tito's motion seemed to be pulled up from the ground and propelled through his whole body, erupting through his muscular back and shoulders, and into the fans. But then he joined me, and with his presence, gathering and scattering his energy through his fan, I could see and feel the energy build up between us. With him as my partner, my movement with the fan felt less like flapping, and more like swirling. Together to the sound of our breath we negotiated space and transferred strength between us. Tito threw his energy out to the end of his arm and into his fan, sending it quivering and arcing over mine. I picked up on his motion and received it into my fan, before spiraling it away to adapt into my own experiments with movement.

On the dance floor, I saw Tito teaching others how to use the fans. People watched him and other fan dancers (there were a hard-core group of about six), and sometimes came up and asked about them. Tito loved to show people how to use the fans, always emphasizing that each person had a unique way of fan dancing just as he or she had of walking. "Look over there," he cried, indicating Chris, "look at the way he stands and spirals as if one line ran from his head into his arms to his feet. He is the only one who can do that." Pride and respect swelled his voice. I watched the novices as they experimented; slowly growing in confidence as they gently stamped out the pulse beat with their feet, finding a rhythm to ride, and on which to soar like a thermal current. Tito described his experience of the community the dancers built among each other through movement:

> At one point, a dancer sees another dancer doing some number [. . .] I was dancing in this position [he demonstrates with an invisible fan, kneeling on the floor and leaning back, spiraling his arms around him all the time]. I let myself go and I realized I had two people in front and two people in the back following each other. The whole body—the four, the five dancers—when they're spread, they come together and pick up the same energy. All the energy in the air and everybody doing the same thing, and coordinating without practicing before [. . .] We see the magic in our hands and it's just—wow! We salute each other, "Thank you."

His description and my experience evoked the power of this dance form to negotiate connections between people on a dance floor. This experience of working together in movement, not upstaging each other, evolved a storehouse of knowledge in which egalitarian and creative interaction between people was acknowledged and valued. Any group of fan dancers was open to those dancing with or without fans, common experiences of movement were shared physically, and dancers were aware of their commonality with each other: their desire to join the movement. It was as if these interactions rehearsed other possible interactions between the individual with HIV and others around him, based on sharing, supporting, and friendship. They also performed a utopian vision in which these types of relationships were the norm, and an alternative to the hoarding of resources and raising of prophylactic barricades against people with HIV and AIDS.

Fan dancing is simply an activity, but the meaning people attach to it at an event such as the Body Positive T-Dance gives it purpose. Being able to identify these meanings deepens an understanding of the ability of the practices at the T-Dance to resonate with the real experience of a gay life with HIV, as well as to rehearse utopic possibilities, which can be practiced outside of the club. However, this must, in turn, be complicated as, in any practice of appropriation, what may be at stake is not freedom, but power.

People revalued the original meaning of lyrics with significance for themselves. Tracks like "You're Free (to Do What You Want to Do)," "Ain't No Mountain High Enough," "Say a Little Prayer," and "Love Hangover" would come up at successive parties and as dancers whooped with pleasure and pushed more energy through their movement, I could sense cultural resonances flowing from their memories and imaginations into the music and back into their bodies. Several dancers said that part of their pleasure on hearing certain classic tracks was their connection with pre-AIDS parties. These tracks became the vehicles for a vast range of private and group associations. The same could be said of any club, and certainly any gay club. But there were important differences in the use-value of the music by the patrons of the Body Positive T-Dance: "I like a theme in the music and DJs do that anyway, but the theme is different. It might be a little more inspirational or uplifting at the Body Positive T-Dance" (Will). In other clubs, the voices of black female singers were cut and sampled in shorter bursts and repeated to such an excess that the meaning became abstract, and the sound became another element of rhythm rather than the discursive or narrative performance of a subject with whom dancers forged an identification. At the Body Positive T-Dance, the girl got to sing her song.

Four types of associations between music and experience in the context of the Body Positive party demonstrated not only acts of appropriation, but also revealed the values used and created around them. First, disco, garage, house, and Hi-NRG music united the dancing of gay men with HIV and AIDS and the voices of black women, both of which groups have consistently been portrayed as weak and culpable victims of their own "hypersexualities." Walter Hughes (1994, 151) recognized that they were also united outside of the discourse of disco by the "epidemiological rhetoric of 'risk groups.'" However, within the Body Positive T-Dance, they were also epistemologically separated because this was a party targeted for men, although several women of color participated regularly, accompanied by men. Outside of the epidemiological rhetoric of risk groups there was little uniting of gay men and women of color with HIV/AIDS. Inside the Body Positive T-Dance a form of drag occurred when dancers lip-synched to the voices of African-American women. But this did not necessarily mean that this practice subverted a perceived construction of gender and race. The power of whiteness to appropriate black voices carried with it the resonances of oppression. The power of men to occupy and appropriate the voices of black women, especially in the cases of gay men lip-synching to women singing about their relationships with other men, enacted identifications of empathy and sympathy with those relationships, not necessarily with other elements in the lives of women of color.

Second, many tracks described physical activity, often in the imperative, such as "Lift Me Up" and "Put Your Lovin' Arms Around Me." To those who are HIV-positive, so often portrayed as feeble and passive, their dynamic response to the energy of house music and such lyrics, defied these representations. When such a track came over the sound system, people previously standing at the bar or sitting with friends snapped to attention and moved to the dance floor. These dancers expressed joy with outstretched arms, spinning, lip-synching, or singing along, clustering together in groups, couples, or remaining alone, inward-focused—a private dance to a personal song. Third, to a community identifying itself around a shared serostatus, lyrics such as these resonated with the emotional and spiritual support of the community—gay or bisexual and HIV-positive.

Lyrics from songs such as the Burt Bacharach and Hal David standard, "Say A Little Prayer," remixed in 1997 and sung by Diana King, are typical. They could describe a personal relationship as the singer describes going about her daily routine thinking of her lover, or a social one, in which members of a group or community think about each other. The poignancy of saying a prayer could also have resonances for listeners who had lost loved ones. Prayer did not have to be vocally performed. Tito saw dancing as a way of praying:

> It's a blessing you send into the universe with your energy when you dance. It's for everyone with AIDS and for all my friends who died. When I asked my friend who was dying in the eighties what this life is all about, he said, "It's all about love." And my dance is my prayer for him and for them all. It's about love.

Love was a lyrical element common to many tracks played in some gay clubs, but whether it was that more tracks with such lyrics were played at the Body Positive T-Dance, or just that I noticed them more in these contexts, the sharing of the music and dance was a function of love and an expression of it.

As I watched Tito and Simon dance together to these lyrics, they embodied their meaning, while simultaneously deepening them with a sense of community-building and with the articulation of its benefits of solidarity and support. The remix of this track I heard at the T-Dance repeated the phrase, *I will love you forever and ever,* the voice of the female singer rich with determination and euphoria.

This particular lyric also resonated with the absence of loved ones. As I watched the dancers moving with each other, heads dropping into the beat, holding themselves in their arms, reaching out and upward either to a present dance partner, or to an absent one, I felt the power of their connections to each other. The dancers were uninhibited in their expression of emotion through dancing. Party organizer Thomas suggested that this was also a result of the safe space created by the support of this peer community:

> Here, everybody allows each other the space of personal freedom, allowing them a couple of hours to do whatever they want [. . .] Dancing allows them really to dance without inhibitions that other guys at the bar might look and see how hideous they might dance, or how crazy, or boring. There's nobody who's judging us here. Because everybody knows it is just great for us to go there and dance [. . .] It's not everywhere. Not even in the gay community.

These tracks carried memories: memories of times shared with those who have passed on, memories of previous parties. Will visibly shuddered with joy when a certain track was played: "This was always Jack's song. We danced to it when we first met." These were memories held not only in the music, but also in the body itself. Tito smiled as he heard Jimmy Ruffin's "Hold On to My Love," a much beloved track at the Saint (the last song played before it closed). He slipped into a memory of dancing to it at the Saint:

> I remember one time [. . .] it was the perfect song, and perfect timing. I finished something with the butterflies [he gestures as if fan dancing] like Swan Lake in the center. These people separated and I was approaching the center—I think at that time there were about five thousand people together. But they gave me the room, and I finished and the DJ stopped the music and came to the center of the dance room and we just embraced and started crying.

When he told me this story, Tito hugged himself, placing his arms once again into the imprint of that hug on his skin, and, through this gesture, he connected again with that person and with that memory. Dancers drew on their own past experiences to construct movement in the present moment. The performative power of dancing at this event derived from its layering, not only with the associations appropriated spaces such as the Roxy and appropriated music and dance styles brought to the individual and to the community. Movement was rendered deeply meaningful by the personal associations both individuals and groups connected with in dancing. At the Body Positive party, DJ Mark Cicero was more likely to sample and mix in such anthems than in other local gay clubs.

The dance space was not only marked out in bricks and mortar, furniture and lights, but with sound. Sound existed while going out of existence. It was dynamic, always in flux, creating its own dimensions moment by moment. In this, it was symptomatic of energy. But at the same time as existing while going out of existence, it was also a means to concretize a moment, turning it and all the desires it contained into an artifact that held and sustained a memory of the abandoned moment. The folding and layering of past experiences onto present ones defied neat distinctions between reality and unreality, presence and absence, and actuality and ideality. These pairings of terms rely upon each other while simultaneously producing excess. This excess is paradoxically embodied by theorist Jacques Derrida (1994) as the ghost: the becoming-body: the articulation of what is no longer and what is not yet. To those men who used music and movement to conjure the presence of absent partners, being with the ghost did not embody being with an other but rather performed a politics of memory.[2] The source of affective power lay not in the content of these memories, but in the retelling. What was the urgency and pleasure of acts of retelling and of the experiences themselves that they were retold? They needed to be retold in the midst of a memory crisis, brought on by the loss of memory and experience through the deaths of PWAs, the indifference of people to AIDS, and the official forgetting in the process of establishing an official history of AIDS.

As well as a mark of love for those who have passed, the urgency of performing these theaters of memory arose from their contingency. So many have died and so many will still die. Dancers needed to connect themselves to a continuum of memory that stretched beyond death to the present in order to reach for a future. As people died, their experiences must not be lost, as Mark expressed:

So many young now act as if AIDS does not exist, as if we and our friends who died did not exist, because maybe they do not know anyone who died, or because less people are dying now. And we have to tell them. They have to know that they can only be this way because so many of us died. And it can happen again. God help us. We don't know how long these drugs will work. We are the guinea pigs. People are having unsafe sex—so many. We have to tell our stories because we thought nothing would happen to us either.

Although memorials may be set up as part of the modern production of national AIDS memory, people also needed "environments of memory," not fixed and static, but dynamic and responsive to the changing demands of the present to reinterpret and restore the past through acts and performances. In these theaters of memory, the past is performed—reinterpreted and restored—through being retold by narrative and by movement. Dancers told their stories to prevent an apocalypse of memories; Tito evoked this when he remembered the death of a close friend by citing a line from Laurie Anderson's *United States,* "When he died, it was as if the whole library burned." Telling these stories was a political intervention by their performers. At the Body Positive T-Dance, the music, movement, and memories together performatively materialized ghosts. And through this materialization, through remembering through the body, the single individual, isolated so much the better to be pathologized, transformed into one that was deeply connected with other bodies—alive and dead.

The men who conjured up those ghosts did not mime dancing with an invisible partner. Their bodies focused intently on a place both beyond the bounds of their skin, and within its experience. Their movement was the embodiment of experience itself, not a pale gesturing or mimicking of an experience with a lover who was no longer there. The first time I went to the Body Positive T-Dance with some friends in early 1996, I sat at the side of the dance floor and watched people dance, overwhelmed—paralyzed maybe—by a great sense of sadness. "This is a hall of ghosts," I remember thinking, "of those who have already departed, and of those whose relationship to death is closer than mine." This was not an uncomplicated feeling for me as an AIDS activist and peer educator versed in the mantra that people live with HIV, rather than die from it. About a year later, when I interviewed one of the organizers of the T-Dance, I was struck by the similarity between my initial reaction to the T-Dance and his. It was a feeling, he relayed, which was very palpable, and yet was overcome by returning to the site of that encounter. To overcome this sense was not to deny or annihilate it. These men did not come to the T-Dance to forget those who were physically absent or to forget their own relationship to death. Many have been close to it on at least one occasion.

The recollection of a ghost of the past was also paradoxically an encounter with a vision of the future. Although improved medication has increased the likelihood of long-term survival for those with HIV, this new prolonged life expectancy entailed some complications. People who five years ago expected to be dead by 1999, were now having to restructure the practices and meaning of their everyday lives. They now knew that they could live for several decades, rather than face rapid deterioration and death within a couple of years of diagnosis, as in the earlier years of the crisis. However, informants saw death from one of the opportunistic infections of AIDS as an unavoidable, albeit delayed reality. Tito reminded himself that he had a nonreturnable ticket. People with HIV monitored themselves for signs of deterioration and had to structure their lives around the routine ingestion of cocktails of awfully powerful drugs (between twenty and fifty a day for those whose voices you hear in this chapter), which ruptured a sense of the everyday with their side effects as Thomas described: "These are so incredible, and so disturbing, and so in the middle of the day." The everyday life of a person with HIV thus included the extraordinary violence of physical reality, a reality Tito knew very well:

> The cocktails . . . it's not a cure, and sometimes, people say, "It's OK if I get it [HIV] because there are the cocktails," and I say "You don't know what it is." Sometimes I say, "This is my last cocktail." I spent two months sleeping in the bathroom with a pillow because the vomiting was too exhausting to get from the bed to the bathroom. And the fevers in the night . . .

At this particular historical moment, there was more than a break with the past, more than a rupture, but an awareness of that rupture. For people with HIV had to incorporate and embody a new sense of time. The hands on the clock slowed down. The initial success of new drug cocktails meant that many felt as if they had a second life—often after a symbolic and often almost literal death. The time given back by these drugs caused another rupture after the rupturing of a sense of time caused by AIDS. Participants expressed that they could not go back to being HIV negative, but now, they could go on. But still, for how long, no one dared say. Infor-

mants like Tito needed to establish a relationship between the present
and the past, which acknowledged and negotiated these ruptures.

> People came from all over the world. And then disappeared because of
> AIDS. For some reason—I don't know—but I'm still alive. But it's not easy
> to witness this new generation doing to itself what we didn't know in 1980.
> This is the problem. And it's very hard to talk when I talk about this. I have
> said before, I will not change anything, I will do everything the same way
> about the Saint, but I will take AIDS away. Because AIDS was the Hitler that
> came and took us to the concentration camp. We were innocent victims.
> We didn't know [he weeps].

All the informants with whom I spoke for this chapter were adamant
in saying, "You must write this down." All seemed to desire to make some
meaning of past and future deaths even in the face of the impossibility
of making meaning from the deaths of so many. They hoped that these
experiences and stories might intervene to change the attitudes and behavior of those who still denied that HIV or AIDS had and could affect
them. Tito and Will wanted their stories written down and read as an ar-
chaeological project: that people would realize that dancing in a club is
a privileged pleasure for which people have died. They wanted the benefits to be in the present and for the future. The memories evoked in
movement and consumption of music at the Body Positive T-Dance were
put to use in building a present and a future. Will observed:

> A lot of these good memories are old memories we try and bring back.
> 'Cos for someone who has HIV, we're looking at another life. And people
> who have had HIV and been sick and on the threshold of going, and com-
> ing back from that feel like it's another life all together. It's totally like your
> second life.

Improvisation may thus be seen as a conversation, not only with the
other participants, but also with the past. I would also argue that improvisation is always a conversation with the future, an articulation between
what has existed and what has not come into existence yet and is performed in the moment-to-moment production of movement. This
movement is this second life.

Dance transformed. Each informant remarked on its health benefits.
For instance, most of the dancers, with or without fans, engaged in
whole body movement, involving the rhythmic, dynamic, and continuous

involvement of the torso. Dancing did not have a formal beginning, middle, and end: participants danced until they wanted to stop. All of the dancers I spoke with who attended the T-Dance went there to exercise. Working up a sweat on the dance floor once a month was cheaper, more expressive, and more fun than going to a gym. Although, for Will, the practice and the words to describe it offered the opportunity for a canny, doubling pun: exercise shook out more than one kind of tension

> It's exercis-cism. Exorcism in the sense of the Catholic Church is the removal of an evil force. So exercising is releasing that. No matter what my problem is, when I dance, I feel better. I just go there. Somehow I'm able to take all these jumbled up feelings that I have inside myself and organize them in some way through my expression and my movement of my body.

On the dance floor, participants rediscovered the joy of shaping and organizing this energy not because it was strange to themselves, but because it *was* themselves. This was part of the appeal of the fans. They materially and visually described the energy and control of the dancer in their environment.

Will indicated a potentially healing effect of the parties:

> You can get to a point where life has no meaning, and this is dangerous. And going to clubs you get new hope, new vision, like a rebirth, seeing yourself in the future. Your T-cells can increase, it happened to a friend of mine.

This may not be as much of a coincidence as it may appear. Tito echoed the others when he attested to the stress-reducing effects of dancing. "I release a lot of the tensions of the week. I shake them off, and dancing helped me do that." Psychologist Mihaly Csikszentmihalyi (1990) has studied states of "optimal experience"—those moments when people experience deep concentration and deep pleasure. He identifies elements of "flow," that is, the pleasurable and total involvement of the individual in an activity for its own sake. This list of flow elements includes thinking less about other things, including problems; making less of an effort to keep a mind on the activity; having more body awareness, more control of the self, more control of the social situation; being less self-conscious and more in harmony with the environment. These are the elements that I have observed and experienced, and that informants have reported to me. Medical and counseling experts working with PWAs report that a psy-

chological state of well-being is an important cofactor in the mainte-
nance and promotion of a healthier lifestyle (Siegel 1986). So the experience of dancing could transform the psychological perception of the
body: the central location of experience, and the generator, not only of
movement, but also of a sense of being together and in the world.

All the dancers were actively making decisions, and informants testified that it felt good to move. How much sweeter when experienced in
moving your body to music was the sense of taking your body back, of
ownership. The location of bodily movement as a way of knowing offered a counterspace of knowledge production to that produced by the
Cartesian split mind/body imperative in Western culture. The body was
freed from its prescribed position as an obstacle to be overcome, and was
of less value in the production of personal and social knowledge. A
whole wealth of experiences filtered through the body to become valued
ways of making meaning. To the individual with HIV, the body was transformed by diagnosis. It became a specialized, medicalized way of knowing: to know one's body was to recognize its physiological and immuno-
logical strengths and weaknesses. But as Tito said, knowing his body this
way, he failed to experience it fully. He used dance to experience himself
fully as well as to give himself a good workout and to shake off all the
frustrations he felt. For him to experience his body did not just mean experiencing its invasion by a retrovirus and subsequent opportunistic infections; it also meant experiencing his body's physical, aesthetic, sexual,
and performative power. By choosing to move in a certain place, in a certain way, we choose to restructure our consciousnesses in vital ways to
which improvisation is central, not only as a personal expressive form,
but as a method of creating a space with a powerful political imperative
and a modeling of a method to achieve personal and political goals.

Several informants were beginning to notice less fear of seroconver-
sion among gay men. New drug treatments of protease inhibitors in
combination with other antiviral drugs were prolonging the lives of
many, making HIV and AIDS manageable infections. This in itself was a
controversial and contingent statement. But even more so was the sug-
gestion, made by Will, that some HIV-negative men welcomed or even
sought HIV infection in order to give their lives a meaning they perceived to be absent:

> Maybe that's one of the things the negative [person] trying to be positive
> is looking for: hope for a new life, a reason to live. Because you're going
> against what the negative says: "Being positive means you're going to die.

AIDS means you're going to die." It's becoming less and less of that today—new drug regimes or whatever. Still, we're not sure about those. Who knows what the hell protease inhibitors are going to do to you five years down the road. We don't know. We're still living the second life based on a really shaky foundation. So here we are trying to get together, trying to have some communion in rejoicing. Still, if you base it on that negative society's foundation it's shaky and could collapse at any minute. So, what do you have? Nothing. Each other. If nothing else, you have each other.

The utopian possibilities of an event such as the Body Positive T-Dance offered a critique of the present, "of *what is,* by casting a picture of what *can and perhaps will be*" (Muñoz 1996, 356). Csikszentmihalyi (1990, 3) grounds this utopian desire to the template of lived body expeience:

> We have all experienced times when, instead of being buffeted by anony-
> mous forces, we do feel in control of our actions, masters of our own fate.
> On the rare occasions that this happens, we feel a sense of exhilaration; a
> deep sense of enjoyment that is long cherished and that becomes a land-
> mark in memory for what life should be like.

These experiences were not only felt, but were also shared by informants who went to the Body Positive T-Dance. They used improvised social dancing to construct templates for relationships with themselves, with others, and with their environment.

Could going to such an event as this really affect change? The transformations affected at the Body Positive T-Dance were not only personal—a transformation of self-image and a potentially healing alleviation of stress, and not only interpersonal—a transformation of a group of individual gay men affected by HIV into a contingent peer community, but I believe that, as well as these, there were possible interventionist transformations of other public consciousnesses. In the visual register of AIDS commentary, the body of the PWA is transformed into what writer and AIDS activist Simon Watney (1994, 66) has called "a signifying husk" of a gay man, alone, passive in the face of his physical destruction, devoid of agency, and the threatening object of the gaze of a presumed seronegative viewer. This othering of PWAs tells us much about major strategies of self-knowledge, rooted in systems of difference and otherness. But, as Watney asserted, even more important, such images serve to justify and validate the continued indifference to the long-term consequences of HIV infection. These representations also affected the self-image of people infected with HIV and PWAs, manifesting themselves in shame, fear of rejection, and isolation. At the Body Positive T-Dance, this dangerously pathetic image was transformed yet again into someone in communion with his peers, active, in control of his body, enjoying his own body, sex-affirming, self-affirming.

Our bodies hold memories: memories of pain, desire, love, of weight and touch, tension and release. In dancing, the body was the location of all these experiences that were not fixed, but that moved and changed as participants moved on the dance floor with the mixing of tracks, rhythms, and samples, rupturing and restructuring time and movement again and again. Improvising dance, participants never moved in an empty space. The space of the dance floor and the practice of dancing were like the body, full of histories. Performance in this case might be both a mobilization and a production in the moment of a space of possibilities in which the future is not described or foreseen, but announced, promised, called for in a performative mode. This production in the moment remained fluid and dynamic by means of the individual and community at play improvising from moment to moment. Walking out of the club was not a reversal of walking in. Something had changed. Sometimes, leaving a club and walking out into the world came as a shock. This shock was revelatory not only of the force of heteronormativity and its fear of those with HIV and AIDS, but also of the sustaining power of cultural practices within events such as the Body Positive T-Dance and their ability to restructure consciousness and to create and celebrate an alternative lifeworld for HIV-positive gay men at the beginning of a new life.

APPENDIXES

A. Method

I. Informant Selection and Recruitment

1. Criteria

Adult men and women who voluntarily identified themselves as "gay," "lesbian," "bisexual," and/or "queer" with some experience of attending dance clubs.

2. Contacting Informants

Step One: Outreach
Most frequently, I used someone I knew as a point of entry. They asked people they knew if they would be interested in participating in this study.

Step Two: Contact and Consent
I provided a copy of my statement to informants by means of description of the project as well as verification of my academic credentials. Potential informants contacted me by telephone, mail, or e-mail. Any such initial contact was not to be understood by the investigator as verbal consent and was to be informant to all the confidentiality procedures outlined below.

(a) The potential informant had the choice to meet me in person at a place of their choosing, and at that time, or prior to that time, received by mail or e-mail
   (i) a copy of my project description,
   (ii) a statement of purpose, including the intent to publish this study as a dissertation and the possibility of the study or any parts of it being published as conference papers, in journals, or as a book,

    (iii) a copy of the types of questions to be asked in the interviews,

    (iv) a copy of the confidentiality procedures as outlined below,

    (v) details of my academic credentials and affiliation with the Department of Performance Studies at New York University, including the contact information of the advisor of the study,

    (vi) contact information of the Office of Sponsored Programs at New York University in order for the potential informant to receive information on the rights of human informants in research projects.

(b) After reviewing the above documentation, as well as having the opportunity to answer any questions the potential informant may have regarding my project and my research procedures, s/he had a cooling off period in which to reflect and consider their consent to this project. I did not recontact the potential informant, but the person was left to contact me by phone, e-mail, or mail. At such point, I gave the individual a copy of the consent form, and was available to answer any questions regarding it.

(c) The individual had the right to refuse to answer any questions and agreed to have interviews tape recorded.

(d) The informant suggested a time and place of their own choosing for the interview.

(e) Informants were assured of anonymity and could choose their own pseudonym. Some gave permission for their own names to be used.

3. Statement to Informants (Distributed to potential participants in the study.)

    Gay and lesbian dance clubs are sometimes written about by journalists and academics; often spoken about by politicians, but before now, no one has carried out a study of these clubs that looks at the improvised dance inside as a valid cultural performance of identity and community. You are being asked to participate in such a study in which you will be asked questions about your reasons for and responses to dancing in these environments.

    I am currently a graduate student in the Department of Performance Studies at New York University, and this study will form the basis of my dissertation as part of my Ph.D.

    You may request not to be asked any questions and your name will not be used in any data or results. A pseudonym will be used to ensure anonymity. These interviews will be recorded but the tapes and transcripts will remain confidential and will be available for review and editing by you. I do not anticipate any benefits or risks to be involved in your participation in this study.

For more information, do not hesitate to contact me.

You are also welcome to contact the supervisor of this research who is on the faculty of the Department of Performance Studies.

If, at any time, you have further questions about your rights as a informant of academic research, you may contact the Office of Sponsored Programs at New York University.

4. Confidentiality

Procedures to protect the confidentiality of informants were as follows:

(a) All audio tapes and transcripts of interviews were stored at the investigator's private residence in a locked filing cabinet drawer to which only the investigator had access.

(b) All tapes were labeled with pseudonyms.

(c) All materials named above were only removed from the investigator's place of residence in the event of a change of residency.

(d) The tapes and transcripts were not reviewed by any party other than the investigator and the informant of the interview.

(e) No informant had access to any information about the identity of another informant or any part of the content of any interview or discussion with any other informant, whether this information was recorded, documented, or verbally relayed.

(f) The informant had the right to review the tapes and transcripts of their interviews with the investigator and request that certain information, any part, or the whole of the content not be used, without the indication of the withdrawal of any such information being recorded in the published study.

(g) If an informant decided to withdraw consent, all tapes and transcripts or records of contact with the investigator would be destroyed and no hard or disk copies kept.

(h) Informants could request possession of any master tapes or transcripts at any time, including the event of their withdrawal from the study.

(i) No informant was identified by name, address, physical description, or any other identifying markers unless full consent was given. Pseudonyms were used to ensure anonymity.

(j) All of the above confidentiality procedures will be followed for three years after the completion of the study, at which point all tapes and transcripts will be destroyed.

II. Procedures Followed

Step One: Selection of Target Sites for Observation

My selection of dance clubs in which to observe was based on the following criteria:

(a) Dance clubs that marked themselves to queer, gay, and/or lesbian communities. These were identified by reviewing gay and/or lesbian entertainment resources: for instance, publications such as *Homo Extra, Dyke Dish, New York Gay and Lesbian News,* and the *Village Voice,* as well as online entertainment listings resources such as *Planet Out.*

(b) Clubs that promoted themselves as clubs for social dance primarily, rather than other activities such as cabaret. Again, attention was paid to advertising and other promotional material such as flyers.

(c) Access. Clubs in the New York City area were possible sites due not only to convenience of access, but also because of New York City's pronounced gay and lesbian cultural history and contemporary culture.

Step Two. Initial Movement Observation in Sites

I attended all of my selected sites at least once in this step and observed improvised social dancing. As I was observing public behavior, which did not involve identifying markers by which anyone could identify the dancers, I did not anticipate the need to obtain consent.

Step Three. Fieldnotes

Fieldnotes were prepared on all these sites with attention to the following:

GEOGRAPHY:
  (a) Where the site was in New York City,
  (b) The size of the club, and
  (c) The layout of the club.

POPULATION:

    (a) How many people in the club at different times of the event, and

    (b) Types of population, i.e. male: female ratio, racial make-up, age distribution.

MOVEMENT:

    (a) Concentration of dancers on the dance floor,

    (b) Use of space,

    (c) Use of body weight,

    (d) Use of shape,

    (e) Use of rhythm,

    (f) Steps, i.e., footwork, and

    (g) Interactions with other dancers, i.e., eye contact, partnering.

Step Four. Preparation of Research Questions to be Asked

My approach was to use primarily open-ended questions with the task to build upon and explore participants' responses to these questions. The goal was to have the participant reconstruct his or her experience within the topic under study. I followed the three-stage interview designed by Dolbeare and Schuman:[1:]

Stage One: Focused Life History
Sample questions asked to establish context:
    Where did you grow up?
    How long have you been in New York?
    Why did you come to New York (if not from the area)?
    When did you first go to a gay/lesbian dance club?
    Did you go by yourself or with friends?
    Why did you go?
    How would you characterize your responses on first going to a club?
    What was the music like?
    Did you dance?
    Do you remember how it felt to dance this first time at a gay/lesbian club?
    How many times (approximately) would you say you have been to gay/lesbian dance clubs since then?

Stage Two: The Details of Experience

Sample questions aimed to focus on the concrete details of the participants' present experience in the topic area of the study. Participants were asked to reconstruct these details.

> *On what occasions do you go to a gay/lesbian club?*
> *How do you decide which one to go to?*
> *What do you do to prepare for going to a gay/lesbian club?*
> *What do you do once you get to the club?*
> *When do you decide to dance?*
> *How long do you dance for?*
> *Do you dance with friends or by yourself?*
> *What do you do to make space for yourself if the dance floor is very crowded?*
> *Typically, what do you do when you are dancing?*
> *What will make you leave the dance floor?*
> *How many times will you return to the dance floor on average over the course of an evening?*

Stage Three: Reflection on the Meaning

I asked questions in order for participants to reflect on the meaning of their experience. Making meaning requires that the participants look at how the factors in their lives interacted to bring them to their present situation. Most of the questions in this section came from responses the participant had given previously.

The number of participants required to make a study representative was based on two criteria:[2]

(a) Sufficiency. Were there sufficient numbers to reflect the range of participants and sites that make up the population so that others outside the sample might have a chance to connect to the experiences of those in it? In this study, I needed to have enough participants to reflect both gay and lesbian experiences, as well as those of race and age.

(b) Saturation of information. This was the point in the study at which I began to hear the same information reported, and was no longer hearing anything new.

Initially I aimed for around 15 to 25 participants.

Step Five. Interviews

These took place at times and places of the interviewee's convenience. Most interviews took on average one and a half hours. The shortest was one hour, the longest three hours. The interviews were open-ended with the emphasis on interviewees telling stories and rendering experiences, rather than answering closed questions.

Step Six. Second Stage of Movement Observation

Repeat observations in selected sites as in step two.

Step Seven. Second Stage of Fieldnotes

Repeat fieldnotes as in step three.

B. Informants

Name[1]	Gender	Age[2]	Race/ethnicity	Occupation	Date(s) interviewed	Location (all NYC)
Will Wright*	M	41	Caucasian[3]	Baker	5/7/96, 10/11/97	His home, East Village
Dana*	F	34	African-American	Teacher	11/3/96	Greenwich Village coffee shop
Thomas Weise	M	29	Caucasian	Volunteer	2/13/97, 10/12/97	My apartment, Chelsea; His home, East Village
Iain*	M	40	Caucasian	Administrator	8/15/97	His office, downtown
Catherine*	F	26	Caucasian	Student	12/2/97, 4/2/98	My apartment, East Village
Mark*	M	42	Caucasian	Freelance Writer	9/14/97	His apartment, Chelsea
Alex*	M	33	Latino	Student/door person	9/24/97, 3/20/98	Greenwich Village restaurant; My apartment, East Village
Roberto "Tito" Mesa	M	51	Latino	On disability	10/13/97, 1/12/98, 7/23/98	His apartment, East Village
Jermaine*	M	35	African-American	New media consultant	1/17/97	Restaurant in Chinatown
Lisa*	F	30	Asian-American	Student	1/17/98	Her apartment, East Village
Stephen*	M	33	African-American	Writer	5/3/98	Restaurant in West Village
Barrel*	M	30	Caucasian	Instructor	4/27/98	His apartment, Greenwich Village
Edie*	F	25	Caucasian	Door person	6/6/98	Coffee shop in East Village
Ariel*	M	26	Caucasian	Student	6/26/98	Coffee shop in East Village
Colin*	M	31	African-American	Administrator	8/24/98	Coffee shop in East Village
Ella*	F	24	Caucasian	Student	8/28/98	East Village bar

1. Names marked with an asterisk are pseudonyms.
2. Not all informants gave their age. I have estimated in those cases that didn't.
3. This term means "white" of European origin.

C. Locations of Clubs

MID-TOWN MANHATTAN
Escuelita, 301 W. 39th St. (8th Ave.)
Octagon, 555 W. 33rd (11th Ave.)
Café con Leche, Club Expo/Kit Kat Klub, 124 W. 43rd St.

WEST-SIDE WATERFRONT
Twilo, 530 W. 27th St. (10th Ave.)
Tunnel, mid-block 27th St. (between 10th and 11th)

CHELSEA
Roxy, 515 W. 18th St.—every night
Splash, 50 W. 17th St. (6th Ave.)—every night
Limelight, 47 West 20th

MEAT-PACKING DISTRICT
Clit Club (event), Mother (name of club), 432 W. 14th St.

GREENWICH VILLAGE
Life, 158 Bleecker St.

WEST VILLAGE
Crazy Nanny's, 21 Seventh Ave. (Leroy St.)
Suspect, Nowbar, 7th Ave. Sth. (Leroy St.)

EAST VILLAGE
Foxy, Velvet, 167 Ave. A (10th St.)—Saturday night. Closed September 1998.
Sugar Babies, Irving Plaza, 17 Irving Place (E. 15th St.)
Meow Mix, 269 E. Houston St. (Suffolk St.)—every night

Pyramid, 101 Ave. A (6th St.)
Salon Wednesdays, Flamingo East, 219 Second Avenue (13th St.)

TRIBECA
Squeezebox, Don Hill's, 511 Greenwich St. (Spring St.)
Angels, 44 Walker St. (Church St.)
Vinyl, 6 Hubert St.
Flava, Club Fahrenheit 349 Broadway (Leonard St.)

QUEENS
Krash, 34–48 Steinway At. Astoria

D. How the City Planning Commission of the City of New York Defines "Adult Establishment"

An "adult establishment" is a commercial establishment where a substantial portion of the establishment includes an adult bookstore, adult eating or drinking establishment, adult theater, or other adult commercial establishment, or any combination thereof, as defined below:

(a) An adult bookstore has a substantial portion of its stock in any one or more of the following:
   (1) books, magazines, periodicals, or other printed matter that are characterized by an emphasis upon the depiction or description of "specified sexual activities" or "specified anatomical areas"; or,
   (2) photographs, films, motion pictures, videocassettes, slides, or other visual representations that are enhanced by an emphasis upon the depiction or description of "specified sexual activities" or "specified anatomical areas."

(b) An adult eating or drinking establishment that regularly features any one or more of the following:
   (1) live performances that are characterized by an emphasis on "specified anatomical areas" or "specified sexual activities" or "specified anatomical areas"; or,
   (2) films, motion pictures, videocassettes, slides, or other photographic reproductions that are characterized by an emphasis upon the depiction or description of "specified sexual activities" or "specified anatomical areas"; or,
   (3) employees who, as part of their employment, regularly expose to patrons "specified anatomical areas."

(c) An adult theater regularly features one or more of the following:

    (1) films, motion pictures, videocassettes, slides, or other photo-graphic reproductions that are characterized by an emphasis upon the depiction or description of "specified sexual activities" or "specified anatomical areas"; or,

    (2) live performances characterized by an emphasis on "specified anatomical areas" or "specified sexual activities" or "specified anatomical areas"; or,

An adult theater shall include commercial establishments where such materials or performances are viewed from individual enclosures.

(d) Another adult commercial establishment is a facility—other than an adult bookstore, adult eating and drinking establishment, adult the-ater, commercial studio, or business or trade school—that features employees who as part of their employment, regularly expose to pa-trons "specified anatomical areas."

For the purpose of defining "adult establishments," "specified sexual ac-tivities" are: (i) human genitals in a state of sexual stimulation or arousal; (ii) actual or simulated acts of human masturbation, sexual intercourse, or sodomy; or (iii) fondling or other erotic touching of human genitals, pubic region, buttock, anus, or female breast.

"Specified anatomical areas" are: (i) less than completely and opaquely concealed: (a) human genitals, pubic region (b) human buttock, anus, or (c) female breast below a point immediately above the top of the areola; or (ii) human male genitals in a discernibly turgid state, even if com-pletely and opaquely concealed.

E. Regulations and Licenses

An establishment must hold a license for on-premises liquor sales. To obtain one, the owner must get approval from the community board, which will consider the nature of the establishment, the owner's reputation, the legal record of any related liquor-serving establishments, and the 500-foot law (if the new business is opening within 500 feet of three or more establishments, the board may deny the license). The community board's recommendation factors in SLA decisions. No alcohol may be served between the hours of 4 A.M. and 8 A.M., or 4 A.M. and midday on Sundays.

Patrons cannot dance in a bar or club that does not have a cabaret license, which is issued by the New York City Department of Consumer Affairs for a fee of $1,000 (as a rule of thumb, more than three people moving rhythmically constitutes dancing). To qualify for a license, the establishment must be in a properly zoned neighborhood and the building itself must have a Use Group 12 overlay, which permits operation as a nighttime dancing and entertainment facility.

Cabaret licenses are granted only after dozens of other permits, certificates, and licenses have been acquired and inspections passed (these are overseen by the Department of Buildings, the municipal electrical department, the Fire Department and Department of Health). The Department of Health must approve the plumbing facilities. Safety requirements include a sprinkler system, two separate and clear means of escape at least 25 feet apart with illuminated exit signs, doors that open outward, a trip switch that will cut off the music if the fire alarm is activated, fire safety lights, and a certified fire warden on the premises. Then the establishment must win approval from the community board and Environmental Control Board, as well as provide them with two affidavits: one stating that background checks on security hires have been performed, and another stating that the space will not be used as a cabaret until the license is granted.

Full nudity is prohibited in establishments that serve alcohol. Topless-ness used to be permitted, but now the rezoning of New York City has re-sulted in this being curtailed. The New York Health Code prohibits es-tablishments from making facilities available for the purpose of sexual activities involving anal intercourse, vaginal intercourse, or fellatio. Such facilities are considered a threat to public health. These rules also have an insidious effect. At J's Hangout—a male sex club—a notice forbade patrons to engage in ball licking as it could lead to fellatio, which is ille-gal. This sign was next to a huge jar full of condoms.

NOTES

Introduction (pp. 1–15)

1. For two excellent discussions of this, see Michael Warner's introduction to Warner 1993 and Steven Seidman's essay in the same volume, "Identity and Politics in a 'Postmodern' Gay Culture: Some Historical and Conceptual Notes." (In Warner 1993, 105–142).

2. In *Public Sphere and Experience: Toward an Analysis of the Bourgeois and Proletarian Public Sphere,* Oskar Negt and Alexander Kluge's critique of Habermas stems from his assumption of a single, central public sphere (1993).

3. As described by Lauren Berlant and Michael Warner, heteronormativity "consists less of norms that could be summarized as a body of doctrine than of a sense of rightness produced in contradictory manifestations—often unconscious—immanent to practice or to institutions" (Berlant and Warner 1998, 548). It refers to the institutions and structures of understanding that make heterosexuality seem not only coherent, but also privileged. It aspires to reproduce an illusion of status quo, insisting upon casting the heterosexual relationship in patriarchal forms with "couples" as the social atom for erotic articulations and ethical priority given to the dichotomies of monogamous/promiscuous and private/public. Materially, it is implicated in a hierarchy of property and propriety and of bearing oneself in the world. It is contingent, sometimes taking contradictory forms.

4. I include the city's definition of an "adult establishment" and its proscribed uses in Appendix D.

5. See Appendix E for a description of the processes of obtaining liquor and cabaret licenses.

6. For a full description of my method, see Appendix A.

Chapter 1 (pp. 16–35)

1. Here, I use Michael de Certeau's distinction between strategies and tactics: "strategies are able to produce, tabulate, and impose these spaces [. . .] whereas tactics can only use, manipulate, and divert these spaces." (1984, 30).

2. Lisa Duggan's theory of homonormativity in *The Incredible Shrinking Public Sphere,* exposes the ways in which conservative and assimilationist gays and lesbians contribute to the privatization of mass culture by subscribing to heteronormative thinking and politics such as the reification of marriage. I work this in the following example to include the impulse to establish dominant linear history, rather than memory in the forms of (dominant) culturally sanctioned places of memory such as plaques and performances or routes such as the Gay Pride parade. However, I do not wish to naturalize these places and practices, as gays and lesbians have had to fight for the right to put up plaques and to have parades or dance clubs. However, what gets placed where or who gets

to walk in whose name can still be read as exclusionary of queer practices or populations, as is evidenced for example in local controversies about changing the title of Lesbian and Gay Pride parades to Lesbian, Gay, Bisexual, and Transgendered Pride.

3. The redevelopment of Times Square from a site of "sleaze" to a Disneyfied shopping and recreation park is a precursor to the process in which the piers are embroiled. Queer activist groups such as Sex Panic! have protested against this loss of queer space.

4. East 5th Street. Open from 1980 to 1988.

Chapter 2 (pp. 36–64)

1. A "house" is a gay male fraternity or alternative kinship group. Each is headed by a "mother."

2. Often, a promoter was somebody known in the club world who proposed a party event at a club and helped organize it, and/or went to other clubs, selecting people to put on the guest list for a party. The promoter also had a contact book of fabulous clubbers and called or sent them invitations offering free or reduced entry at their event. Promoters sometimes also hired people to stand outside clubs and hand out flyers advertising events.

3. For a "full disclosure" of the Studio 54 experience, see Anthony Haden-Guest (1997). Studio 54's heyday was 1977 to 1980, and then it reopened from 1982 to 1986. Celebrities who gave the New York nightlife its cachet "would let loose all night in a post-Vietnam, post-Watergate sybaritic whirl" (Foderaro 1994).

4. These incidents occurred at Vinyl in January 1997. One was a freak accident. As there were also several drug-related arrests and a citation for selling alcohol to a minor, the club has its beer and wine license revoked pending a hearing.

5. Victor Turner characterizes liminality as "necessarily ambiguous."

> Liminal entities are neither here nor there: they are betwixt and between the positions assigned and arrayed by law, custom, convention, and ceremonial. [. . .] Their [neophytes] behavior is normally passive or humble. [. . .] It is [as] though they are being reduced or ground down to a uniform condition to be fashioned anew and endowed with additional powers to enable them to cope with their new station in life. Among themselves, neophytes tend to develop an intense comradeship and egalitarianism. (in Turner 1994, 94)

6. From "Clubs" listing. *Time Out* October 18–25, 1995:33

7. From "Gay and Lesbian" listing. *Time Out* October 18–25, 1995:51

8. A call-out was a moment when typically the DJ, or maybe an MC, asked the crowd to shout out in appreciation of the DJ or the performer. Sometimes, the crowd was also cued to call out in allegiance to their local or regional point of origin. For instance, "Brooklyn in the house, shout out!"

Chapter 3 (pp. 65–85)

1. Opened by DJ Nicky Siano and his brother in a loft on 22nd Street, it later moved to 172 Mercer after a series of Fire Department raids that closed several dance spots.

2. Anthony Thomas presents a useful mapping of the development of house music in black gay clubs in Chicago in his essay "The House the Kids Built: The Gay Black Imprint on American Dance Music" (1995). This essay is particularly helpful in charting the "Africanness" of house music, and how its rhythmic qualities encourage dance. See also John Miller Chernoff's classic ethnomusicological analysis of these aspects in *African Rhythm and African Sensibility* (1979).

3. DJ headphones only have one earpiece so that DJs can simultaneously hear the record being played through the club and the crowd responding and the track on the turntable being cued up.

4. For an excellent analysis of house music produced and mixed by club DJs, see Kai Fikentscher, *"You Better Work!"*: Underground Dance Music of New York City (2000).

5. The back beats are the second and fourth beats in a four-beat measure. Emphasis on the back beat intensifies its pull away from the strong beats and therefore provides an important target point for improvisers who want to play with the beat. For a musicological elaboration of this, see Berliner 1994, 149–51.

6. Paul Connerton suggests that what is important to a group or an individual is committed to the body and performed as habit:

> Our bodies [. . .] keep the past in an entirely effective form in their continuing ability to perform certain skilled actions. We may not remember how or when we first learned to swim, but we can keep on swimming successfully—remembering how to do it—without any representational activity on our part at all [. . .]. Many forms of habitual skilled remembering illustrate a keeping of the past in mind that, without ever adverting to its historical origin, nevertheless re-enacts the past in our present conduct. In habitual memory, the past is, as it were, sedimented in the body. (Connerton 1989: 72)

Chapter 4 (pp. 86–110)

1. The context of "postmodern dance" in which much of this work took place is described in Sally Banes' classic text, *Terpsichore in Sneakers: Post-Modern Dance* (1980). Cynthia Novack also investigates contact improvisation and its political resonances of personal freedom from the restraints of formal choreography, emphasizing the creative autonomy of the dancer, and by association, of disco dancing as its freedom from the restraints of formal gender-determined partnering in her essay "Looking at Movement as Culture: Contact Improvisation to Disco" (1988).

2. For a history of opposition to dancing in Western society, see Ann Louise Wagner's *Adversaries of Dance: from the Puritans to the Present* (1997).

3. For example, Jack Newfield's columns in the *New York Post* throughout 1997–99.

4. In "Pedro Zamora's *Real World* of Counterpublicity: Performing an Ethics of the Self," José Esteban Muñoz considers the minoritarian ethics of the self as a care of the self. "To work on oneself is to veer away from models of the self that correlate with socially prescribed identity narratives. The rejection of these notions of the self is not simply an individualistic rebellion: resisting dominant modes of subjection entails not only contesting dominant modalities

of governmental and state power but also opening up a space for new social formations." In Sasha Torres, ed., *Living Color: Race and Television in the United States* (Durham and London: Duke University Press: 198). Here, I assert we can see the possibility for an ethics of sociality in new social formations that grow out of an ethics of the self—that by rejecting dominant modalities people simultaneously embrace others who also reject them and who want to work out new ways of being together that may not be the norm.

Chapter 5 (pp. 111–127)

1. See Appendix D: How the City Defines an "Adult Establishment."

Chapter 6 (pp. 128–158)

1. Source: Audience Research and Analysis for the New York Nightlife Association.
2. Owen 1997: 34–37.
3. Reported in Bastone 1997.
4. See Appendix D: How the City Planning Commission of the City of New York Defines "Adult Establishment."
5. Licenses for dancing and cabaret were initiated in New York City in 1926 in order to restore a measure of control over the city's huge prohibition-era nightclubs. In Chauncey 1994: 352.
6. Source: Audience Research and Analysis for the New York Nightlife Association.
7. From 1996–97, the New York Anti-Violence Project reports a 40% increase in charges of public lewdness against men seeking men. Men have been arrested by the New York Police Department, Port Authority police, parks police, Metro North, and Long Island Railroad police.
8. In comparison to New York, in Miami's South Beach, the city and the police realize that nightlife is a big part of the reason why a formerly dilapidated resort town is now thriving. A collective policy of cooperation has been actively developed. In New York City in 1997, Andrew Rasiej of Irving Plaza co-founded The New York Nightlife Association—an organization of club owners—to replace the current discord between clubs and communities with dialogue.
9. At the height of his career, Peter Gatien operated four of the largest nightclubs in New York City: The Tunnel, the Palladium, Limelight, and Club USA. On May 15 1996, he was roused from his bed by four Drug Enforcement agents and held on $1 million bail, accused of turning his clubs into "drug supermarkets." In addition, the Manhattan district attorney's office conducted a full-scale audit of his finances looking for tax evasion (Studio 54's owners Steve Rubell and Ian Schrager were brought down this way). All charges were subsequently dropped or dismissed. At the time of writing, Michael Alig, Gatien's front man, club kid, and promoter of notorious parties such as Disco 2000 at Limelight, is awaiting trial for the grisly murder of Angel Melendez, another fixture on the club scene.
10. In particular, the columnist has written polemics against nightclub owner Peter Gatien, in the cause of protecting kids from drugs. Newfield claims he allegedly profiteered from the sale of drugs to kids at his clubs: "What does it take in this town for the SLA to do its job and revoke a liquor license? A liquor license

is not a constitutional right, like free speech or freedom of religion. It's a privilege, conditioned on obeying the law, being a good neighbor, not seducing kids into drug use, and not ruining the quality of life for a community."

11. Citations include: Limelight, August 1996: closed by police on four narcotics-related disorderly premises charges; reopened Spring 1998. Pyramid, April 1996–April 1997: Community Board 3 hears complaints. Charges pending for sales to minors and overcrowding. Rome, March 1997: citation for unlicensed dancing (go-go boys) and assorted noise complaints. Crowbar, March 1997: citations for unlicensed dancing, closed. Vinyl, January 1997: two charges for assault, one for a controlled substance, and one for sale to a minor. Beer and wine license revoked. Many of these citations were subsequently dismissed. Sources: club managers, Community Board Records, State Liquor Authority.

12. Gays and lesbians had dance parties in these locations for many years previous to gay liberation of the late 1960s and early 1970s. However, as George Chauncey writes in his excellent history of gay nightlife in New York City from 1890–1940, a new wave of policing in the 1930s sought to contain homosexuality by prohibiting its presence in the public sphere where authorities feared it threatened to disrupt public order and the reproduction of "normal" gender and sexual arrangements (Chauncey 1994: 9).

13. In a 1993 essay in the *New Republic,* Andrew Sullivan calls on gays to abandon "the notion of sexuality as cultural subversion" which, he says, alienates "the vast majority of gay people who not only accept the natural origin of their sexual orientation, but wish to be integrated into society as it is." For these people, a 'queer' identity is precisely what they want to avoid," and a responsible gay politics should be about helping. Quoted in Mendelsohn 1996: 30.

14. GHB or gamma-hydroxybutrate is a synthetic hormone affecting the central nervous system. It is used by some clubgoers to break down inhibitions.

15. D'Emilio stresses that the new forms of gay identity and patterns of group life for which capitalism created the material conditions reflected the differentiation of people according to gender, race, and class. For instance, women were more likely to remain economically dependent on men. The Kinsey studies of the 1940s and 1950s showed a positive correlation between years of schooling and lesbian activity. College-educated women, far more able than their working class sisters to support themselves, could survive more easily without intimate relationships with men (Kinsey 1948; Kinsey et al. 1953).

16. Cited in Mendelsohn 1996, 29.

Chapter 7 (pp. 159–183)

1. Within Body Positive's roster of peer workshops and outreach programs, several targeted HIV-positive people of color. Stand Up Harlem, a support organization based on West 130th Street in uptown Manhattan, is dedicated to support people with HIV in its predominantly African-American neighborhood, although it also attracts African-Americans with HIV from other parts of the city. Stand Up Harlem attempts to appeal to the black HIV+ communities that have been disenfranchised from some central posts of black community structure, particularly church and family, due to drug use, incarceration, homosexuality, and/or their seropositive status.

2. In his 1996 essay, "Ghosts of Public Sex: Utopian Longings, Queer Memories," José Esteban Muñoz suggests that queer memory is always political as

"queer memories of utopia and the longing that structures them [. . .] help us carve out a space for actual, living sexual citizenship." (356.) Muñoz focuses on what he calls the ritualized tellings of remembrances through film, video, performance, writing, and visual culture. To this list, I include improvised social dancing in queer clubs as a particular way to recall not only utopias, but the dystopic stories of separation, illness, and death. The utopic imagination is both critique and conjuration of an absent and longed for reality. In this instance, it is also a conjuration of absent friends and lovers.

Appendix A (pp. 185–191)

1. Dolbeare and Schuman, *Analysis, education and everyday life.* Lexington, MA: Heath, 1982.
2. I. E. Seidman, *Interviewing as Qualitative Research* (New York: Teachers College, Columbia University, 1991): 45.

BIBLIOGRAPHY

Books

Abu-Lughod, Lila. *Writing Women's Worlds: Bedouin Stories.* Berkeley: University of California Press, 1993.

Anderson, Benedict. *Imagined Communities: Reflections on the Origin and Spread of Nationalism.* London: Verso, 1983.

Apel, Willi. *Harvard Dictionary of Music.* Second edition. Cambridge, Mass: Harvard University Press, 1969.

Attali, Jacques. *Noise: the Political Economy of Music.* Translated by Brian Massumi. Minneapolis: University of Minnesota Press, 1985.

Banes, Sally. *Terpsichore in Sneakers: Post-Modern Dance.* Boston: Houghton Mifflin, 1980.

———. *Writing Dancing in the Age of Postmodernism.* Hanover and London: University Press of New England/Wesleyan University Press, 1994.

Bateson, Gregory and Margaret Mead. *Balinese Character: a Photographic Analysis.* Special Publications of the New York Academy of Sciences, Vol. II, 1942.

Behar, Ruth and Deborah A. Gordon, eds. *Women Writing Culture.* Berkeley: University of California Press, 1995.

Benjamin, Walter. *Illuminations.* Edited by Hannah Arendt. Translated by Harry Zohn. New York: Schocken Books, 1968.

———. *The Origin of German Tragic Drama.* London: New Left Books, 1977.

Benthall, J. and T. Polhemus, eds. *The Body as a Medium of Expression.* London: Allen Lane, 1975.

Berliner, Paul. *Thinking in Jazz.* Chicago: University of Chicago Press, 1994.

Birdwhistell, Ray L. *Kinesics and Context: Essays on Body Motion Communication.* Philadelphia: University of Pennsylvania Press, 1970.

Blom, Lynne Anne, and L. Tarin Chaplin. *The Moment of Movement: Dance Improvisation.* Pittsburgh: University of Pittsburgh Press, 1988.

Boyer, M. Christine. *The City of Collective Memory: Its Historical Imagery and Architectural Entertainments.* Cambridge, Mass: MIT Press, 1996.

Brake, Mike. *Comparative Youth Cultures: the Sociology of Youth Cultures and Youth Subcultures in America, Britain, and Canada.* London: Routledge and Kegan Paul, 1985.

Certeau, Michel de. *The Practice of Everyday Life.* Translated by Steven F. Rendall. Berkeley: University of California Press, 1984.

———. *L'Invention du quotidien.* Paris: Gallimard, 1990.

Chambers, Iain. *Urban Rhythms: Pop Music and Popular Culture.* New York: St. Martin's Press, 1985.

———. *Popular Culture: the Metropolitan Experience.* London: Methuen, 1986.

Chauncey, George. *Gay New York: Gender, Urban Culture, and the Making of the Gay Male World 1890–1940.* New York: Basic Books, 1994.

Chernoff, John Miller. *African Rhythm and African Sensibility: Aesthetics and Social Action in African Musical Idioms.* Chicago: University of Chicago Press, 1979.

Clifford, James. *The Predicament of Culture: Twentieth-Century Ethnography, Literature, and Art.* Cambridge, Mass.: Harvard University Press, 1988.

Clifford, James and George E. Marcus, eds. *Writing Culture: The Poetics and Politics of Ethnography.* Berkeley: University of California Press, 1986.

Connerton, Paul. *How Societies Remember.* Cambridge, U.K., Cambridge University Press, 1989.

Creekmur, Corey K. and Alexander Doty, eds. *Out in Culture: Gay, Lesbian, and Queer Essays on Popular Culture.* Durham and London: Duke University Press, 1995.

Csikszentmihalyi, Mihaly. *Flow: The Psychology of Optimal Experience.* New York: Harper and Row, 1990.

D'Emilio, John. *Sexual Politics, Sexual Communities: The Making of a Homosexual Minority in the United States, 1940–1970.* Chicago: University of Chicago Press, 1983.

Derrida, Jacques. *Specters of Marx: The State of Debt, the Work of Mourning and the New International.* Translated by Peggy Kamuf. New York: Routledge, 1994.

Drewel, Margaret Thompson. *Yoruba Ritual: Performers, Play, Agency.* Bloomington: Indiana University Press, 1992.

Durkheim, Emile. *The Rules of Sociological Method.* Lukes, S., ed. London: Macmillan, 1982.

Dyer, Richard. *Only Entertainment.* Routledge: London and New York, 1992.

Fabian, Johannes. *Time and the Other: How Anthropology Makes Its Object.* New York: Columbia University Press, 1983.

Fikentscher, Kai. *"You Better Work!": Underground Dance Music in New York City.* Middletown, Conn.: Wesleyan University Press, 2000.

Foster, Susan Leigh, ed. *Corporealities: Dancing, Knowledge, Culture and Power.* New York and London; Routledge, 1996.

Foucault, Michel. *The History of Sexuality,* Volumes 1 and 2. New York: Vintage. 1980.

Frith, Simon. *Sound Effects: Youth, Leisure, and the Politics of Rock 'n' Roll.* London: Constable, 1983.

Goffman, Erving. *The Presentation of Self in Everyday Life.* Harmondsworth, U.K.: Penguin, 1969.

Gramsci, Antonio. *Selections from the Prison Notebooks.* Ed. and trans. Quentin Hoare and Geoffrey Nowell-Smith. London: Lawrence and Wishart, 1971.

Habermas, Jurgen. *The Structural Transformation of the Public Sphere: An Inquiry into a Category of Bourgeois Society.* Translated by Thomas Burger with Frederick Lawrence. Cambridge, Mass.: MIT Press, 1989.

Haden-Guest, Anthony. *The Last Party: Studio 54, Disco, and the Culture of the Night.* New York: William Morrow, 1997.

Halbwachs, Maurice. *Les cadres sociaux de la memoire.* Paris: F. Alcan, 1925.

——. *On Collective Memory.* Edited, translated, and with an introduction by Lewis A. Coser. Chicago: University of Chicago Press, 1992.

Hall, Edward T. *The Hidden Dimension*. Garden City, New York: Doubleday, 1996.

Hall, Stuart and Tony Jefferson, eds. *Resistance Through Rituals: Youth Subcultures in Post-War Britain*. London: Harper and Collins, 1991.

Hanna, Judith Lynne. *Dance, Sex and Gender: Signs of Identity, Dominance, Defiance and Desire*. Chicago: University of Chicago Press, 1988.

Harris, Daniel. *The Rise and Fall of Gay Culture*. New York: Hyperion, 1997.

Hazzard-Gordon, Katrina. *Jookin': The Rise of Social Dance Formations in African-American Culture*. Philadelphia: Temple University Press, 1990.

Hebdige, Dick. *Subculture: The Meaning of Style*. London: Methuen, 1979.

Huizinga, Johan. *Homo Ludens: A Study of the Play Element in Culture*. Boston: Beacon Press, 1950

Ingram, Gordon Brent, Anne-Marie Bouthillette, and Yolanda Retter. *Queers in Space: Communities, Public Places, Sites of Resistance*. Seattle: Bay Press, 1997.

Jennings, Michael W. *Dialectical Images: Walter Benjamin's Theory of Literary Criticism*. Ithaca: Cornell University Press, 1987.

Kant, Immanuel. *The Critique of Judgement*. New York: Hafner Publishing Co., [1790] 1966.

Kinsey, Alfred et al. *Sexual Behavior in the Human Male*. Philadelphia: W. B. Saunders, 1948.

——. *Sexual Behavior in the Human Female*. Philadelphia: W.B. Saunders, 1953.

Klein, Alan M. *Little Big Men: Bodybuilding Subculture and Gender Construction*. Albany: State University of New York Press, 1993.

Lévi-Strauss, Claude. *Tristes Tropiques*. New York: Atheneum 1961.

Lomax, Alan, ed. *Folk Song Style and Culture*. Washington, D.C.: American Association for the Advancement of Science, Pub. No. 88, 1968.

MacIver, R. M. and Charles H. Page. *Society: An Introductory Analysis*. Macmillan Co., 1961:8–10.

Malinowski, Bronislaw. *Argonauts of the Western Pacific*. New York: E. P. Dutton, 1961.

Malone, Jaqui. *Steppin' on the Blues: The Visible Rhythms of African American Dance*. Champaign: University of Illinois Press, 1996.

Marcus, George E. and Michael M. J. Fischer. *Anthropology as Culture Critique*. Chicago: University of Chicago Press, 1986.

Mead, Margaret and F. C. Macgregor. *Growth and Culture*. New York: Putnam, 1951.

Mullaney, Stephen. *The Place of the Stage: License, Play, and Power in Renaissance England*. Chicago: University of Chicago Press, 1988.

Muñoz, José Esteban. *Disidentifications: Queers of Color and the Performance of Politics*. Minneapolis and London: University of Minnesota Press, 1999.

Negt, Oskar and Alexander Kluge. *Public Sphere and Experience: Toward an Analysis of the Bourgeois and Proletarian Public Sphere*. Trans. Peter Labanyi, Jamie Owen Daniel, and Assenka Oksiloff. Minneapolis and London: University of Minnesota Press, 1993.

Ness, Sally Ann. *Body, Movement, and Culture: Kinesthetic and Visual Symbolism in a Philippine Community*. University of Pennsylvania Press, 1992.

Pillich, William F. *Social Dance*. Dubuque, Iowa: W. C. Brown, 1967.

Pratt, Ray. *Rhythm and Resistance: Explorations in the Political Uses of Popular Music*. New York and Westport, Conn.: Praeger, 1990.

Roach, Joseph. *Cities of the Dead: Circum-Atlantic Performance.* New York: Columbia University Press, 1996.

Robbins, Bruce, ed. *The Phantom Public Sphere.* Minneapolis and London: University of Minnesota Press, 1993.

Rosaldo, Renato. *Culture and Truth: The Remaking of Social Analysis.* Boston: Beacon Press, 1989.

Ross, Andrew and Tricia Rose, eds. *Microphone Fiends: Youth Music and Youth Culture.* New York: Routledge, 1994.

Rotello, Gabriel. *Sexual Ecology: AIDS and the Destiny of Gay Men.* New York: Dutton, 1997.

Sanders, Joel, ed. *Stud: Architectures of Masculinity.* Princeton Architectural Press, 1996.

Savigliano, Marta. *Tango and the Political Economy of Passion.* Boulder: Westview Press, 1995.

Schechner, Richard. *Between Theater and Anthropology.* Philadelphia: University of Pennsylvania Press, 1985.

Soja, Edward W. *Postmodern Geographies: The Reassertion of Space in Critical Social Theory.* London, New York: Verso, 1989.

Sterns, Marshall and Jean Sterns. *Jazz Dance: the Story of American Vernacular Dance.* New York: Da Capo Press, 1994.

Stoller, Paul. *The Taste of Ethnographic Things: the Senses in Anthropology.* Philadelphia: University of Pennsylvania Press, 1989.

Sullivan, Andrew. *Virtually Normal: an Argument about Homosexuality.* New York: Alfred A. Knopf, 1995.

Thomas, Helen, ed. *Dance, Gender, and Culture.* New York: St. Martin's Press, 1995.

Thornton, Sara. *Club Cultures: Music, Media and Subcultural Capital.* Cambridge, U.K.: Polity Press, 1995.

Tierney, William G. *Academic Outlaws: Queer Theory and Cultural Studies in the Academy.* London: Sage Publications, 1997.

Turner, Victor. *The Ritual Process: Structure and Anti-Structure.* New York: Aldine de Gruyter, 1969, 1994.

Wagner, Ann Louise. *Adversaries of Dance: from the Puritans to the Present.* Urbana: University of Illinois Press, 1997.

Wallace, Michele. *Black Popular Culture: a Project.* Edited by Gina Dent. Seattle: Bay Press, 1992.

Warner, Michael, ed. *Fear of a Queer Planet: Queer Politics and Social Theory.* Minneapolis and London: University of Minnesota Press, 1993.

Watney, Simon. *Practices of Freedom: Selected Writings on HIV/AIDS.* Durham, N.C.: Duke University Press, 1994.

Williams, Raymond. *The Country and the City.* New York: Oxford University Press, 1973.

Articles

Barber, Charles. "AIDS Apartheid." *NYQ,* no. 2, November 3, 1991: 42–68.

Bastone, William. "Quality of (Night) Life Issues." *Village Voice,* February 18, 1997: 36–38.

Berlant, Lauren and Michael Warner. "Sex in Public." *Critical Inquiry* 24, Winter 1998: 547–566.

Birdwhistell, Ray L. "It Depends on the Point of View." In Schechner, Richard and Mady Schuman, eds. *Ritual, Play, and Performance.* New York: Seabury Press, 1976.

Butler, Judith. "Desire." Lentricchia, Frank and Thomas McLaughlin, eds. *Critical Terms for Literary Study,* Second Edition. Chicago and London: University of Chicago Press, 1995: 369–386.

Califia, Pat. "San Francisco: Revisiting 'The City of Desire.'" In Ingram, Gordon Brent, Anne-Marie Bouthillette, and Yolanda Retter. *Queers in Space: Communities, Public Places, Sites of Resistance.* Seattle: Bay Press, 1997: 177–196.

Certeau, Michel de. "Practices of Space." In Blonsky, Marshall, ed. *On Signs.* Baltimore: The Johns Hopkins University Press, 1985: 124.

Clifford, James. "On Ethnographic Allegory." In James Clifford and George E. Marcus, eds. *Writing Culture: The Poetics and Politics of Ethnography.* Berkeley: University of California Press, 1986: 98–121.

Colter, Ephen Glenn. "Fruits of Repression." *http://ww.citysearchnyc.com/nyc/nightlife/Underground_Gay_Clubs.html,* February 21, 1997.

Daly, Ann. "To Dance Is 'Female.'" *TDR* 33, 4(T124), Winter: 23–27.

D'Emilio, John. "Capitalism and Gay Identity." Harry Abelove, Michele Aima Barale, David M. Halperin, eds. *The Lesbian and Gay Studies Reader.* New York: Routledge, 1993.

DeFrantz, Thomas. "Popular Music Movement Styles: Empowerment and Rap Music." *UCLA Journal of Dance Ethnology* 17, 1993: 17–22.

De Lauretis, Teresa. "Queer Theory: Lesbian and Gay Sexualities, An Introduction." *Differences* 3:2, summer 1991: iii–xviii.

Duggan, Lisa. "Queering the State." *Social Text* 39, summer 1994: 1–14.

Dunlap, David W. "As Disco Faces Razing, Gay Alumni Share Memories." *New York Times,* August 31, 1995: B3.

Flores, Juan and George Yudice. "Living Borders: Buscando America: Languages of Latino Self-Formation." *Social Text* 24, 1990: 57–85.

Foderaro, Lisa W. "Party, Party, Party All the Time." *New York Times.* Feb 27, 1994, section 9. L.2.

Foucault, Michel. "Nietzsche, Genealogy, History." In Donald F. Bouchard, ed., *Language, Counter-Memory, Practice: Selected Essays and Interviews.* Ithaca: New York: Cornell University Press, 1977: 139–64.

Fraser, Nancy. "Rethinking the Public Sphere: A Contribution to the Critique of Actually Existing Democracy." In Robbins, ed., 1993.

Friedland, LeeEllen. "Disco: Afro-American Vernacular Performance." *Dance Research Journal* 15, 2, Spring 1983: 27–35.

Fusco, Coco. "Who's Doin' the Twist?: Notes Towards a Politics of Appropriation." In *English is Broken Here: Notes on Cultural Fusion in the Americas.* New York: Norton, 1995.

Goldstein, Richard. "Whose Quality of Life Is It, Anyway?" *Village Voice,* Feb. 18, 1997: 38–39.

Goldstone, Adam. "Dance At Your Own Risk." *Time Out* May 8–15, 1997: 7–14.

Hall, Stuart. "Notes on Deconstructing 'The Popular.'" Samuel Raphael, ed. *People's History and Socialist Theory.* London: Routledge, 1981: 227–240.

——. "On Postmodernism and Articulation: An Interview." *Journal of Communication Inquiry.* 10, 1986: 58–72.

Hanna, Judith Lynne. "Moving Messages: Identity and Desire in Popular Music and Social Dance." James Lull, ed., *Popular Music and Social Dance,* Second Edition, London and New Delhi: Sage Publications, 1992: 176–195.

Hazzard-Gordon, Katrina. "Afro-American Core Culture Social Dance: An Examination of Four Aspects of Meaning." *Dance Research Journal* 15, 2 (Spring) 1983: 21–26.

Hughes, Walter. "In the Empire of the Beat: Discipline and Disco." In Ross, Andrew, and Tricia Rose, eds. *Microphone Fiends: Youth Music and Youth Culture.* New York: Routledge, 1994.

"Introduction to a critique of urban geography" *Situationist International Anthology,* 5, 1955. Edited and translated by Ken Knabb. Berkeley, Calif.: Bureau of Public Secrets, 1981.

Kaplan, Alice and Kristin Ross. Introduction to "Everyday Life." *Yale French Studies,* 73, 1987: 1–6.

Keil, Charles. "Participatory Discrepancies and the Power of Music." *Cultural Anthropology* 2, 3, 1987: 275–83.

Langlois, Tony. "Can You Feel It? DJs and House Music Culture in the UK." *Popular Music,* 1992, volume 11/2: 229–38.

Levin, David Michael. "The Embodiment of Performance." *Salmagundi.* 31–32, Fall 1975/Winter 1976: 120–142.

Lukes, S., "Political Ritual and Social Integration," *Sociology,* 9 (1975), 289–308.

McKinley, Jesse. 'Dirty Dancing.' *Out* May 1998: 90–95.

McRobbie, Angela. "Dance and Social Fantasy." In McRobbie, A. and M. Nava, eds. *Gender and Generation.* London: Macmillan, 1984.

Mauss, Marcel. "Techniques of the Body." *Economy and Society,* Vol. II, No. 1, 1973: 70–88.

Mendelsohn, Daniel. "We're Here! We're Queer! Let's Get Coffee!" *New York.* September 30 1996: 25–31.

Miller, D.A. "Anal Rope." In *Inside/Out: Lesbian Theories, Gay Theories,* ed. Fuss, Diana. New York and London: Routledge 1991.

Muñoz, José Esteban. "Ghosts of Public Sex: Utopian Longings, Queer Memories." In *Policing Public Sex: HIV Prevention and the Future of Queer Activism.* Dangerous Bedfellows, eds. Boston: South End Press, 1996: 355–73.

——. "Pedro Zamora's *Real World* of Counterpublicity: Performing an Ethics of the Self." In Torres, Sasha, ed. *Living Color: Race and Television in the United States.* Durham and London: Duke University Press, 1998: 193–218.

Nora, Pierre. "Between Memory and History: *Les Lieux de Mémoire.*" *Representations,* Spring 1989, no. 25:7–25: 7–25.

Novack, Cynthia. "Looking at Movement as Culture: Contact Improvisation to Disco." *TDR* 32, 4 (T120), Winter 1988: 102–19.

Owen, Frank. "Sleepless in Manhattan." *Village Voice,* March 28, 1995: 27–31.

——. "What Is Special K? How an Animal Tranquilizer Became New York's Latest Drug Craze." *Village Voice,* July 11, 1995: 25–27.

——. "Crackdown in Clubland." Village Voice, Feb 18, 1997: 34–37.

Riggs, Marlon. "Black Macho Revisited: Reflections of a SNAP! Queen." In

INDEX

access, 4, 8, 130, 139; denied, 3
accessories, 41
ACT-UP (AIDS Coalition to Unleash
    Power), xvii–xviii, xix, xxiv, 142
"adult establishments," xxi, 130, 197–
    198
"adult materials," xxi
"adult performances," xxi
adult venues, xvii, 8
advertising, 139, 140
affectiveness, 1, 9
agency, 5, 6, 78–79; surrender of, 87
AIDS, 32, 49, 53, 68, 134, 136, 159;
    "Apartheid," 164–165; deaths from,
    xvi, xvii, xviii, xix, xx, xxi, xxii, xxiii,
    xxiv, 31, 176–179; denial of, 170; ef-
    fect on body, 164–168; effect on
    club scene, 163, 173; fear of, 172;
    history of, 176; industry, 165; life
    with, 159, 160, 162, 164, 165, 166–
    168, 169, 177–179, 180–183; the
    media, xxii, 146, 169; panic, 146;
    philanthropy, 138; pre-AIDS, 163,
    173; resources, 161, 169; Quilt, xviii,
    xxii
AIDS Drug Assistance Program (ADAP),
    xxii
alcohol, 11, 42, 91
Alex, 23–25, 31, 38, 41, 49, 53, 60, 62–
    63, 101–102, 106, 108, 139, 140,
    141, 142–146
alienation, 89, 97
Alig, Michael, xxii–xxiii, 133, 147
American Airlines, xxiii, 137
American Psychiatric Association, xiv
amyl nitrate, xvi
Angels, 113–114
anthropology, 9
anticipation, 101
Anti-Violence Project of New York, xxiii,
    44, 133

anxiety, 47, 49–50, 99–100
appropriation, 55–57, 69, 74–75, 99,
    173–174, 176; temporal, 57
archaeology, 2, 21, 30, 32
Area, 24, 49, 63, 142, 145
Arena, 57, 76–77, 98, 139, 163
Ariel, 33–34, 42–43, 123–125, 140–
    141
arrests, xviii, xxiii, 133
articulation, 3
assimilation, 142
Atlanta, xvii, 137
Atlantic Monthly, 136
Atkins, Juan, xvi
audience, 9, 16, 18, 21, 27, 38–39, 40,
    41, 68, 115–118
Aviance, Kevin, 48
AZT, xvii

backroom, xvii, 135, 148. *See also* sex
Bambaataa, Afrika, xiv
Barrel, 39, 42, 86, 100–101, 139, 148
bars, xi, xvii, 8; leather, 17, 30, 146, 168;
    transvestite, xxiii, 132
Basquiat, Jean-Michel, 63
bathhouses, xvii
beat, xiv, 10, 62, 66, 172. *See also* music
belonging, 47, 89, 141, 168
BET (Black Entertainment Television),
    7, 62, 86
Better Days, xiii
Billy the Kid, 149
binarism, 6
Black Party, 137. *See also* circuit parties
Black and Blue Party, 137. *See also* circuit
    parties
Board of Health, 130
body, 17, 122, 125; buffness, 139–141;
    care of, 42, 166; critical mass of, 46,
    48, 57, 104, 143, 166; dancing, 1, 4,
    9–10, 33–35, 61–62, 71–85, 91–92,

215

body *(continued)*
94–105, 107, 113, 115–122, 123–
125, 128, 151, 159, 169–177; desirable, 139–141; enjoyment of, 37,
152; image, 139–140; knowledge,
10, 95–96, 102–103, 172; memory,
18; mind, 92; politics, 8, 122; search,
51; sensations of, 9–10
Body & SOUL, 77
Body Positive, xxi, xxiv, 161, 164
Body Positive T-Dance, xxi, 10, 13, 16,
54, 159, 160–162, 161, 164, 165,
166, 167–171, 172–175, 176, 177–
180, 182–183; closure of, xxiv, 159,
160–162, 163
Bond, Justin, 128, 147
boundaries, 9, 56
Boy Bar, 23, 49, 108, 144–145
Bratton, William, 132
Brody, Michael, xiv
Bronx, xiv, xix, 131, 149
Brooklyn, 31

Café Con Leche, 98
Cake, xxiii, 135, 147
California, 24
capitalism, 9, 89, 92–93, 106, 134, 141,
144
Catherine, 41, 46, 57, 90, 91, 115
celebration, 1, 2, 16, 47, 55, 107, 160
Centers for Disease Control, xvi, xxii
Central Park, 22
chairs, 55
Chelsea, 17, 23, 30, 44, 45, 89, 130, 133,
143, 149, 168; boys, 148; Chelsea
Piers, 23
Cherry Jubilee, 137
chewing gum, 41–42
Chicago, xiv, xv, 67, 68
chill-out area, 56
choreography, 13, 18, 26, 90–91, 94,
110
Christopher Street, 29, 45, 130
Cicero, Mark, 165, 176
cigarettes, 41–42
circuit parties, 137–139, 147; corporate
sponsorship of, xxiii–xxiv, 137–138
circulation, 37, 54, 59
citations, xxiii, 131, 133

citizenship, 133, 157
City of New York Planning Council, 8,
130
class, 5, 106, 108–109, 138, 147–149,
154–155
Clinton, Bill, xx, xxii
Clit Club, xix, xx, 56, 109, 117, 145,
151, 154
closeness, 104–106
clothes, 17, 33, 38–41, 72
Club Farenheit, 51, 150
Club USA, xx
Clubzilla, 47, 60
coat check, 56
cocaine, 43, 170. *See also* drugs
Cocksuckers & Buttfuckers, 147
cognitive maps, 13, 17, 21–22, 29, 31,
155, 168
Colin, 61–62, 102–103, 118–119, 149–
150, 153
Colorado, xx
coming out, 58, 163, 166–167
commemoration, xiii, 28, 29
commodification, 21, 54, 141, 143, 157
commodity, 21, 115, 117
community, xv, 1, 2, 4, 13, 29, 38, 47,
60, 86–90, 101, 106–107, 108–110,
122, 133, 153, 157, 165, 172, 174–
175, 176, 182; imagined, 47, 75
Community Boards, xxi, xxii, xxiii, 129,
131, 132, 134
composition, 1, 6, 7, 66, 71, 72, 73, 82,
84, 85, 126
confidence, 37, 82, 95, 172
connection, 18, 107–108, 166, 172, 176
consent, 11, 185–187
consumption, 28–29, 141
Continental Baths, xiii, 67
control, 1, 78–79, 182, 183
conversation, 42
co-option, 23
crackdown, xxiii, 8, 13, 129–135
Crawford, Cindy, xx
Crazy Nanny's, 151
creativity, 3, 9, 172
crime, xxiii, 130, 132–134
criminalization, 13, 129, 134
Crowbar, 46, 56, 86, 104–105, 106, 119,
134, 135, 146, 148, 155

crowd, 10
cruising, 22, 42, 59, 104, 111, 113, 132, 133, 145–146; arrests for, xxiii
cryptosporidium, 162
Cybotron, xvi

Dana, 94, 120, 151
dance clubs, 36–37; after-hours, xii; black, xiii, xiv, 51, 52, 61–62, 67, 69, 135–136, 148–155; center, 58; closures of, xxiii xvii, xxiii, 51, 129–130, 133, 134, 157; dissatisfaction in, 52–53; dressing for, 7, 17, 33, 38–41, 72 (*see also* clothes; dressing); end of the night, 6, 183; entry into, 50, 55–56, 58, 167; gay, xi–xxiv, 2, 8, 10, 16–17, 24, 34, 36, 45, 46–47, 50, 52, 53, 57–58, 60, 61–63, 67, 69, 72–73, 76–77, 89, 98, 101, 102, 105, 107, 111, 118, 123, 139, 149, 159, 170, 176; for HIV-positive gay men, 160, 161–162, 163, 165–170, 171–178; Latino, 51, 61, 67, 69, 98–99, 121, 135, 149–151; lesbian, 2, 10, 50, 56, 81–82, 94, 95, 103, 104, 109, 112–117, 120, 145, 147, 150–152, 156–157; location, 44, 195–196; policing, 48, 50, 51; profits, 42, 50, 51, 134; queer, 41, 46, 104, 106, 128, 134–135, 139, 142–145, 146–147, 148, 154–155, 158; regulars, 48, 106; traveling to and from, 7, 44–46; underground, xiii, 129, 148, 149
dance crazes, xii. *See also* Twist, the
dance floor, 1, 17, 18, 32, 58, 90, 94, 96, 113, 118, 152, 171, 177, 183
dancers, 1, 4, 9–10, 33–35, 61–62, 71–85, 91–92, 94–105, 107, 113, 115–122, 123–125, 128, 151, 152, 159, 169–177; DJs, 13, 166, 173–176; interactions with each other, 13, 36, 96–99, 100–106, 166, 172, 175; suspicion of, 91–92
Danceteria, 24, 25, 60, 101, 142, 145
danger, 8, 17, 25, 45–46
Daughters of Bilitis, xii
David, 48
Davis, Rick, xvi
Defense of Marriage Act 1996, xxii

desire, 3, 4, 13, 37, 78, 86–87, 93–94, 100–101, 102, 104, 106–107, 112, 122, 139–140, 172, 176
Detroit, xvi
deviance, 9
difference, 1, 5, 62, 97, 140, 143, 150, 155
disco, xiv, 60, 173; backlash, xv, 68; commercialization, xiii, 67
disco nap, 42
discrimination, 50, 162
Disney, 131, 133
disorientation, 56, 59, 66, 73
diversity, 29–30, 37, 69, 140
DJs, xiii, 62, 69, 131, 138, 147, 165; artistry, 69–70; booth, 59, 69; dancers, xiii, 13, 66, 69–71, 73–74, 76–77, 79, 80, 95; music performance, xii–xiii, 67, 69; style, xix; technique, 69–71, 73–74
door, 46, 47, 54, 56, 168; policy, 49–53, 143, 165
door people, 41, 46, 48–52, 63
drag, 142, 143, 144–146; balls, xix; kings, 145–146; queens, xii, 47, 51, 160
dressing, 7, 17, 33, 38–41, 72, 150, 155, 165, 166. *See also* clothes; dance clubs, dressing for
drugs, xvi, xxii, xxiii, 8, 10, 11, 16, 42–43, 58, 91, 132, 134, 135, 136, 137, 163, 165, 166; exhaustion, 53; overdoses, 9, 138; prescription, xvii, xviii, 162, 167–168, 178. *See also* cocaine; Ecstasy; ketamine; protease inhibitors; Special K

East Village, 16, 23, 41, 45, 54, 106, 132, 146, 149, 155, 160; gentrification, 106
Ecstasy, 42, 43
economy, 4, 21, 47, 156; beauty, 4, 164; desirability, 4, 164; PINK, 30, 142
Edelweiss, xxiii, 132
Edie, 50, 113–114, 120, 151, 156–157
egalitarianism, 3, 120, 172
Electric Circus, 45
elitism, 138–139, 164
Ella, 114, 151

embodiment, 2, 3, 9, 12, 17–18, 19, 21, 34, 65, 106
empowerment, 36, 37, 64, 65, 92–93, 107
energy, 1, 2, 9, 94, 95, 118, 155, 163, 170, 172, 173, 174, 176
entrance, 55–56, 58, 167
entry, 3; fee, 4, 47, 69, 138, 147, 149, 164–165
eroticisation, 146
escape, 8, 86, 91, 126
Escuelita, 51, 56, 98–99, 117, 135, 149, 150
ethnicity, 5, 9, 157
ethnography, 5, 9–12, 18, 21, 160–161, 179
everyday life, 5, 21, 27, 30, 63, 65, 85, 87, 91, 93, 102, 126, 162, 178
excess, 41, 61, 152, 153, 176
exchange, 2, 36–37, 66, 100, 106, 126
excitement, xv, 68, 79–80
Exhibitchionist, 81
expression, 1, 8
eye contact, 98, 100–101, 111, 119, 121

fabulousness, 12, 36–37, 53, 56, 64, 85
family, 36, 38, 52, 106, 108, 131, 133, 148
family values, xx, 108
fans, 160, 169–173; fan-dancing, 169–173
fantasy, 25, 63
Farley "Jackmaster" Funk, xvii
femininity, 150–151, 153
feminism, 9, 113–114, 151
field-notes, 10
fierceness, 12, 84–85, 152
Fierman, Michael, xviii
fines, xxiii, 135
Fire Island, xi, 137; Morning Party, xiii, 9, 137, 138. See also circuit parties
fire regulations, xxiii
fitting in, 6
five-hundred-foot rule, 132
Flamingo East, 148
Flava, 51, 56, 150
flow, 10, 180
Food and Drug Administration (FDA), xviii, xxii

footwear, 1, 2. See also clothes; dressing
Foxy, 41, 143, 147
freakiness, 143, 144, 156
Freda's Hideaway, 149
freedom, 3, 86, 90–91, 103, 107, 136, 166
Friday, 61
friendship, 2, 12, 42, 100–101, 172
fun, 37, 38
funding, xxii, 137
future, 1, 9, 27, 160, 179

Gaiety, 25
Galaxy 21, xiii
Gallery, xiii, xv, 67
garage music, xiv
Gatien, Peter, xxii–xxiii, xxiv, 133
gay; activism, 9, 142; assimilation, 136–137, 138; businesses, 30–31; clubs, xi–xxiv, 2, 8, 10, 16–17, 24, 34, 36, 45, 46–47, 50, 52, 53, 57–58, 60, 61–63, 67, 69, 72–73, 76–77, 89, 98, 101, 102, 105, 107, 111, 118, 123, 139, 149, 159, 170, 176; and lesbian sexuality, 137; marriage, xx, xxii; men of color, 148–155; neoconservatives, 136–137, 146; politics, 92, 137; and queer, 23, 137; youth, xxi
"gay cancer," xvi
Gay Men's Health Crisis, xvi, xvii, xxiii, 138, 164; Dance-A-Thon, xix
Gay Pride, 29–30, 47–48
gaze, 113–114, 118–119
gentrification, 130. See also East Village
gesture, 21, 26, 56, 83
GHB (gamma-hydroxybutrate), xxiii
ghettoization, 29
go-go dancers, 8, 13, 58, 65, 90, 112, 113–120, 131, 147, 169
Grasso, Francis, xii, xiii
Greenwich Village, 149
guest list, 45, 47–50
Guiliani, Rudolph, xx, xxi, xxiii, 8, 118, 128, 130, 134
guns, xxiii
gym, 72

habit, 21, 30
Happyland, xix, 131

Haring, Keith, 63
Harlem, xi, xix; drag balls, xx
Harmony, 113
Haven, xiii
Hawaii Supreme Court, xx
healing, 13, 180-182
health hazards, xvii
heat, 10, 74
hedonism, 16, 65, 91, 138
Hell Ball, 137
Helms, Jesse, xxi
Her/she Bar, 114, 150-151, 154
He's Gotta Have It, xxi, 146
heteronormativity, 5, 9, 18, 19, 57, 89, 92, 106, 113, 183
heteroorthodoxy, 6, 40-41
heterosexuality, xvii, 6
heterosexualization of gay culture, 142
Hi-NRG, xv 68, 70, 75, 173
hip-hop, xxiii, 62, 71, 129, 135, 136, 149, 154, 150
HIV, xvi, 8, 10; community, 161-163, 165, 172; gay men, 160, 161; life with, 162; number of Americans living with, xxiv; prevention, xx. *See also* AIDS
home, 3, 7, 43, 52, 108, 148
Homo Extra, 140, 167
homonormativity, 28, 40-41, 89, 157
homophobia, 5, 40, 75, 77, 91, 134, 135, 153
homosexualization of straight culture, 142
Hotlanta, 137. *See also* circuit parties
house music, xiv, xvii, 60, 150, 173, 174. *See also* music
Hudson, Rock, xvii

Iain, 44, 86, 99-100, 138, 140, 141
ID, xxiii, 50, 136
identifications, 4, 23, 37, 75, 141, 162, 167, 174
identity, 2, 4, 5, 29, 60, 108-110, 157, 158
identity politics, 4, 5, 29, 87-88, 157
imagination, 1, 3, 5, 7, 9, 24, 86, 110, 122, 173; kinetic, 81, 83; political, 35, 65, 181; utopian, 3, 65, 66, 157
immersion, 10

impossibility, 2, 3
improvisation, 4, 21, 34-35, 71-72, 82-84, 90-91, 93-95, 172, 179, 181, 183
improvised social dancing, 1, 6, 29, 33, 34, 70-74, 80-85, 91, 94, 120-121, 126, 183; context, 7; history, 68; prejudices, 78
individual, 1, 3; and group, 95, 34, 102, 121-122
informants, 6, 11, 12, 18, 19, 185-191, 193
insider, 5, 161
International Conference of AIDs, xix
interviews, 11, 12, 16, 22, 32, 189-191
Irving Plaza, 130

Jackie, xx, 60, 135, 146, 147
Jermaine, 30-31, 39-40, 149
joy, xv, 40
Juniorverse, xxiii, 139
juxtaposition, 12, 33, 38, 57

Karposi's Sarcoma, 162, 163
Kenny Scharf Room, 50
ketamine (Special K), 42
kinesphere, 79, 94, 98; group, 78
knowledge, 2, 10, 22, 172; embodied, 10, 95-96, 102-103, 172, 181; self, 4, 32, 37, 65, 122-123; shared, 2, 10, 100-102, 122, 172, 182; physical, 2, 10, 95, 181
Knuckles, Frankie, xiii, xiv, 67
Kramer, Larry, xvi, xvii, xxiv
Krash, 51, 98-99, 149, 150

Laboratory, 127
lang, k.d., xx
laws: sex, xii; licensing public dancing, xxiii, 8, 130, 131, 134, 199-200; liquor licensing, xxi, 8, 130, 132, 134, 199-200; New York State, xii; zoning, xxiii, 8, 113, 130
layering, 21, 71, 176
Le Jardin, xiii
lesbian: chic, xx; of color, 147, 150-151, 148, 150-151, 154; dance clubs, 2, 10, 50, 56, 81-82, 94, 95, 103, 104, 109, 112-117, 120, 145, 147, 150-152, 156-157; sexuality, 156

Leslie, Robbie, xviii
Levan, Larry, xiii, xiv, xx, 67, 77
license: cabaret 8, 131, 134, 199–200;
    liquor, xxi, 8, 130, 132, 134, 199–200
Life, 49
lifeworlds, 2–6, 9, 14, 18–19, 22–25,
    27–28, 31, 34, 36–38, 45, 52, 65–
    66, 69, 74, 85, 87, 91, 93, 104, 106,
    110, 112, 126–127, 144, 158; differ-
    ence from community, 4; difference
    from identity, 4–5. See also queer life-
    worlds
lights, 10, 56, 59
Limelight, xvi, xxii, 47–48, 49, 56, 57,
    59, 60, 111, 117
liminality, 57
limitations of language, 2
line, 46–47, 48, 51
Lisa, 104, 107, 109, 113, 117, 119, 145,
    147, 151, 154, 155
Loft, xiii
Los Angeles, xi
loss, 31, 176–179
Love Machine, 39
LSD, xvi
lyrics, xiii, 70, 74–76, 151, 173–175

Madonna, xix, 73, 129
Mailman, Bruce, xv, xxi, 52, 105
Mancuso, David, xiii
Manilow, Barry, xiii
maps, 3, 22, 23, 25, 29, 30, 56, 69
marginalization, 6, 8, 149
Mark, 57, 58, 120, 156, 170, 176–177
masculinity, 61–62, 153
mass-production, 21, 67–68
materialization, 3, 18
Mattachine Society, xi–xii
May, Derrick, xvi
meaning, 3, 6, 23, 26, 84, 123, 172–176
Meat Packing District, 146
media, xvii, xxi, xxii, 8, 133–134, 140,
    162; and AIDS, xxii; gay, xxiii, 9, 138,
    139; mass, 24; and sensationalization,
    9; underground, 24
Melendez, Angel, xxii
membership, xvii, 52
memorial, xxii, 16, 160, 175–178
memory, 1, 12, 17, 19–22, 24, 26–27,

32–33, 157, 173, 175, 179; body, 18;
    collective, 23, 34; embodied, 17, 32,
    102, 175–178; environments of
    memory, 20–21, 27, 177; perfor-
    mance, 19, 32, 176; physical, 18;
    places of memory, 20–21; social, 22,
    32, 75; theater of, 18, 30, 40, 177
Meow Mix, 50, 114, 147, 150
merengue, 98–99, 121, 150
Miami, 137
Midler, Bette, xiii, 129, 142
Midtown, xxiii
Milk, Harvey, xv
mimesis, 1, 97, 100–101, 106, 117, 140
mindlessness, 87, 92, 95
Mineshaft, 16
Mistress Formika, 135
mixing: of bodies, 155, 169; DJs, xii, xiii,
    176; heterosexual and gay and/or
    lesbian, xvii; music, 10, 66, 175; ra-
    cial, xiii, 155; sexual, xiii, 155. See also
    DJs, technique
Mo. B. Dick, 145
monogamy, xxiii, 136
moral panic, xxi, 136
Morales, David, 79
Morning Party, xxiii, 137, 138. See also
    circuit parties
mourning, 1
movement, 1, 3, 5, 4, 9–10, 18, 33–35,
    56, 61–62, 64, 71–85, 91–92, 94–
    105, 107, 113, 115–122, 123–125,
    128, 151, 159, 169–177, 179; affec-
    tivity, 34, 170–173; attitude, 84–85;
    contact, 96, 171; cues, 79, 83, 117;
    development, 80–84; diversity of, 35,
    171; effort, 72, 170–171; everyday
    life, 3; exchange, 2, 36–37, 66, 100,
    100, 106, 126, 171–173; flow, 70,
    171–172; freeze, 84; gesture, 21, 26,
    56, 83; health benefits, 179–181; in-
    corporation, 25, 34, 87, 99–100,
    106; intensity, 83–84, 95; involve-
    ment, 18, 78–80, 94–95; knowledge,
    10, 95–96, 102–103, 172, 181; mass
    of, 10, 59, 60, 72, 79–80, 90; motifs,
    80–82, 94; phrasing, 71, 74, 81–82,
    84; range, 77; repertoire, 21, 34, 60,
    79, 82–84; repetition, 80–82;

sharing, 35; style, 9, 33, 35, 61–62, 94–95, 171; teaching, 35, 100; tempo, 10, 71–72, 76; transmission, 100, 171–172; using other people's, 1, 34, 97, 100–101, 106, 117, 140; variation, 71, 80–82, 117; whole body, 81, 83, 171, 179–180
MTV, xvi, xvii, xxi, 7, 62; *Yo! MTV Raps,* xix
Mudd Club, xv, xvi
murder, xxii, 133
music, 59, 65, 70, 177, 179; African-American, 69; beat, xiv, 62, 66, 172; business, xvi; disco, xiv, 60, 173; garage, xiv, 60, 67, 75, 77, 173; hardhouse, 58, 60, 75, 77; Hi-NRG, xv, 68, 70, 75, 173; hip-hop, xxiii, 62, 71, 129, 135, 136, 149, 154, 150; history, 68; house, xiv, xvii, 60, 150, 173, 174; identification with, 68; Latin, 69; lyrics, 70, 74–76, 151, 173–175; melody, xv, 68; mixing, 69–70; and movement, 71–85, 101; percussion, xiv, 67; pop, 60; process, 78–79; programming, 66; rap, xv, 151; r'n'b, 61, 67, 71, 151; rock, 60, 157; role in everyday life, 1; tempo, 10, 62; texture, 78; underground, xvi; vocals, xiv, xv, 67, 68, 75–76, 77, 173

Nam June Paik, 63
National AIDS Fund, 137
negative society, 169
New Jersey, 24, 31, 58, 167
New Republic, 136
New York, xx
New York City, 2, 17, 25, 68–69, 91, 129, 136, 146, 155, 163, 164, 168; administration, xxi, 13, 129; attraction of, 31, 163, 164; coming to, 16, 22, 163, 164; fiscal crisis, xiv
New York Department of Buildings, 131
New York Department of Consumer Affairs, 131
New York Department of Health, 131
New York Fire Department, xix, 130, 131, 134, 135
New York Gay and Lesbian History Archive, 20
New York Nightlife Association, 130

New York Post, 133
New York Times, xvi, xxii, 25, 136, 163
New York University, xxiv, 2, 147
Newfield, Jack, 133
Newsweek, xxii
Next, 140, 167
noise, 132, 134, 136
normativity, 5, 156. *See also* heteronomativity; homonormativity
novelty, 63

objectification, 113–114, 151
observation, 2, 11
obstruction of view, xxiii
Octagon, 61–62, 89, 102–103, 149, 152, 153
One Magazine, xii
opposition, 2, 6, 20, 144
oppression, 37, 50, 125
order, 59, 65, 66, 67, 70, 77, 96, 125
orientation, 56–57, 58–60, 62, 66, 102–103
Out, 137
outsider, 5, 12, 86, 106, 132, 161
outing, xix
Outweek, xix
overcrowding, xxiii

Padavan, Frank, xxi, 132
Paik, Nam June. *See* Nam June Paik
Palladium, xvii, 49, 56, 76, 139; closure of, xxiii, xxiv; demolition of, xxiv
Pansy Division, xxi
Paradise Garage, xiv, xix, 67, 101–102; closure, xviii
Paris Is Burning, xx
participants, 1, 5, 6, 40
participation, 3, 9, 10, 37, 59, 65, 70, 78–79, 94, 165
partnering, 98–99, 103–104, 121
past, 1, 9, 32, 160, 176–179; performance of, 20; reinterpretation of, 18; restoration of, 18, 177
peers, 37, 47, 166, 167, 175
performance, 3, 7, 12, 16, 17, 18, 21, 26, 27, 40, 80–81, 142, 143, 145, 183; consciousness, 18, 27, 56
Performance Studies, 2, 9
Philip Morris, 137

plaques, xxii, 20
play, 1, 7, 17, 22, 37, 56, 60, 61, 66, 84–
    85, 91, 106, 119, 122, 125, 141, 145,
    151, 155
pleasure, 1, 2, 3, 6, 8, 9, 21, 23, 37, 60,
    65, 66, 79, 80, 85, 110, 123, 142,
    144, 150, 157, 173, 179
podium, 90, 113, 115, 116, 117, 118,
    119, 131
point-of-entry, 11
police, xxii, 50, 130; raids, xxii, 50–51,
    129, 133, 134; stop and seach, xxiii,
    135; surveillance, 52, 133, 136
political activism, 36, 37
polyrhythms, 71
polyvocality, 3
porn houses, xxiii
pornography, 139, 157
power, 9, 69
Poz, xxiv
prejudice, 140
preparation, 13, 37, 54. *See also* dressing;
    drugs
present, 1, 9, 160, 179
promoters, 47–49, 62, 138, 147
prostitution, xxiii, 132, 133, 157
protease inhibitors, xxii
proximity, 54
psychogeography, 24, 28, 44
public dancing, xxiii, 8, 131, 134
public lewdness, xxiii
public sphere, 3, 4–5
punk, xv, 23, 25, 143, 147, 154
Pyramid, xvi, 23, 89, 144, 156

quality of life, 13, 129–130, 131, 133,
    136, 157
Queens, 31, 40, 51, 98, 149
queer, 5–6, 154; drag, 144–146; life-
    world, 2–6, 9, 12, 14, 18–19, 22–25,
    27–28, 31, 34, 36–38, 45, 52, 63,
    65–66, 69, 74, 85, 87, 91, 93, 104,
    106, 110, 112, 126–127, 134, 144,
    158; people of color, 133, 134; per-
    formance of queerness, 38; self-
    identification as, 4, 148; sexuality,
    146; style, 40–41, 143–144, 148;
    theory, 5–6; world-making, 6, 19, 37,
    77, 85, 94, 112, 121–122

queercore, xxi
Queer Nation, xix
queerness, 18, 144, 155
Quinn, Christine, 133
quotidian, 3, 7, 12, 17, 22, 30, 63

race, 5, 9, 108–109, 148–155, 157,
    173–174
racism, 5, 89, 134, 135, 136
raids, xi, xxii, xxiii
Rasiej, Andrew, 130
reality, 5, 7, 9, 43–44, 57, 63, 113, 176
realization, 3, 110
Real World, xxi
reappropriation, 5
rehearsal, 35, 65, 126–127, 129, 172,
    173
relaxation, 62, 71
release, 8, 180
repetition, 2, 21, 56, 66, 75, 80–82, 85,
    123, 165, 173
representation, 7, 8, 9, 12, 66, 112, 122,
    157, 182–183
reproduction, 21
residents, 45
resistance, 6, 37, 129, 157
restored behavior, 27
retelling, 17, 32. *See also* storytelling
rezoning, 8. *See also* zoning laws
rhythm, 2, 10, 71, 73–74, 79, 80, 166,
    172
ritual, 32, 42–43
rock and roll, 60, 147
Rolling Stone, xxi
Ross, Diana, xiii
Rotello, Gabriel, xxiii
Roxy, xv, 160, 163, 168, 176
recreation, 3
redevelopment, 28
Ruffin, Jimmy, xix
rules, 7, 53, 66, 90, 96, 97, 99–100, 103
Run-D.M.C., xvii
rupture, 178–179
Ryan White CARE Act, xx

"same sex lover," 4, 154
safety, 26, 44–45
safety regulations, xix
Saint, xv, xxi, 16, 31, 32, 36, 38, 45–46,

52, 53, 63, 68, 105, 107, 149, 159, 179; closure of, xviii–xix; dance floor, xv; demolition of, xxii

Saint Mark's Baths, xv, xvii, xxi, 31, 47

salsa, 150

samples, 56, 173, 176

Sanctuary, xiii

San Francisco, xii, xv, 136, 137, 170

San Francisco Society for Individual Rights, xii

Sanitary Codes, xvii

saquinavir, xxii

Saturday, xxiii

Saturday Night Live, 24, 38

Save Avenue A Society, 132

Scharf, Kenny, 129. *See also* Kenny Scharf Room

security, 45, 133; search, 51, 133

selection, 23, 34, 41, 48–49, 50, 89

self-consciousness, 123–125, 141, 180

self-esteem, 37, 140

self-fashioning, 3, 5, 7, 19, 27, 36, 38–41, 44, 62, 87, 112, 158

separation, 12, 43–44

sex, 8, 22–23, 86, 111–112, 120, 123, 128, 136, 157, 162, 163, 166, 169, 183; performance, 112, 115–118; public, 131; safer, xvii, 167; unsafe, xxi, 181–182

sex clubs, xxi, 16, 146

Sex Panic!, 29, 130

sexism, 89; and gay men, xii

Sheridan Square, xiii, 20

Siano, Nicky, xiii

Signorile, Michaelangelo, xix, xxiii

Silverados, 103

similarity, 62

Skin, 147

sleaze, 25, 146–147

Social Club Task Force, 131

social dance, 136; score, 7

Social Task Force, xix

Social Toilet, 147

socialization, 1, 25, 99–100, 101

Soho, xviii, 136

S.O.S., 103, 121

sound, 2

soundscape, 10, 56, 70–71; and dancers, 71–77

Sound Factory, xix, 72; closure of, xxii

Sound Factory Bar, xxi, 56, 97, 159, 167, 168, 169

space, 4, 16, 22, 37, 94, 95, 96, 102–103, 166; claiming of, 13, 53–54, 170; contestation of, 48; conversion of, 53; host, 19, 23; ownership, 58; for people of color, 51–52, 61–62, 148–155; politics of, 8, 157; safe, 11, 50, 52, 134, 148, 156, 175; separate, 43; small, 61, 104–105, 143, 169; territorialization of, 50; use of, 10, 13, 18, 23, 60–61, 72–73, 79–80, 133

Special K, 42, 43

Splash, 149

Squeezebox, 25, 139, 142–144, 156

stage-management, 62

Stand Up, 164

State Liquor Authority, xi, xxi, 132

Stephen, 36, 37, 38, 40, 46, 56, 85, 104–106, 107, 120, 134, 141, 146, 148, 152, 155

Stiles, B.J., 137

Stonewall, xii, 20, 28, 135; commemoration of, xiii, xxi

storytelling, 12, 16–17, 21–22, 26–27, 29, 123, 176–178, 179

straights, 48, 50, 53, 156

strategies, 5, 19, 59, 157

"Strategy '97," xxiii

street, 12, 17, 39, 152; parties, xv

strip clubs, xxiii, 113–117

strippers, 13, 112, 113–117

Studio 54, xiv, xv, xvi, xvii, 24, 48, 49, 67, 146–147

Studio Filthy Whore, 143, 146

style, 142–144, 157

stylization, 27

subversion, 66, 145, 148

Sugarhill Gang, xv

Sunday, xxiii, 61

survival, 160, 163, 178

Suspect, 61, 149–150, 152, 154

sweat, 10, 106, 180

tactics, 5, 19, 50

taxes, xxii

tea dances, 161

Tenaglia, Danny, 60, 77

tension, 8, 9, 35, 48, 73, 180
Terrel, Charles, xv
theater, 3, 22, 39, 120, 126; of memory, 18
theme parties, 63
third body, 3, 37
third space, 7, 43–44, 93, 108, 148
Thomas, 90
time, 43, 67, 178–179
Time, xix
Time Out, 57–58, 135
Times Square, 24, 130, 132
Tito, 16–18, 22–23, 25, 26, 27, 30, 31, 32, 36, 38, 46–47, 50, 52, 53, 63, 90, 96–97, 105–106, 107, 159, 160–161, 163, 164, 165–166, 169–172, 175–176, 177, 178–179, 181
togetherness, 3
Tompkin, Susan, 105
touch, 55, 98–99, 104–106
"tourists," 48, 50, 57–58
Trannie Chasers, 147
transcendence, 1, 6, 13, 66, 122–126
transformation, 1, 23, 27, 55, 177, 179–181, 182–183; of self, 65, 182–183
transgendered, 5
transgression, 144–146
translation, 2
transmission, 21, 35, 87, 106
traveling, 7, 44–46
Tribeca, 51, 63, 113, 136
trivialization, 8, 37, 92
Trocadero, 170
Tunnel, xvii, xxii, xxiii, 42, 45, 50, 57–60, 72, 102, 135
12 West, 23, 36
Twilo, xxii, xxiii, 10, 42, 45, 56, 57, 69, 72, 78–80, 89, 98, 104, 117, 139, 147, 163, 165, 166
Twist, the, xii, 129, 136
Twisted, 147
2i, 95

U+Me, 61–62
utopia, 3, 4, 5, 47, 87, 88–89, 93, 109, 125, 127, 154, 182

Valenti, Chi Chi, 146
value, 3, 6, 12–13, 66, 108, 173; shared, 84, 172
Vanity Fair, xx
Vasquez, Junior, xix, xxiii, 57–58, 76–77, 134
Velvet, 41, 104, 128
velvet rope, 164, 168
Village Voice, 25, 167
Vinyl, 42, 77, 136
violation, 8, 51, 131
violence, 9, 17, 22, 26, 134, 178
VIP, 52, 144; passes, 49; room, 49, 58
vocals, xiv, xv, 67, 68, 75–76, 77, 173
voguing, xix

walking, 54–55
Wall Street Journal, The, xxii
Warehouse, xiv, 67, 149
Washington, DC, xxiv, 137; National March on, xv, xviii
water, 42
weapons, 51
Webster Hall, 160, 167, 168, 169
Weekly Standard, The, 136
Weise, Thomas, 162, 165, 168, 175, 178
West Village, 23, 28, 29, 44, 61, 130, 149
White Party, 137. *See also* circuit parties
Winter Party, 137. *See also* circuit parties
Wizard of Oz, The, 63
word of mouth, 7, 148, 149
work, 3, 7, 43, 52
world-making, 2–6, 9, 13, 14, 18–19, 22–25, 27–28, 31, 34, 36–38, 45, 52, 65–66, 69, 74, 85, 87, 91, 93, 104, 106, 110, 112, 126–127, 144, 158
Wright, Will, 163, 165, 166, 167, 169, 175, 180, 181–182

youth, 49

Zamora, Pedro, xxi
Zone DK, xxi, 146
zoning laws, xxiii, 8, 113, 130

About the author: Fiona Buckland received her Ph.D. in Performance Studies at New York University. She has published essays and review articles in *New Theatre Quarterly* and *Women and Performance*.